Kubernetes for Serverless Applications

Implement FaaS by effectively deploying, managing, monitoring, and orchestrating serverless applications using Kubernetes

Russ McKendrick

BIRMINGHAM - MUMBAI

Kubernetes for Serverless Applications

Commissioning Editor: Gebin George
Acquisition Editor: Prateek Bharadwaj
Content Development Editor: Nithin Varghese
Technical Editor: Khushbu Sutar
Copy Editor: Safis Editing
Project Coordinator: Virginia Dias
Proofreader: Safis Editing
Indexer: Francy Puthiry
Graphics: Tania Dutta
Production Coordinator: Aparna Bhagat

First published: January 2018

Production reference: 1170118

Published by Packt Publishing Ltd.
Livery Place
35 Livery Street
Birmingham
B3 2PB, UK.

ISBN 978-1-78862-037-6

www.packtpub.com

Mapt

Contributors

About the author

Russ McKendrick is an experienced solution architect who has been working in IT and related industries for over 25 years. During his career, he has had varied responsibilities, from looking after an entire IT infrastructure to providing first-line, second-line, and senior support in both client-facing and internal teams for large organizations.

Russ supports open source systems and tools on public and private clouds at Node4 Limited, where he heads up the Open Source Solutions team.

I would like to thank my family and friends for their support and for being so understanding about all the time I have spent in front of the computer, writing. I would also like to thank my colleagues at Node4 and our customers for their kind words of support and encouragement throughout the writing process.

About the reviewer

Paul Adamson has worked as an Ops engineer, a developer, a DevOps Engineer, and all variations and mixes of all of these. When not reviewing this book, Paul keeps busy helping companies embrace the AWS infrastructure. His language of choice is PHP for all the good reasons and even some of the bad.

Jeeva S. Chelladhurai has been working as a DevOps specialist at the IBM GTS Labs for the last 10 years. He is the coauthor of *Learning Docker* by Packt Publishing. He has more than 20 years of IT industry experience and has technically managed and mentored diverse teams across the globe in envisaging and building pioneering telecommunication products. He is also a strong proponent of the agile methodologies, DevOps, and IT automation. He holds a master's degree in computer science from Manonmaniam Sundaranar University and a graduation certificate in project management from Boston University.

Packt is searching for authors like you

If you're interested in becoming an author for Packt, please visit `authors.packtpub.com` and apply today. We have worked with thousands of developers and tech professionals, just like you, to help them share their insight with the global tech community. You can make a general application, apply for a specific hot topic that we are recruiting an author for, or submit your own idea.

Table of Contents

Preface

Kubernetes has been one of the standout technologies of the last few years; it has been adopted as a container clustering and orchestration platform by all the major public cloud providers, and it has quickly become the standard across the industry.

Add to this that Kubernetes is open source, and you have the perfect base for hosting your own Platform as a Service or PaaS across multiple public and private providers; you can even run it on a laptop and, due to its design, you will get a consistent experience across all of your platforms.

Its design also makes it the perfect platform for running serverless functions. In this book, we will look at several platforms that can be both deployed on and integrated with Kubernetes, meaning that not only will we have PaaS but also a robust Function as a Service platform running in your Kubernetes environment.

Who this book is for

This book is primarily for operations engineers, cloud architects, and developers who want to host their serverless functions on a Kubernetes cluster.

What this book covers

`Chapter 1`, *The Serverless Landscape*, explains what is meant by serverless. Also, we will get some practical experience of running serverless functions on public clouds using AWS Lambda and Azure Functions.

`Chapter 2`, *An Introduction to Kubernetes*, discusses what Kubernetes is, what problems it solves, and also takes a look at its backstory, from internal engineering tool at Google to an open source powerhouse.

`Chapter 3`, *Installing Kubernetes Locally*, explains how to get hands-on experience with Kubernetes. We will install a local single node Kubernetes cluster using Minikube and interact with it using the command-line client.

`Chapter 4`, *Introducing Kubeless Functioning*, explains how to launch your first serverless function using Kubeless once the Kubernetes is up and running locally.

`Chapter 5`, *Using Funktion for Serverless Applications*, explains the use of Funktion for a slightly different take on calling serverless functions.

`Chapter 6`, *Installing Kubernetes in the Cloud*, covers launching a cluster in DigitalOcean, AWS, Google Cloud, and Microsoft Azure after getting some hands-on experience using Kubernetes locally.

`Chapter 7`, *Apache OpenWhisk and Kubernetes*, explains how to launch, configure, and use Apache OpenWhisk, the serverless platform originally developed by IBM, using our newly launched cloud Kubernetes cluster.

`Chapter 8`, *Launching Applications Using Fission*, covers the deploying of Fission, the popular serverless framework for Kubernetes, along with a few example functions.

`Chapter 9`, *Looking at OpenFaaS*, covers OpenFaaS. While it's, first and foremost, a Functions as a Service framework for Docker, it is also possible to deploy it on top of Kubernetes.

`Chapter 10`, *Serverless Considerations*, discusses security best practices along with how you can monitor your Kubernetes cluster.

`Chapter 11`, *Running Serverless Workloads*, explains how quickly the Kubernetes ecosystem is evolving and how you can keep up. We also discuss which tools you should use, and why you would want your serverless functions on Kubernetes.

To get the most out of this book

Operating Systems:

- macOS High Sierra
- Ubuntu 17.04
- Windows 10 Professional

Software:
We will be installing several command-line tools throughout this book; each of the tools will have installation instructions and details of its requirements in the chapters. Note that while instructions for Windows systems are provided, a lot of the tools we will be using were originally designed to run primarily on Linux/Unix based systems such as Ubuntu 17.04 and macOS High Sierra, and the book will favor these systems. While every effort has been made at the time of writing to verify that the tools work on Windows-based systems, as some of the tools are experimental builds, we cannot guarantee that they will continue to work on updated systems, because of this, I would recommend using either a Linux- or Unix-based system.

Hardware:

- **Windows 10 Professional and Ubuntu 17.04 system requirements**:
    - Systems using processors (CPUs) launched in 2011 or later with a 1.3 GHz or faster core speed, except Intel Atom processors or AMD processors based on the *Llano* and *Bobcat* micro-architectures
    - 4 GB RAM minimum with 8 GB RAM or more recommended
- **Apple Mac system requirements**:
    - **iMac**: Late 2009 or newer
    - **MacBook/MacBook (Retina)**: Late 2009 or newer
    - **MacBook Pro**: Mid-2010 or newer
    - **MacBook Air**: Late 2010 or newer
    - **Mac mini**: Mid-2010 or newer
    - **Mac Pro**: Mid-2010 or newer

Access to at least one of the following public cloud services:

- **AWS**: `https://aws.amazon.com/`
- **Google Cloud**: `https://cloud.google.com/`
- **Microsoft Azure**: `https://azure.microsoft.com/`
- **DigitalOcean**: `https://www.digitalocean.com/`

Download the example code files

You can download the example code files for this book from your account at `www.packtpub.com`. If you purchased this book elsewhere, you can visit `www.packtpub.com/support` and register to have the files emailed directly to you.

You can download the code files by following these steps:

1. Log in or register at `www.packtpub.com`.
2. Select the **SUPPORT** tab.
3. Click on **Code Downloads & Errata**.
4. Enter the name of the book in the **Search** box and follow the onscreen instructions.

Once the file is downloaded, please make sure that you unzip or extract the folder using the latest version of:

- WinRAR/7-Zip for Windows
- Zipeg/iZip/UnRarX for Mac
- 7-Zip/PeaZip for Linux

The code bundle for the book is also hosted on GitHub at `https://github.com/PacktPublishing/Kubernetes-for-Serverless-Applications`. We also have other code bundles from our rich catalog of books and videos available at `https://github.com/PacktPublishing/`. Check them out!

Download the color images

We also provide a PDF file that has color images of the screenshots/diagrams used in this book. You can download it here: `https://www.packtpub.com/sites/default/files/downloads/KubernetesforServerlessApplications_ColorImages.pdf`.

Conventions used

There are a number of text conventions used throughout this book.

`CodeInText`: Indicates code words in text, database table names, folder names, filenames, file extensions, pathnames, dummy URLs, user input, and Twitter handles. Here is an example: "This contains a single file called `index.html`."

A block of code is set as follows:

```
apiVersion: apps/v1beta1
kind: Deployment
metadata:
  name: cli-hello-world
  labels:
    app: nginx
```

When we wish to draw your attention to a particular part of a code block, the relevant lines or items are set in bold:

```
apiVersion: apps/v1beta1
kind: Deployment
metadata:
  name: cli-hello-world
  labels:
    app: nginx
```

Any command-line input or output is written as follows:

```
$ brew cask install minikube
```

Bold: Indicates a new term, an important word, or words that you see onscreen. For example, words in menus or dialog boxes appear in the text like this. Here is an example: "At the bottom of the page, you will have a button that allows you to create an **Access Token** and **Access Token Secret** for your account."

Warnings or important notes appear like this.

Tips and tricks appear like this.

Get in touch

Feedback from our readers is always welcome.

General feedback: Email `feedback@packtpub.com` and mention the book title in the subject of your message. If you have questions about any aspect of this book, please email us at `questions@packtpub.com`.

Errata: Although we have taken every care to ensure the accuracy of our content, mistakes do happen. If you have found a mistake in this book, we would be grateful if you would report this to us. Please visit `www.packtpub.com/submit-errata`, selecting your book, clicking on the Errata Submission Form link, and entering the details.

Piracy: If you come across any illegal copies of our works in any form on the Internet, we would be grateful if you would provide us with the location address or website name. Please contact us at `copyright@packtpub.com` with a link to the material.

If you are interested in becoming an author: If there is a topic that you have expertise in and you are interested in either writing or contributing to a book, please visit `authors.packtpub.com`.

Reviews

Please leave a review. Once you have read and used this book, why not leave a review on the site that you purchased it from? Potential readers can then see and use your unbiased opinion to make purchase decisions, we at Packt can understand what you think about our products, and our authors can see your feedback on their book. Thank you!

For more information about Packt, please visit `packtpub.com`.

1
The Serverless Landscape

Welcome to the first chapter of *Kubernetes for Serverless Applications*. In this chapter, we are going to be looking at and discussing the following:

- What do we mean by serverless and Functions as a Service?
- What services are out there?
- An example of Lambda by Amazon Web Services
- An example of Azure Functions
- Using the serverless toolkit
- What problems can we solve using serverless and Functions as a Service?

I think it is important we start by addressing the elephant in the room, and that is the term serverless.

Serverless and Functions as a Service

When you say serverless to someone, the first conclusion they jump to is that you are running your code without any servers.

This can be quite a valid conclusion if you are using one of the public cloud services we will be discussing later in this chapter. However, when it comes to running in your own environment, you can't avoid having to run on a server of some sort.

Before we discuss what we mean by serverless and Functions as a Service, we should discuss how we got here. As people who work with me will no doubt tell you, I like to use the *pets versus cattle* analogy a lot as this is quite an easy way to explain the differences in modern cloud infrastructures versus a more traditional approach.

Pets, cattle, chickens, insects, and snowflakes

I first came across the *pets versus cattle* analogy back in 2012 from a slide deck published by Randy Bias. The slide deck was used during a talk Randy Bias gave at the cloudscaling conference on architectures for open and scalable clouds. Towards the end of the talk, he introduced the concept of pets versus cattle, which Randy attributes to Bill Baker who at the time was an engineer at Microsoft.

The slide deck primarily talks about scaling out and not up; let's go into this in a little more detail and discuss some of the additions that have been made since the presentation was first given five years ago.

Randy's slide deck can be found at `https://www.slideshare.net/randybias/architectures-for-open-and-scalable-clouds`.

Pets

Pets are typically what we, as system administrators, spend our time looking after. They are traditional bare metal servers or virtual machines:

- We name each server as you would a pet. For example, `app-server01.domain.com` and `database-server01.domain.com`.
- When our pets are ill, you will take them to the vets. This is much like you, as a system administrator, would reboot a server, check logs, and replace the faulty components of a server to ensure that it is running healthily.
- You pay close attention to your pets for years, much like a server. You monitor for issues, patch them, back them up, and ensure they are fully documented.

There is nothing much wrong with running pets. However, you will find that the majority of your time is spent caring for them—this may be alright if you have a few dozen servers, but it does start to become unmanageable if you have a few hundred servers.

Cattle

Cattle are more representative of the instance types you should be running in public clouds such as **Amazon Web Services** (**AWS**) or Microsoft Azure, where you have auto scaling enabled.

- You have so many cattle in your herd you don't name them; instead they are given numbers and tagged so you can track them. In your instance cluster, you can also have too many to name so, like cattle, you give them numbers and tag them. For example, an instance could be called `ip123067099123.domain.com` and tagged as `app-server`.
- When a member of your herd gets sick, you shoot it, and if your herd requires it you replace it. In much the same way, if an instance in your cluster starts to have issues it is automatically terminated and replaced with a replica.
- You do not expect the cattle in your herd to live as long as a pet typically would, likewise you do not expect your instances to have an uptime measured in years.
- Your herd lives in a field and you watch it from afar, much like you don't monitor individual instances within your cluster; instead, you monitor the overall health of your cluster. If your cluster requires additional resources, you launch more instances and when you no longer require a resource, the instances are automatically terminated, returning you to your desired state.

Chickens

In 2015, Bernard Golden added to the pets versus cattle analogy by introducing chickens to the mix in a blog post titled *Cloud Computing: Pets, Cattle* and *Chickens?* Bernard suggested that chickens were a good term for describing containers alongside pets and cattle:

- Chickens are more efficient than cattle; you can fit a lot more of them into the same space your herd would use. In the same way, you can fit a lot more containers into your cluster as you can launch multiple containers per instance.
- Each chicken requires fewer resources than a member of your herd when it comes to feeding. Likewise, containers are less resource-intensive than instances, they take seconds to launch, and can be configured to consume less CPU and RAM.
- Chickens have a much lower life expectancy than members of your herd. While cluster instances can have an uptime of a few hours to a few days, it is more than possible that a container will have a lifespan of minutes.

Unfortunately, Bernard's original blog post is no longer available. However, The New Stack have republished a version of it. You can find the republished version at `https://thenewstack.io/pets-and-cattle-symbolize-servers-so-what-does-that-make-containers-chickens/`.

Insects

Keeping in line with the animal theme, Eric Johnson wrote a blog post for RackSpace which introduced insects. This term was introduced to describe serverless and Functions as a Service.

Insects have a much lower life expectancy than chickens; in fact, some insects only have a lifespan of a few hours. This fits in with serverless and Functions as a Service as these have a lifespan of seconds.

Later in this chapter, we will be looking at public cloud services from AWS and Microsoft Azure which are billed in milliseconds, rather than hours or minutes.

Eric's blog post can be found at `https://blog.rackspace.com/pets-cattle-and-nowinsects/`.

Snowflakes

Around the time Randy Bias gave his talk which mentioned pets versus cattle, Martin Fowler wrote a blog post titled *SnowflakeServer*. The post described every system administrator's worst nightmare:

- Every snowflake is unique and impossible to reproduce. Just like that one server in the office that was built and not documented by that one guy who left several years ago.
- Snowflakes are delicate. Again, just like that one server—you dread it when you have to log in to it to diagnose a problem and you would never dream of rebooting it as it may never come back up.

Martin's post is available at `https://martinfowler.com/bliki/SnowflakeServer.html`.

Summing up

Once I have explained pets, cattle, chickens, insects, and snowflakes, I sum up by saying:

> *"Organizations who have* ***pets*** *are slowly moving their infrastructure to be more like* ***cattle****. Those who are already running their infrastructure as* ***cattle*** *are moving towards* ***chickens*** *to get the most out of their resources. Those running* ***chickens*** *are going to be looking at how much work is involved in moving their application to run as* ***insects*** *by completely decoupling their application into individually executable components."*

Then finally I say this:

> *"No one wants to or should be running* ***snowflakes****."*

In this book, we will be discussing insects, and I will assume that you know a little about the services and concepts that cover cattle and chickens.

Serverless and insects

As already mentioned, using the word serverless gives the impression that servers will not be needed. Serverless is a term used to describe an execution model.

When executing this model you, as the end user, do not need to worry about which server your code is executed on as all of the decisions on placement, server management, and capacity are abstracted away from you—it does not mean that you literally do not need any servers.

Now there are some public cloud offerings which abstract so much of the management of servers away from the end user that it is possible to write an application which does not rely on any user-deployed services and that the cloud provider will manage the compute resources needed to execute your code.

Typically these services, which we will look at in the next section, are billed for the resources used to execute your code in per second increments.

So how does that explanation fits in with the insect analogy?

Let's say I have a website that allows users to upload photos. As soon as the photos are uploaded they are cropped, creating several different sizes which will be used to display as thumbnails and mobile-optimized versions on the site.

In the pets and cattle world, this would be handled by a server which is powered on 24/7 waiting for users to upload images. Now this server probably is not just performing this one function; however, there is a risk that if several users all decide to upload a dozen photos each, then this will cause load issues on the server where this function is being executed.

We could take the chickens approach, which has several containers running across several hosts to distribute the load. However, these containers would more than likely be running 24/7 as well; they will be watching for uploads to process. This approach could allow us to horizontally scale the number of containers out to deal with an influx of requests.

Using the insects approach, we would not have any services running at all. Instead, the function should be triggered by the upload process. Once triggered, the function will run, save the processed images, and then terminate. As the developer, you should not have to care how the service was called or where the service was executed, so long as you have your processed images at the end of it.

Public cloud offerings

Before we delve into the core subject of this book and start working with Kubernetes, we should have a look at the alternatives; after all, the services we are going to be covering in upcoming chapters are nearly all loosely based off these services.

The three main public cloud providers all provide a serverless service:

- AWS Lambda from AWS (`https://aws.amazon.com/lambda/`)
- Azure Functions by Microsoft (`https://azure.microsoft.com/en-gb/services/functions/`)
- Cloud Functions from Google (`https://cloud.google.com/functions/`)

Each of these services has the support of several different code frameworks. For the purposes of this book, we will not be looking at the code frameworks in too much detail as using these is a design decision which has to based on your code.

We are going to be looking at two of these services, Lambda from AWS and Functions by Microsoft Azure.

AWS Lambda

The first service we are going to look at is AWS Lambda by AWS. The tagline for the service is quite a simple one:

> *"Run code without thinking about servers."*

Now those of you who have used AWS before might be thinking the tagline makes it sound a lot like the AWS Elastic Beanstalk service. This service inspects your code base and then deploys it in a highly scalable and redundant configuration. Typically, this is the first step for most people in moving from pets to cattle as it abstracts away the configuration of the AWS services which provide the scalability and high availability.

Before we work through launching a hello world example, which we will be doing for all of the services, we will need an AWS account and its command-line tools installed.

Prerequisites

First of all, you need an AWS account. If you don't have an account, you can sign up for an account at `https://aws.amazon.com/`:

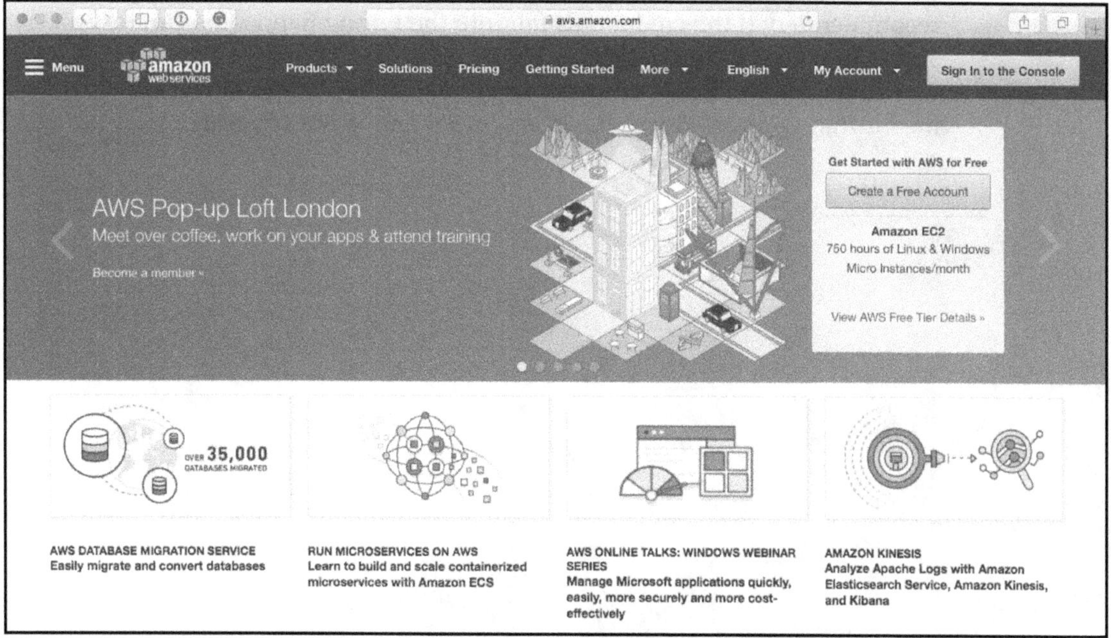

While clicking on the **Create a Free Account** and then following the onscreen instructions will give you 12 months' free access to several services, you will still need to provide credit or debit card details and it is possible that you could incur costs.

For more information on the AWS free tier, please see `https://aws.amazon.com/free/`. This page lets you know which instance sizes and services are covered by the 12 months of free service, as well as letting you know about non-expiring offers on other services, which include AWS Lambda.

Once you have your AWS account, you should create a user using the AWS **Identity and Access Management** (**IAM**) service. This user can have administrator privileges and you should use that user to access both the AWS Console and the API.

For more details on creating an IAM user, see the following pages:

- **Getting started with IAM**: `http://docs.aws.amazon.com/IAM/latest/UserGuide/getting-started.html`
- **IAM best practices**: `http://docs.aws.amazon.com/IAM/latest/UserGuide/best-practices.html`

Using your AWS root account to launch services and access the API is not recommended; if the credentials fall into the wrong hands you can lose all access to your account. Using an IAM rather than your root account, which you should also lock down using multi-factor authentication, means that you will always have access to your AWS account.

The final prerequisite is that you need access to the AWS command-line client, where I will be using macOS, but the client is also available for Linux and Windows. For information on how to install and configure the AWS command-line client, please see:

- **Installing the AWS CLI**: `http://docs.aws.amazon.com/cli/latest/userguide/installing.html`
- **Configuring the AWS CLI**: `http://docs.aws.amazon.com/cli/latest/userguide/cli-chap-getting-started.html`

When configuring the AWS CLI, make sure you configure the default region as the one you will be accessing in the AWS web console, as there is nothing more confusing than running a command using the CLI and then not seeing the results in the web console.

Once installed, you can test that you can access AWS Lambda from the command-line client by running:

```
$ aws lambda list-functions
```

This should return an empty list of functions like the one shown in the following screenshot:

```
1. russ (bash)
russ in ~
⚡ aws lambda list-functions
{
    "Functions": []
}
russ in ~
⚡
```

Now that we have an account set up, created, and logged in using a non-root user, and we have the AWS CLI installed and configured, we can look at launching our first serverless function.

Creating a Lambda function

In the AWS Console, click on the **Services** menu in the top-left of the screen and select **Lambda** by either using the filter box or clicking on the service in the list. When you first go to the Lambda service page within the AWS Console, you will be presented with a welcome page:

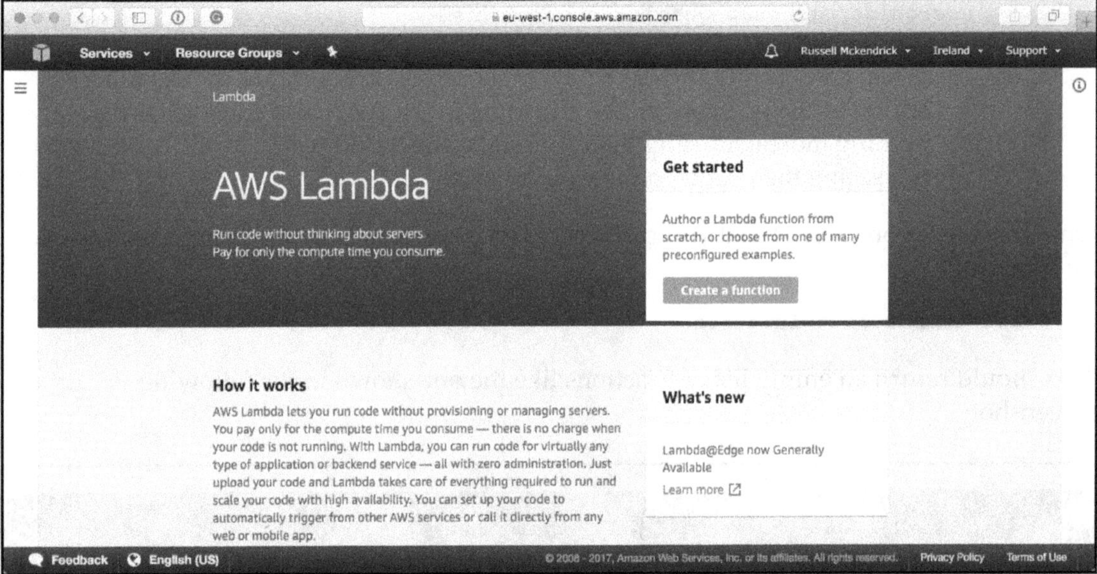

Clicking on the **Create a function** button will take us straight to the process of launching our first serverless function.

There are four steps to creating a function; the first thing we need to do is select a blueprint:

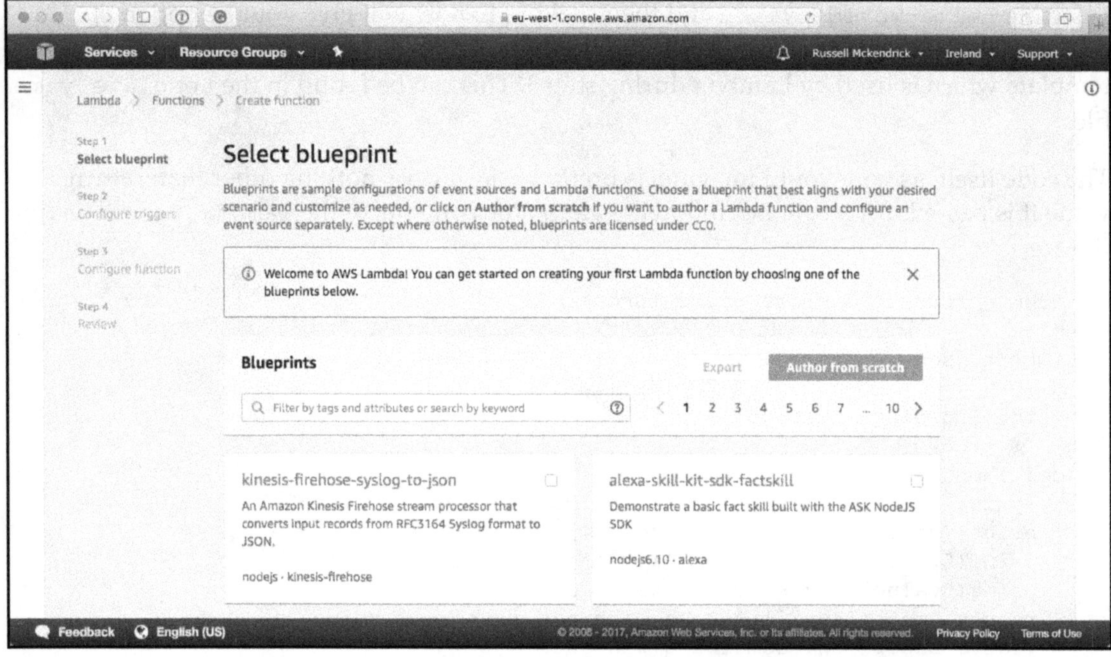

For the basic hello world function, we are going to be using a pre-built template called `hello-world-python`; enter this into the filter and you should be presented with two results, one is for Python 2.7 and the second uses Python 3.6:

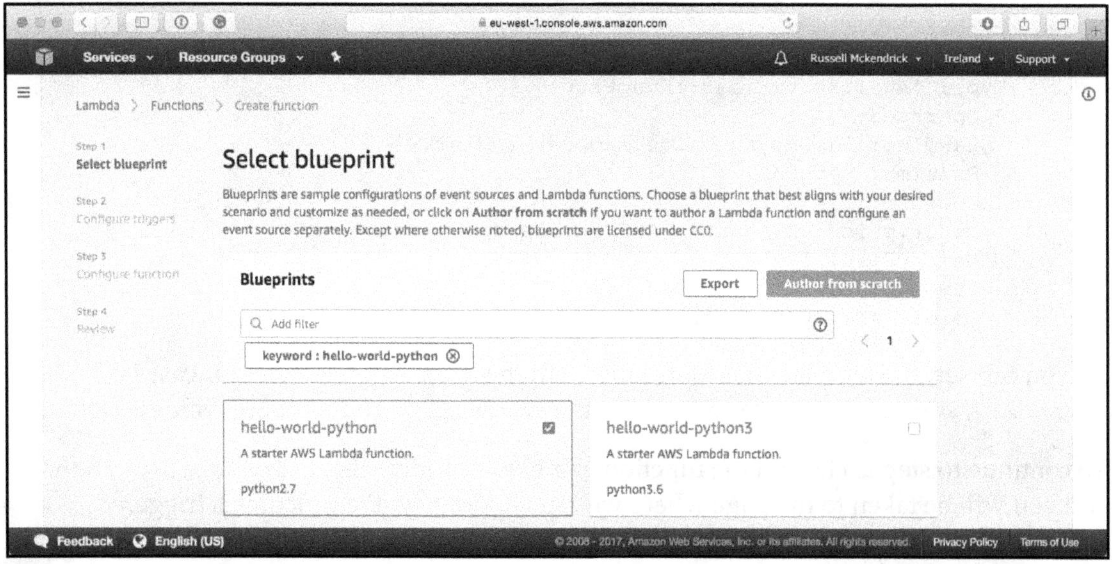

Selecting `hello-world-python` and then clicking **Export** will give you the option of downloading the code used in the function in the `lambda_function.py` file and the template which is used by Lambda during step 3. This can be found in the `template.yaml` file.

The code itself, as you would imagine, is pretty basic. It does nothing other than return a value it is passed. If you are not following along, the contents of the `lambda_function.py` file are:

```
from __future__ import print_function

import json

print('Loading function')

def lambda_handler(event, context):
  #print("Received event: " + json.dumps(event, indent=2))
  print("value1 = " + event['key1'])
  print("value2 = " + event['key2'])
  print("value3 = " + event['key3'])
  return event['key1'] # Echo back the first key value
  #raise Exception('Something went wrong')
```

The `template.yaml` file contains the following:

```
AWSTemplateFormatVersion: '2010-09-09'
Transform: 'AWS::Serverless-2016-10-31'
Description: A starter AWS Lambda function.
Resources:
  helloworldpython:
    Type: 'AWS::Serverless::Function'
    Properties:
      Handler: lambda_function.lambda_handler
      Runtime: python2.7
      CodeUri: .
      Description: A starter AWS Lambda function.
      MemorySize: 128
      Timeout: 3
      Role: !<tag:yaml.org,2002:js/undefined> ''
```

As you can see, the template file configures both the `Runtime`, which in our case is `python2.7`, and some sensible settings for the `MemorySize` and `Timeout` values.

To continue to step 2, click on the function name, which for us is `hello-world-python`, and you will be taken to the page where we can choose how the function is triggered:

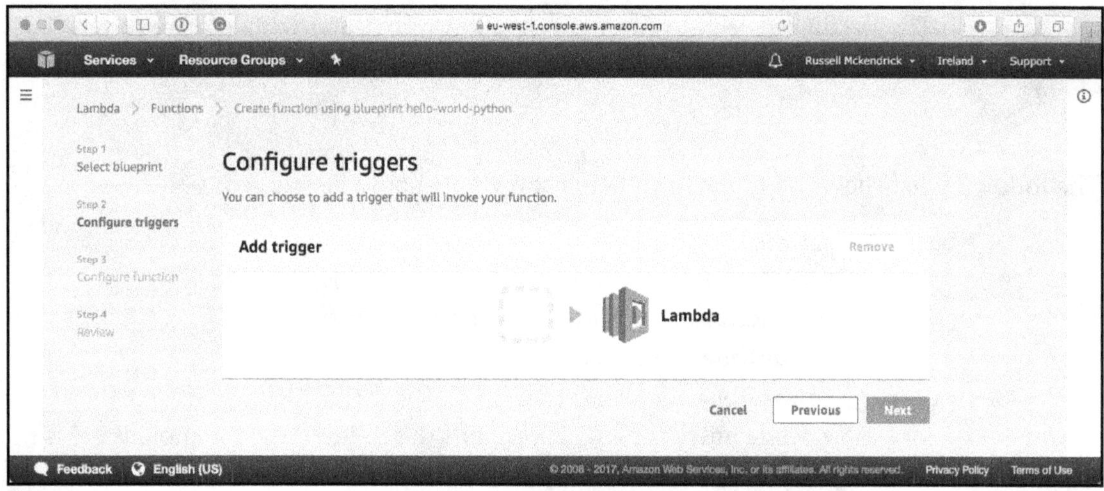

We are not going to be using a trigger just yet and we will look at these in a little more detail in the next function we launch; so for now, click on **Next**.

Step 3 is where we configure our function. There is quite a bit of information to enter here, but luckily a lot of the detail we need to enter has been pre-populated from the template we looked at earlier, as you can see from the following screenshot:

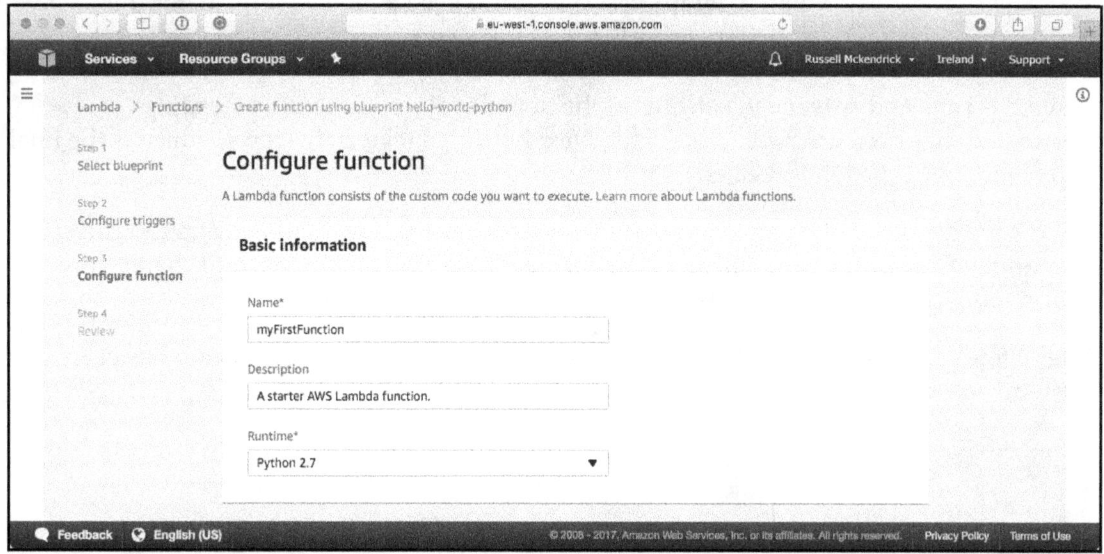

The details we need to enter are as follows: anything with a * is required and the *information* in italics was pre-populated and can be left as-is.

The following list shows all of the form fields and what should be entered:

- **Basic information**:
  - **Name***: `myFirstFunction`
  - **Description**: *A starter AWS Lambda function*
  - **Runtime**: *Python 2.7*
- **Lambda function code**:
  - **Code entry type**: This contains the code for the function, there is no need to edit this
  - **Enable encryption helpers**: Leave unticked
  - **Environment variables**: Leave empty
- **Lambda function handler and role**:
  - **Handler***: *lambda_function.lambda_handler*
  - **Role***: Leave *Create new role from template(s)* selected
  - **Role name***: *myFirstFunctionRole*
  - **Policy templates**: We do not need a policy template for this function, leave blank

Leave the **Tags** and **Advanced settings** at the default values. Once the preceding information has been entered, click on the **Next** button to take us to step 4, which is the final step before our function is created.

Review the details on the page. If you are happy that everything has been entered correctly, click on the **Create function** button at the bottom of the page; if you need to change any information, click on the **Previous** button.

After a few seconds, you will receive a message confirming that your function has been created:

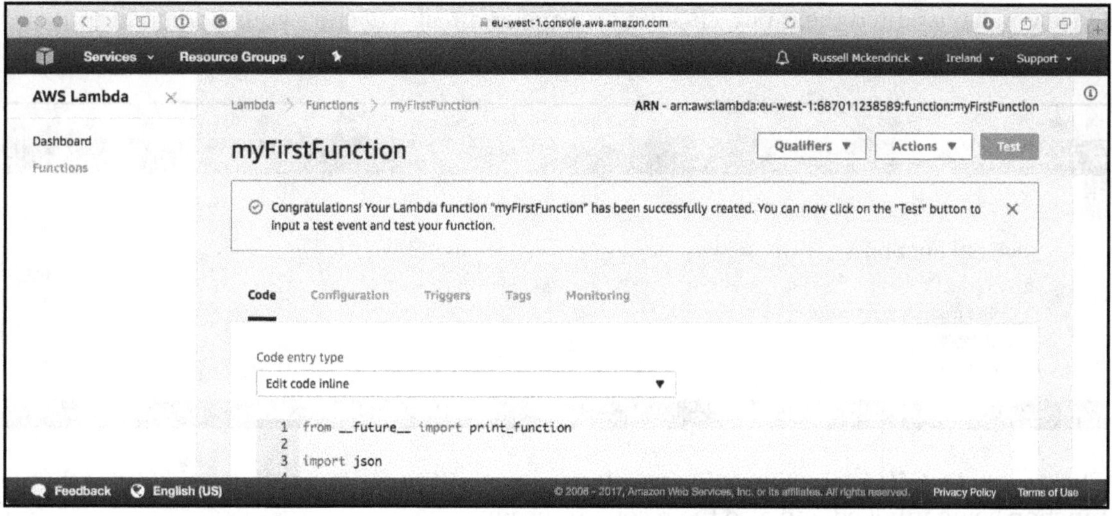

In the preceding screenshot, there is a **Test** button. Clicking this will allow you to invoke your function. Here you will be able to customize the values posted to the function. As you can see from the following screenshot, I have changed the values for `key1` and `key2`:

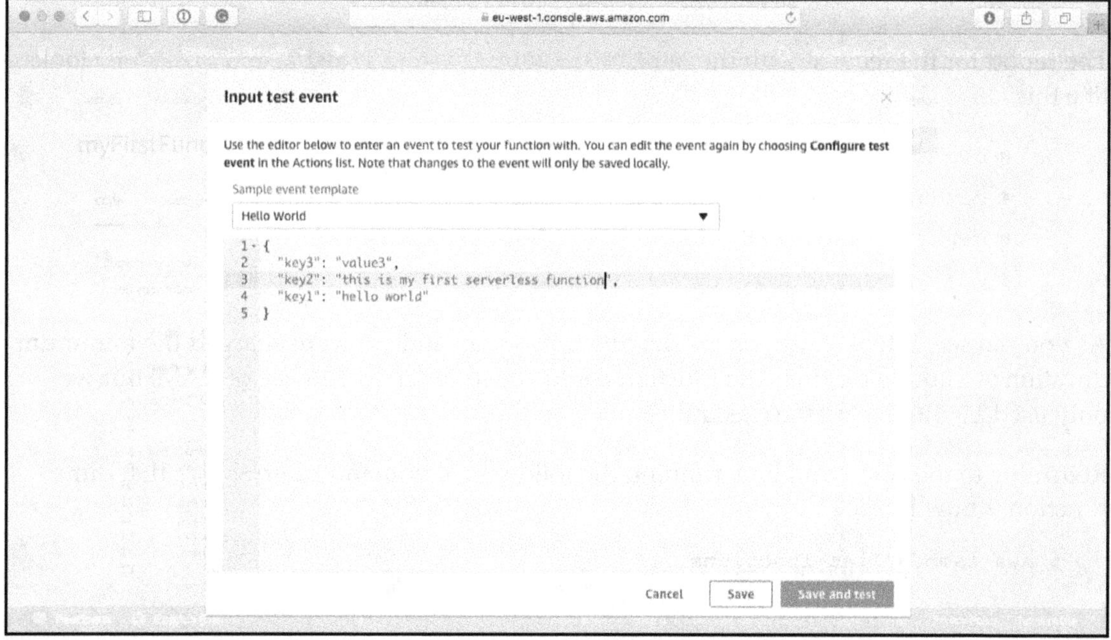

Once you have edited the input, clicking on **Save and test** will store your updated input and then invoke the function:

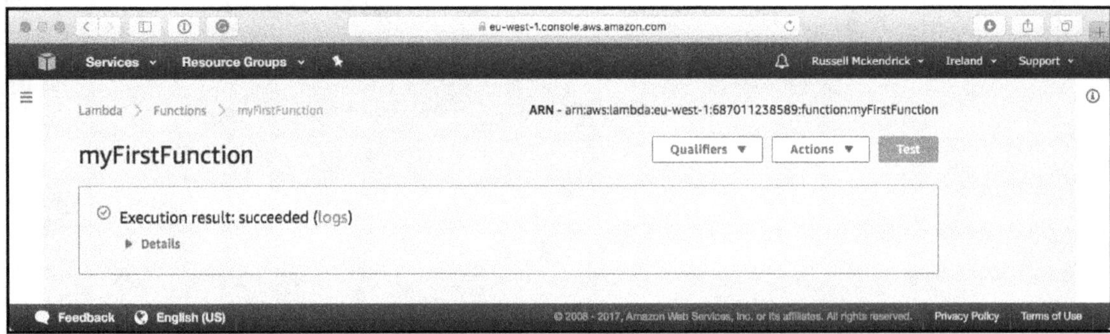

Clicking on **Details** in the **Execution result** message will show you both the results of the function being invoked and also the resources used:

```
START RequestId: 36b2103a-90bc-11e7-a32a-171ef5562e33 Version: $LATEST
value1 = hello world
value2 = this is my first serverless function
value3 = value3
END RequestId: 36b2103a-90bc-11e7-a32a-171ef5562e33
```

The report for the request with the `36b2103a-90bc-11e7-a32a-171ef5562e33` ID looks like this:

- `Duration: 0.26 ms`
- `Billed Duration: 100 ms`
- `Memory Size: 128 MB`
- `Max Memory Used: 19 MB`

As you can see, it took `0.26 ms` for the function to run and we were charged the minimum duration of `100 ms` for this. The function could consume up to `128 MB` of RAM, but we only used `19 MB` during the execution.

Returning to the command line, running the following command again shows that our function is now listed:

```
$ aws lambda list-functions
```

The output of the preceding command is as follows:

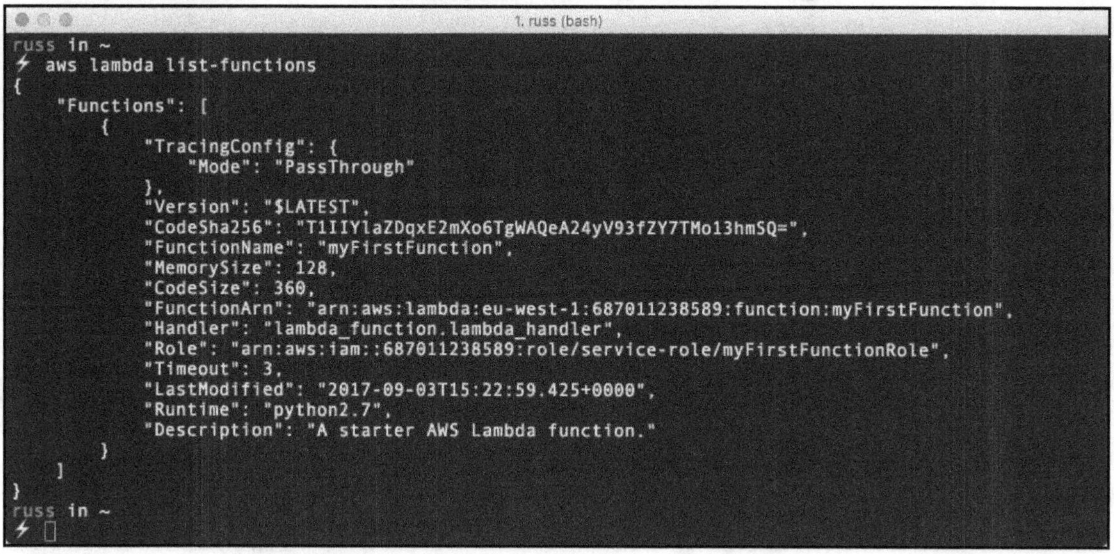

```
1. russ (bash)
russ in ~
⚡ aws lambda list-functions
{
    "Functions": [
        {
            "TracingConfig": {
                "Mode": "PassThrough"
            },
            "Version": "$LATEST",
            "CodeSha256": "T1IIYlaZDqxE2mXo6TgWAQeA24yV93fZY7TMo13hmSQ=",
            "FunctionName": "myFirstFunction",
            "MemorySize": 128,
            "CodeSize": 360,
            "FunctionArn": "arn:aws:lambda:eu-west-1:687011238589:function:myFirstFunction",
            "Handler": "lambda_function.lambda_handler",
            "Role": "arn:aws:iam::687011238589:role/service-role/myFirstFunctionRole",
            "Timeout": 3,
            "LastModified": "2017-09-03T15:22:59.425+0000",
            "Runtime": "python2.7",
            "Description": "A starter AWS Lambda function."
        }
    ]
}
russ in ~
⚡
```

We can also invoke our function from the command line by running the following command:

```
$ aws lambda invoke \
    --invocation-type RequestResponse \
    --function-name myFirstFunction \
    --log-type Tail \
    --payload '{"key1":"hello", "key2":"world", "key3":"again"}' \
    outputfile.txt
```

As you can see from the preceding command, the `aws lambda invoke` command requires several flags:

- `--invocation-type`: There are three types of invocation:
    - `RequestResponse`: This is the default option; it sends the request, which in our case is defined in the `--payload` section of the command. Once the request has been made, the client waits for a response.

    - `Event`: This sends the request and triggers an event. The client does not wait for a response and instead you receive an event ID back.
    - `DryRun`: This calls the function, but never actually executes it—this is useful when testing that the details used to invoke the function actually have the correct permissions.
- `--function-name`: This is the name of the function we want to invoke.
- `--log-type`: There is currently a single option here, `Tail`. This returns the result of the `--payload`, which is the data we want to send the function; typically this will be JSON.
- `outputfile.txt`: The final part of the command defines where we want to store the output of the command; in our case it is a file called `outputfile.txt` which is being stored in the current working directory.

When invoking the command from the command line, you should get something like the following result:

```
1. russ (bash)
russ in ~
⚡ aws lambda invoke \
→     --invocation-type RequestResponse \
→     --function-name myFirstFunction \
→     --log-type Tail \
→     --payload '{"key1":"hello", "key2":"world", "key3":"again"}' \
→     outputfile.txt
{
    "LogResult": "U1RBU1QgUmVxdWVzdElkOiA2OTFlZDFjYi05MGJmLTExZTctOTdhNC1iYjhjODJjODg3NTUgVmVyc2lvbjogJExBVEVTVAp2YWx1ZTEgPSBoZWxsbwp2YWx1ZTIgPSB3b3JsZAp2YWx1ZTMgPSBhZ2FpbgpFTkQgUmVxdWVzdElkOiA2OTFlZDFjYi05MGJmLTExZTctOTdhNC1iYjhjODJjODg3NTUKUkVQT1JUIFJlcXVlc3RJZDogNjkxZWQxY2ItOTBiZi0xMWU3LTk3YTQtYmI4YzgyYzg4NzU1CUR1cmF0aW9uOiAzLjIzIG1zCUJpbGxlZCBEdXJhdGlvbjogMTAwIG1zIAlNZW1vcnkgU2l6ZTogMTI4IE1CCU1heCBNZW1vcnkgVXNlZDogMTkgTUIJCg==",
    "StatusCode": 200
}
russ in ~
⚡
```

Returning to the AWS Console and remaining on the `myFirstFunction` page, click on **Monitoring** and you will be presented with some basic statistics about your function:

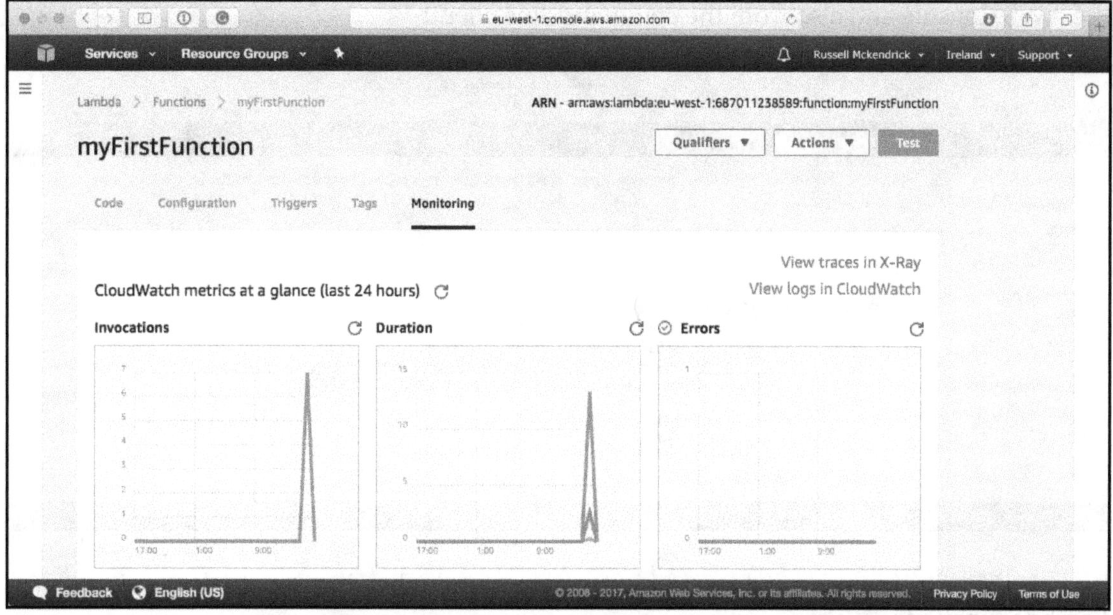

As you can see from the preceding graphs, there are details on how many times your function has been invoked, how long it takes, and also if there are any errors.

Clicking on **View logs in CloudWatch** will open a new tab which lists the log streams for `myFirstFunction`. Clicking on the name of the log stream will then take you to a page which gives you the results for each time the function has been invoked both as testing in the AWS Console and also from the command-line client:

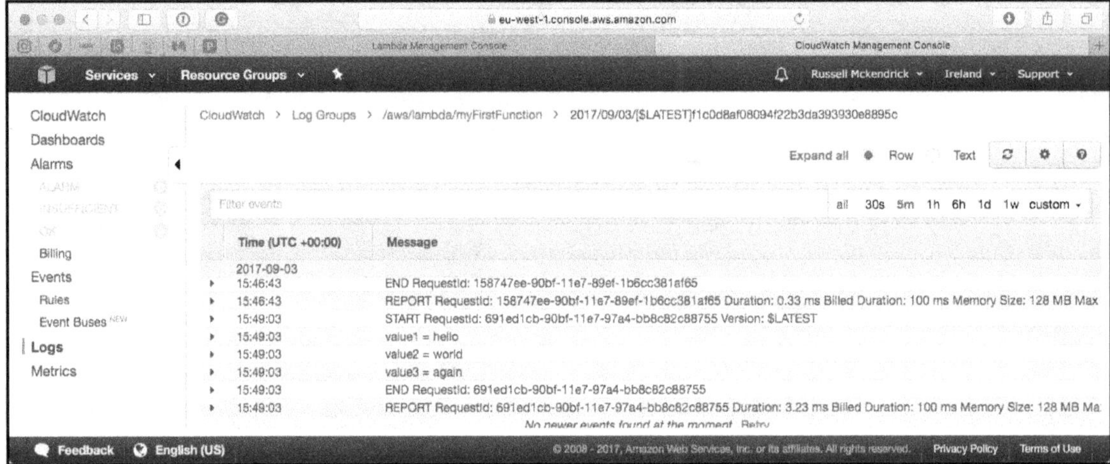

Both the **Monitoring** page and logs are extremely useful when it comes to debugging your Lambda functions.

Microsoft Azure Functions

Next up, we are going to take a look at Microsoft's serverless offering, Azure Functions. Microsoft describes this service as:

> *"Azure Functions is a solution for easily running small pieces of code, or "functions," in the cloud. You can write just the code you need for the problem at hand, without worrying about a whole application or the infrastructure to run it."*

Like Lambda, there are several ways your Function can be invoked. In this quick walkthrough, we will be deploying a Function which is called using an HTTP request.

Prerequisites

You will need an Azure account to follow along with this example. If you don't have an account, you can sign up for a free account at `https://azure.microsoft.com/`:

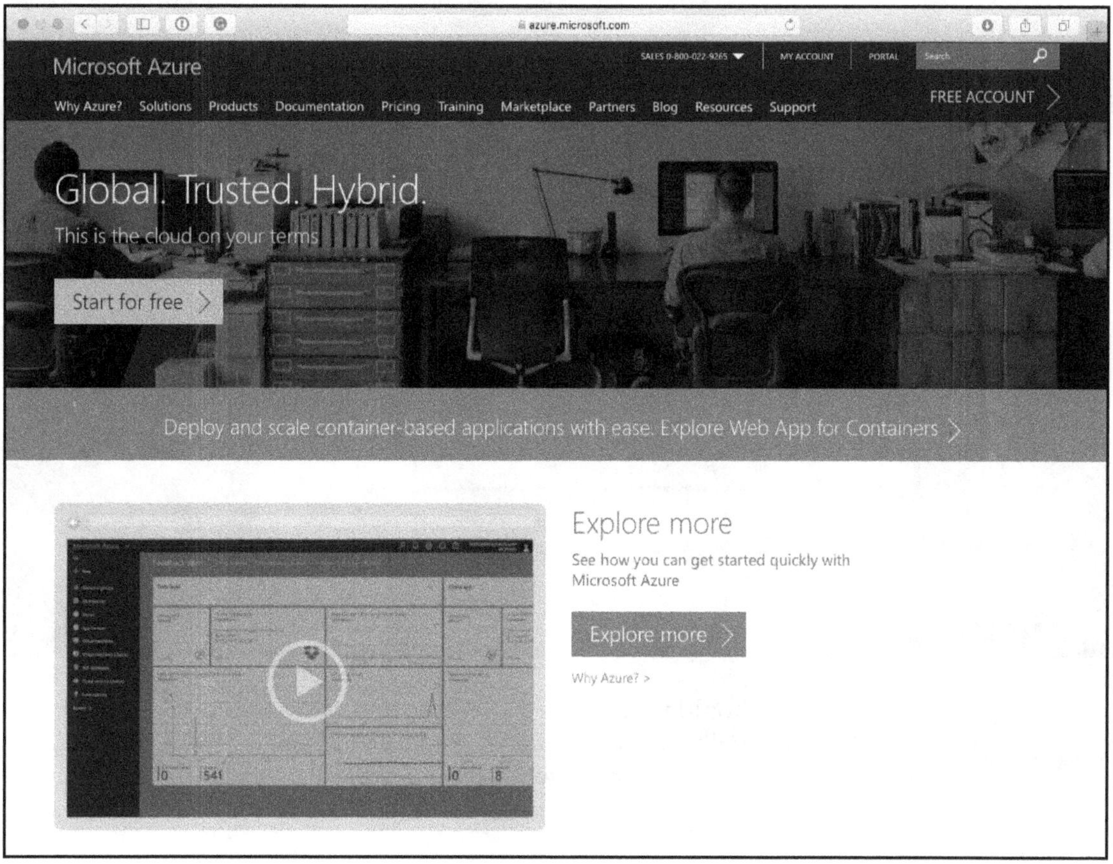

At the time of writing, Microsoft is crediting all new accounts with $200 to spend on Azure services, and like AWS, several services have a free tier.

While you are credited with $200, you will still need to provide credit card details for verification purposes. For more information on the services and limits in the free tier, please see `https://azure.microsoft.com/en-gb/free/pricing-offers/`.

Creating a Function app

All of the work we are going to be doing to create our first Function app will be using the web-based control panel. Once you have your account, you should see something like the following page:

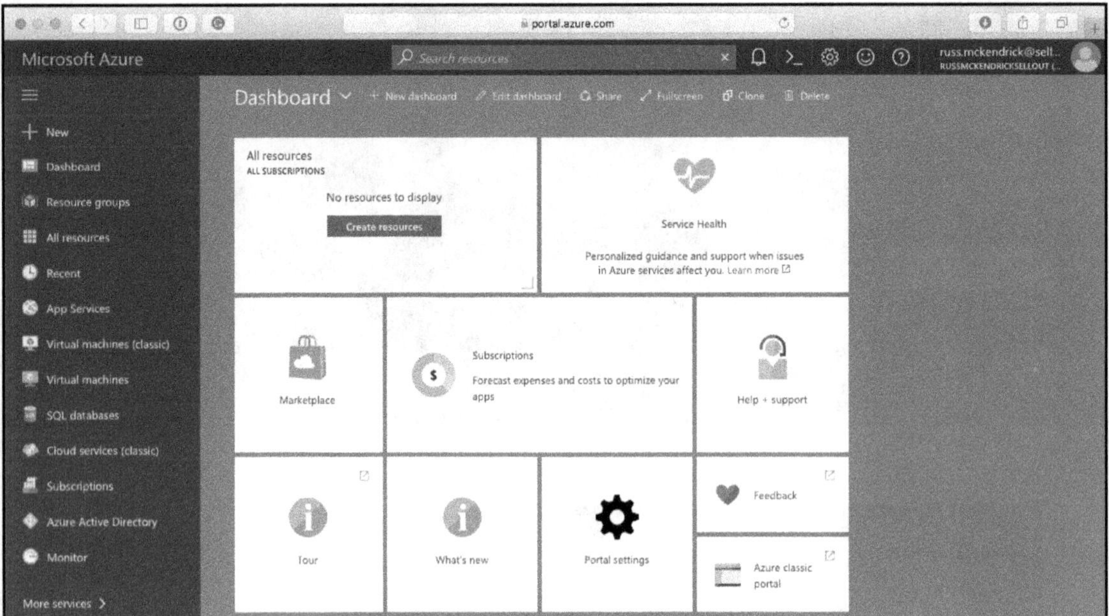

One thing you should note about the Microsoft Azure control panel is that it scrolls horizontally, so if you lose where you are on a page you can typically find your way back to where you need to by scrolling to the right.

As you can see from the preceding screenshot, there are quite a few options. To make a start creating your first Function, you should click on **+ New** at the top of the left-hand side menu.

From here, you will be taken to the Azure **Marketplace**. Click on **Compute** and then in the list of featured marketplace items you should see **Function App**. Click on this and you will be taken to a form which asks for some basic information about the Function you want to create:

- **App name**: Call this what you want; in my case I called it `russ-test-version`. This has to be a unique name and, if your desired **App name** has already been used by another user, you will receive a message that your chosen **App name** is not available.
- **Subscription**: Choose the Azure subscription you would like your Function to be launched in.
- **Resource Group**: This will be automatically populated as you type in the **App name**.
- **Hosting Plan**: Leave this at the default option.
- **Location**: Choose the region which is closest to you.
- **Storage**: This will automatically be populated based on the **App name** you give, for our purpose leave **Create New** selected.
- **Pin to dashboard**: Tick this as it will allow us to quickly find our Function once it has been created.

If you are not following along in your account, my completed form looks like the following screenshot:

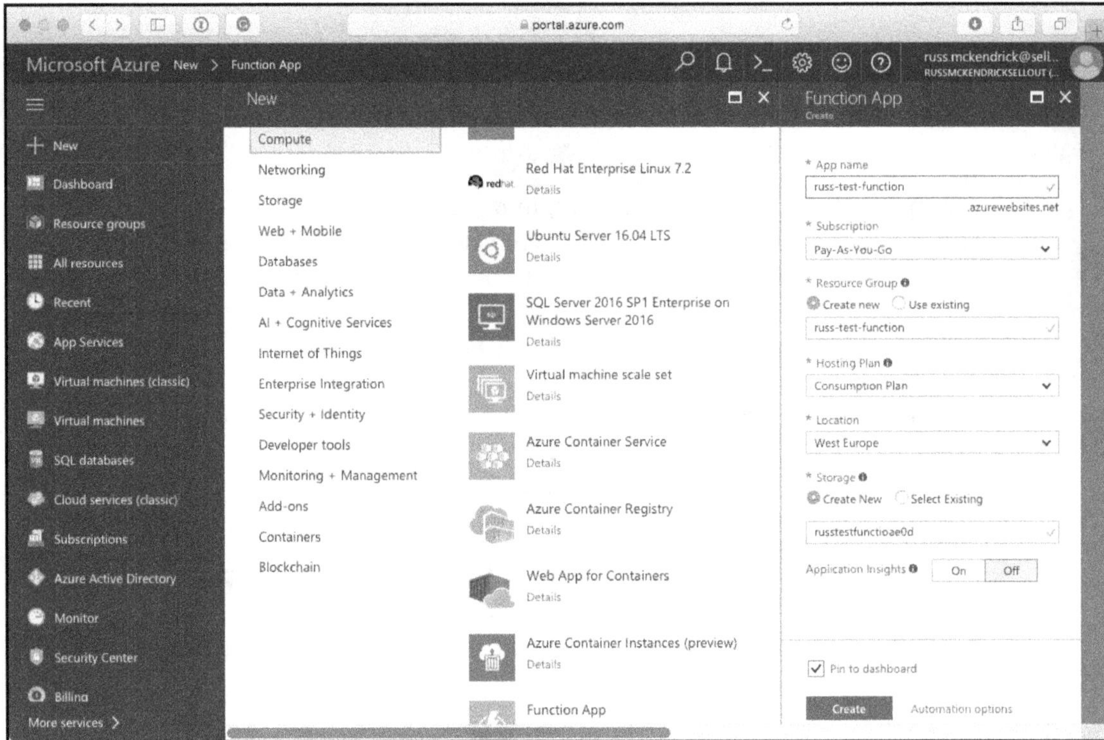

Once you have filled out the form, click on the **Create** button at the bottom of the form and you will be taken back to your **Dashboard**. You will receive a notification that your Function is being deployed as you can see from the box at the right-hand side in the following screenshot:

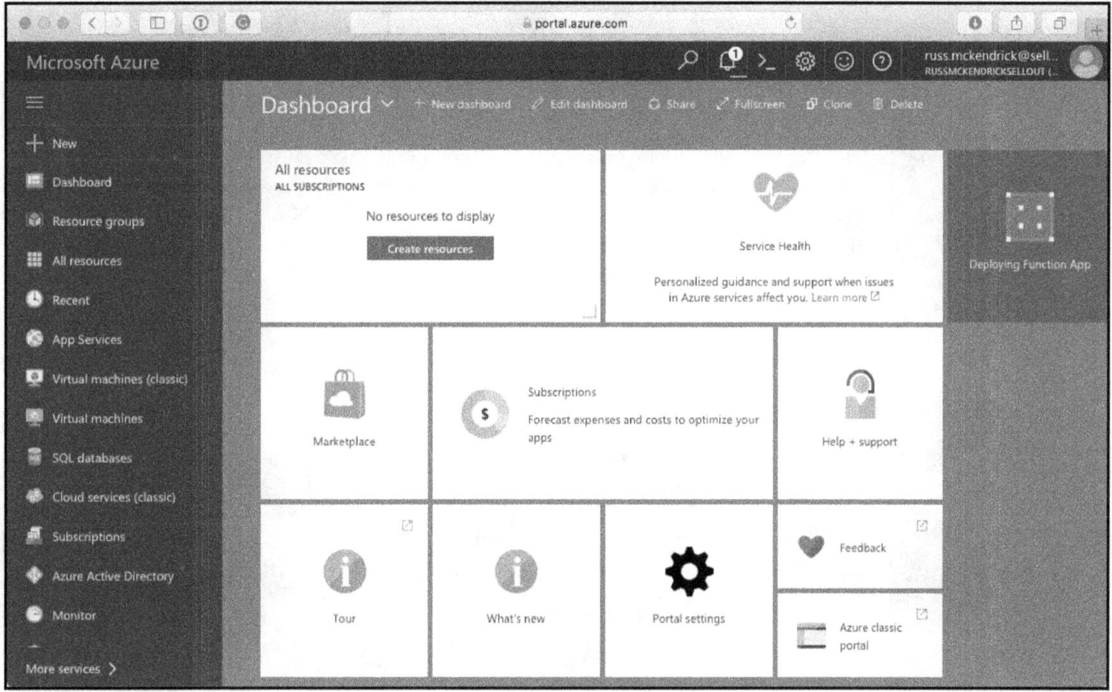

Clicking on the square in the **Dashboard** or on the notification in the top menu (the bell icon with the **1** on it) will take you to an **Overview** page; here you can view the status of the deployment:

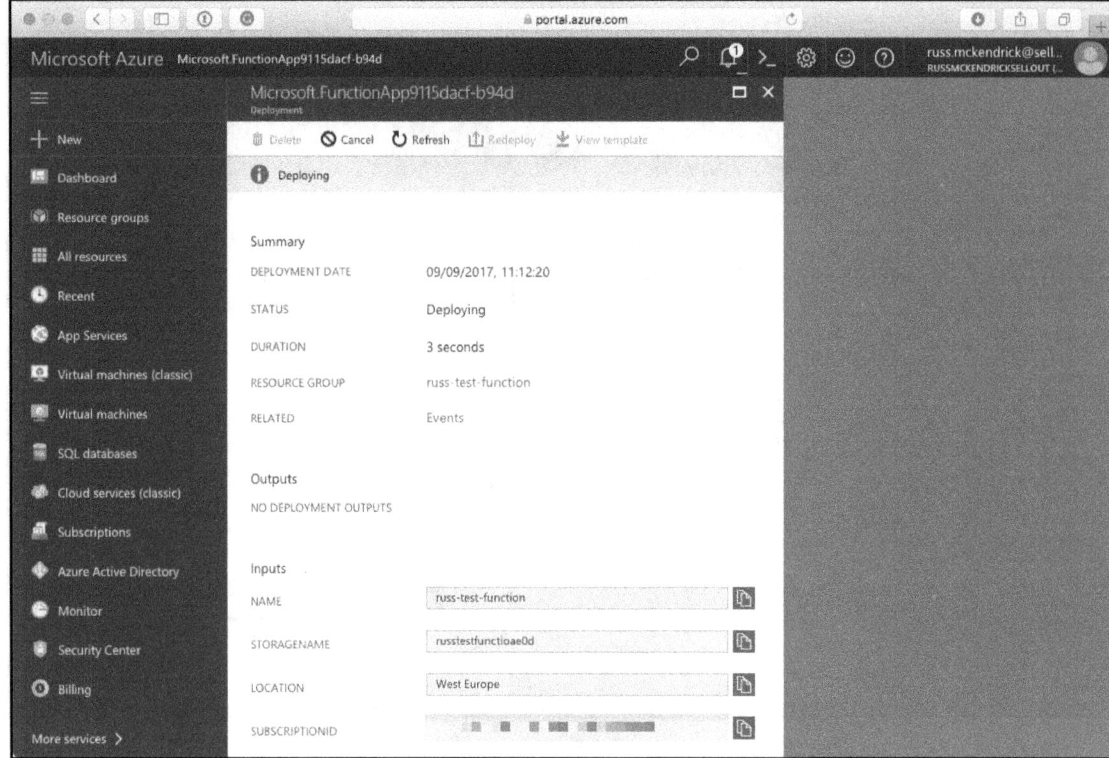

Once deployed, you should have an empty Function app ready for you to deploy your code into:

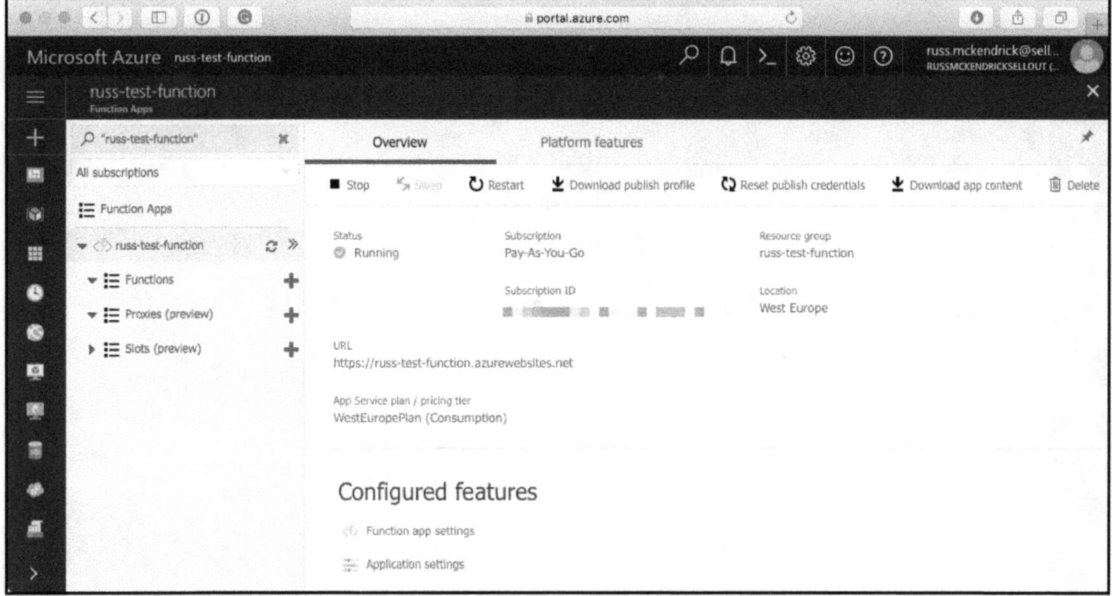

To deploy some test code, you need to click on the + icon next to **Functions** in the left-hand side menu; this will take you to the following page:

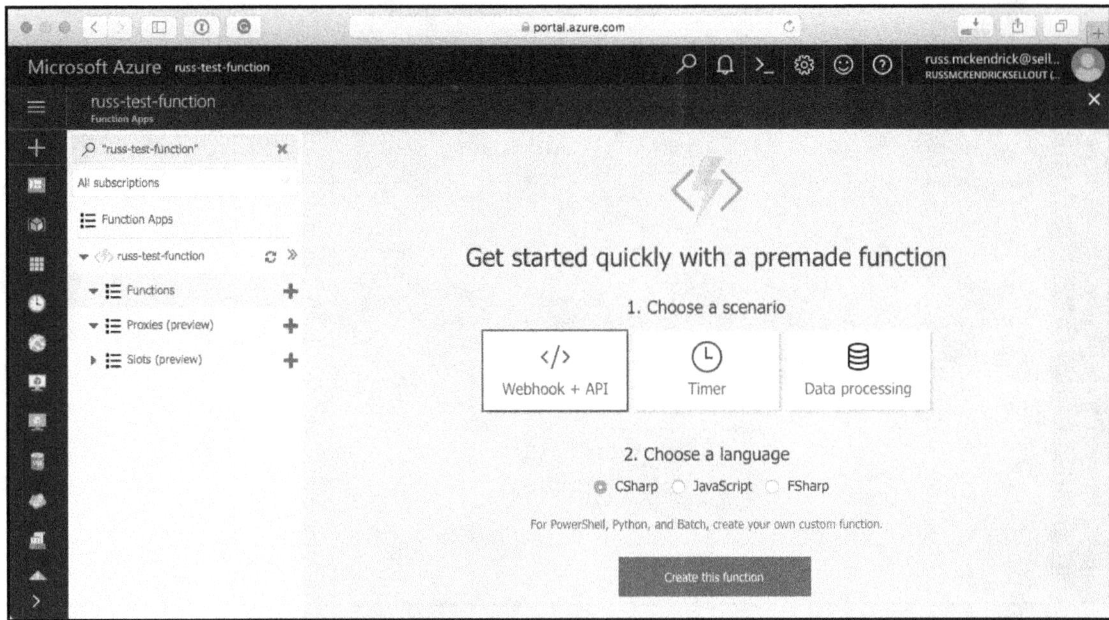

With **Webhook + API** and **CSharp** selected, click on **Create this function**; this will add the following code to your Function app:

```
using System.Net;

public static async Task<HttpResponseMessage> Run(HttpRequestMessage req,
TraceWriter log)
{
    log.Info("C# HTTP trigger function processed a request.");

    // parse query parameter
    string name = req.GetQueryNameValuePairs()
        .FirstOrDefault(q => string.Compare(q.Key, "name", true) == 0)
        .Value;

    // Get request body
    dynamic data = await req.Content.ReadAsAsync<object>();

    // Set name to query string or body data
    name = name ?? data?.name;
```

```
        return name == null
            ? req.CreateResponse(HttpStatusCode.BadRequest, "Please pass
            a name on the query string or in the request body")
            : req.CreateResponse(HttpStatusCode.OK, "Hello " + name);
    }
```

This code simply reads in the variable `name`, which it has passed via the URL and then prints back to the user as `Hello <name>`.

We can test this by clicking on the **Run** button at the top of the page. This will execute our Function as well as giving you the output and logs:

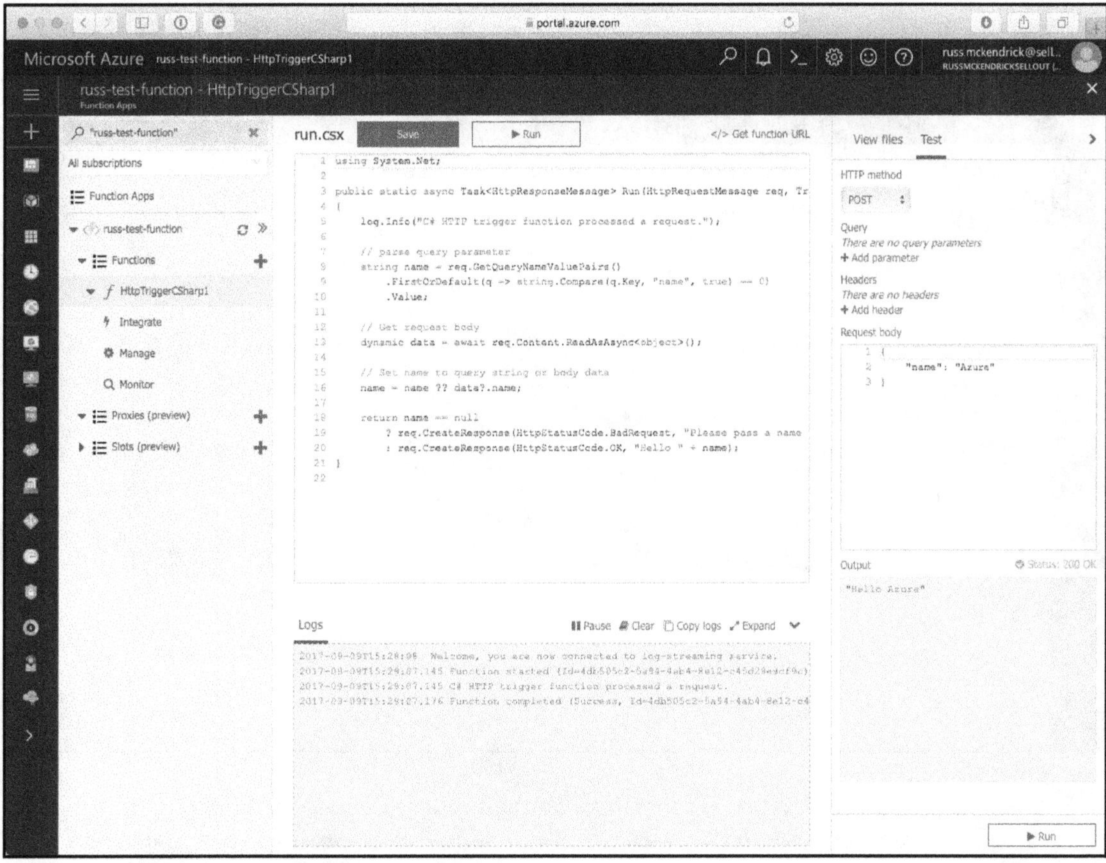

The logs for the test run look like this:

```
2017-09-09T15:28:08 Welcome, you are now connected to log-streaming
service.2017-09-09T15:29:07.145 Function started
(Id=4db505c2-5a94-4ab4-8e12-c45d29e9cf9c)2017-09-09T15:29:07.145 C# HTTP
trigger function processed a request.2017-09-09T15:29:07.176 Function
completed (Success, Id=4db505c2-5a94-4ab4-8e12-c45d29e9cf9c, Duration=28ms)
```

You can also view more information on your Function app by clicking on **Monitor** in the inner left-hand side menu. As you can see from the following screenshot, we have details on how many times your Function has been called, as well as the status of each execution and the duration for each invocation:

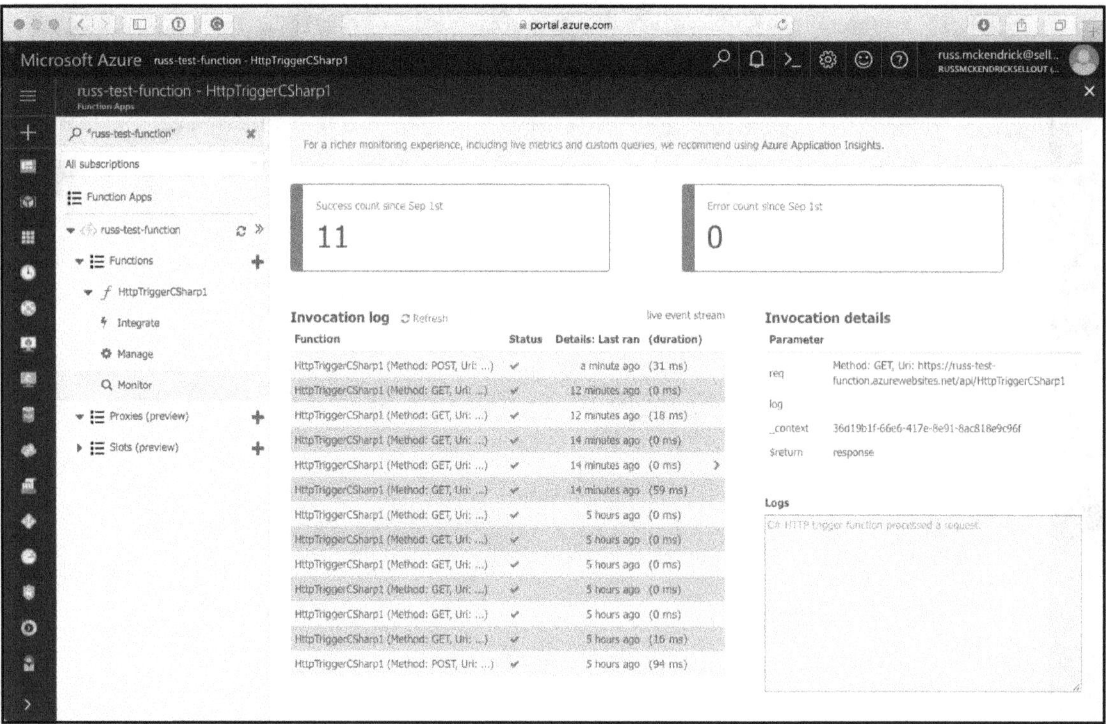

For more detailed information on the invocation of your Function app, you can enable Azure Application Insights, and for more information on this service, please see `https://azure.microsoft.com/en-gb/services/application-insights/`.

Being able to test within the safety of the Azure **Dashboard** is all well and good, but how do you directly access your Function app?

If you click on **HttpTriggerCSharp1**, which will take you back to your code, above the code block you will have a button which says **Get function URL**, and clicking on this will pop up an overlay box with a URL in it. Copy this:

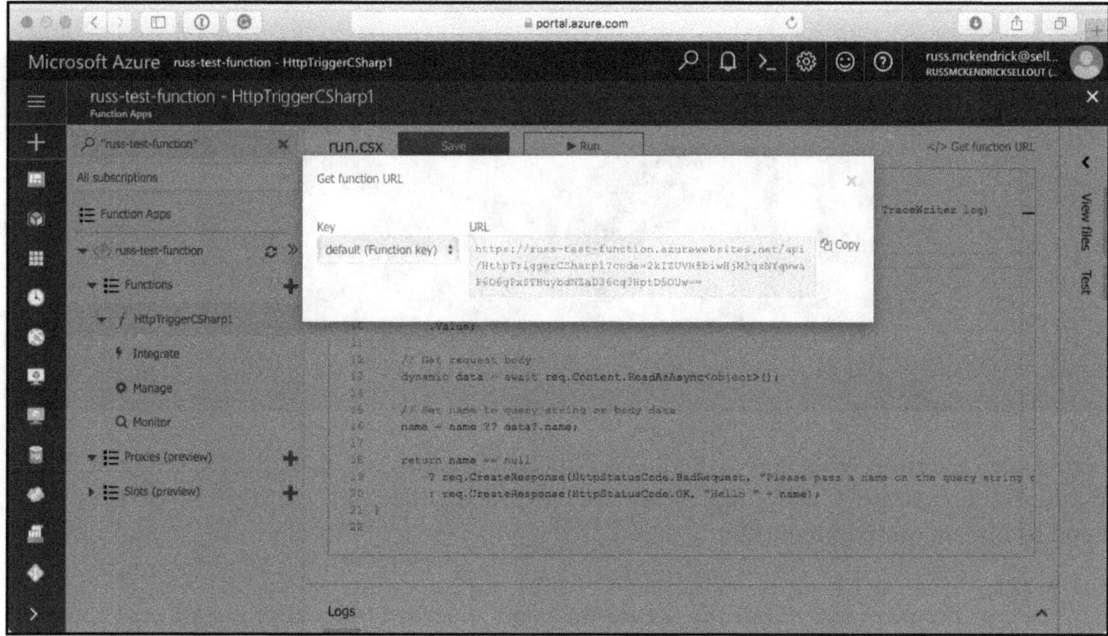

For me, the URL was:

```
https://russ-test-function.azurewebsites.net/api/HttpTriggerCSharp1?cod
e=2kIZUVH8biwHjM3qzNYqwwaP6O6gPxSTHuybdNZaD36cq3HptD5OUw==
```

The preceding URL will no longer work as the Function has been removed; it has been provided for illustration purposes only, and you should replace it with your URL.

To interact with URLs on the command line, I am going to be using HTTPie, which is a command-line HTTP client. For more detail on HTTPie, see the project's homepage at `https://httpie.org/`.

Call that URL on the command line using HTTPie with the following command:

```
$ http
"https://russ-test-function.azurewebsites.net/api/HttpTriggerCSharp1?code=2
kIZUVH8biwHjM3qzNYqwwaP6O6gPxSTHuybdNZaD36cq3HptD5OUw=="
```

This gives us the following result:

```
1. russ (bash)
russ in ~
⚡ http "https://russ-test-function.azurewebsites.net/api/HttpTriggerCSharp1?code=2kIZUVH8biwHjM3qzN
YqwwaP6O6gPxSTHuybdNZaD36cq3HptD5OUw=="
HTTP/1.1 400 Bad Request
Cache-Control: no-cache
Content-Length: 63
Content-Type: application/json; charset=utf-8
Date: Sat, 09 Sep 2017 15:44:09 GMT
Expires: -1
Pragma: no-cache
Server: Microsoft-IIS/8.0
X-AspNet-Version: 4.0.30319
X-Powered-By: ASP.NET

"Please pass a name on the query string or in the request body"

russ in ~
⚡
```

As you can see from what is returned, our Function app has returned the HttpStatusCode BadRequest message. This is because we are not passing the `name` variable. To do this, we need to update our command to:

```
$ http
"https://russ-test-function.azurewebsites.net/api/HttpTriggerCSharp1?code=2
kIZUVH8biwHjM3qzNYqwwaP6O6gPxSTHuybdNZaD36cq3HptD5OUw==&name=kubernetes_for
_serverless_applications"
```

As you would expect, this returns the correct message:

```
1. russ (bash)
⚡ http "https://russ-test-function.azurewebsites.net/api/HttpTriggerCSharp1?code=2kIZUVH8biwHjM3qzN
YqwwaP6O6gPxSTHuybdNZaD36cq3HptD5OUw==&name=kubernetes_for_serverless_applications"
HTTP/1.1 200 OK
Cache-Control: no-cache
Content-Encoding: gzip
Content-Length: 160
Content-Type: application/json; charset=utf-8
Date: Sat, 09 Sep 2017 10:24:44 GMT
Expires: -1
Pragma: no-cache
Server: Microsoft-IIS/8.0
Vary: Accept-Encoding
X-AspNet-Version: 4.0.30319
X-Powered-By: ASP.NET

"Hello kubernetes_for_serverless_applications"

russ in ~
⚡
```

You can also enter the URL in your browser and see the message:

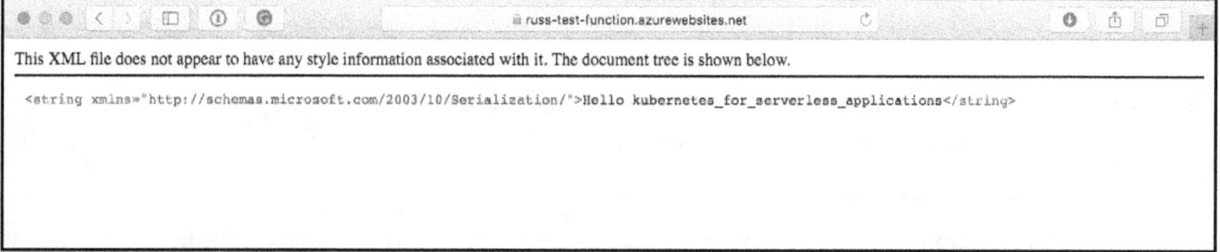

The serverless toolkit

Before we finish this chapter, we are going to take a look at the serverless toolkit. This is an application that aims to provide a consistent experience when it comes to deploying your serverless functions across different cloud providers. You can find the service's homepage at `https://serverless.com/`.

As you can see from the home page, it supports both AWS and Microsoft Azure, as well as the Google Cloud Platforms and IBM OpenWhisk. You will also notice that there is a **Sign Up** button; click on this and follow the onscreen prompts to create your account.

Once signed up, you will receive some very simple instructions on how to install the tool and also deploy your first application; let's follow these now. First of all, we need to install the command-line tool by running:

```
$ npm install serverless -g
```

The installation will take a few minutes, and once it is installed you should be able to run:

```
$ serverless version
```

This will confirm the version that was installed by the previous command:

```
1. russ (bash)
russ in ~
⚡ serverless version
1.21.1
russ in ~
⚡
```

Now that the command-line tool is installed and we have confirmed that we can get the version number without any errors, we need to log in. To do this, run:

```
$ serverless login
```

This command will open a browser window and take you to a login page where you will need to select which account you wish to use:

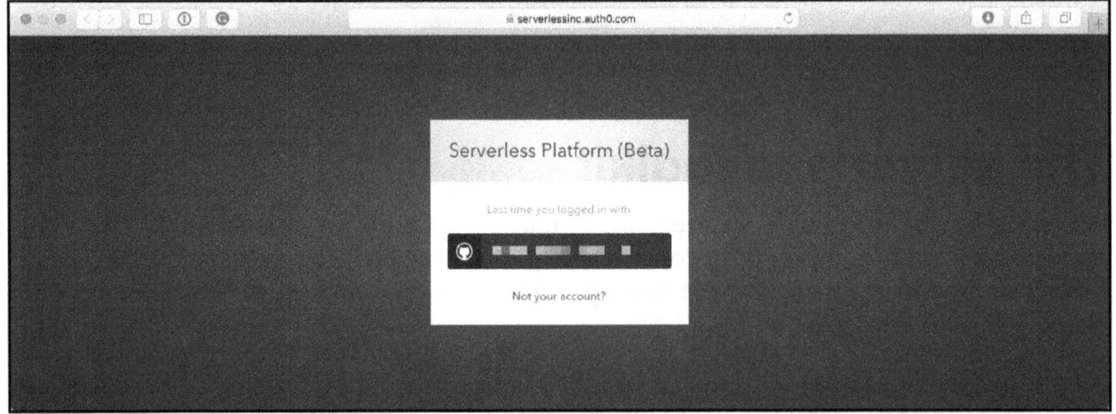

As you can see in the preceding screenshot, it knows I last logged into serverless using my GitHub account, so clicking this will generate a **Verification Code**:

Pasting the code into your Terminal at the prompt and pressing *Enter* on your keyboard will then log you in:

```
1. russ (bash)
Serverless: The Serverless login will open in your default browser...
Serverless: Opening browser...
Please enter the verification code here:
Serverless: You are now logged in
russ in ~
```

Now that we are logged in, we can create our first project, which is going to be another `hello-world` application.

To launch our `hello-world` function in AWS, we must first create a folder to hold the artifacts created by the serverless toolkit and change to it; I created mine on my `Desktop` using:

```
$ mkdir ~/Desktop/Serverless
$ cd ~/Desktop/Serverless
```

To generate the files needed to launch our `hello-world` application, we need to run:

```
$ serverless create --template hello-world
```

This will return the following message:

```
1. Severless (bash)
russ in ~/Desktop/Severless
⚡ serverless create --template hello-world
Serverless: Generating boilerplate...

                 The Serverless Application Framework
                              serverless.com, v1.21.1

Serverless: Successfully generated boilerplate for template: "hello-world"
Serverless: NOTE: Please update the "service" property in serverless.yml with your service name
russ in ~/Desktop/Severless
⚡
```

Opening `serverless.yml` in my editor, I can see the following (I have removed the comments):

```
service: serverless-hello-world
provider:
  name: aws
  runtime: nodejs6.10
functions:
  helloWorld:
    handler: handler.helloWorld
    # The `events` block defines how to trigger the handler.helloWorld code
    events:
      - http:
          path: hello-world
          method: get
          cors: true
```

I updated the service to be `russ-test-serverless-hello-world`; you should choose something unique as well. Once I had saved my updated `serverless.yml` file, I ran:

```
$ serverless deploy
```

This, as you may have already guessed, deployed the `hello-world` application to AWS:

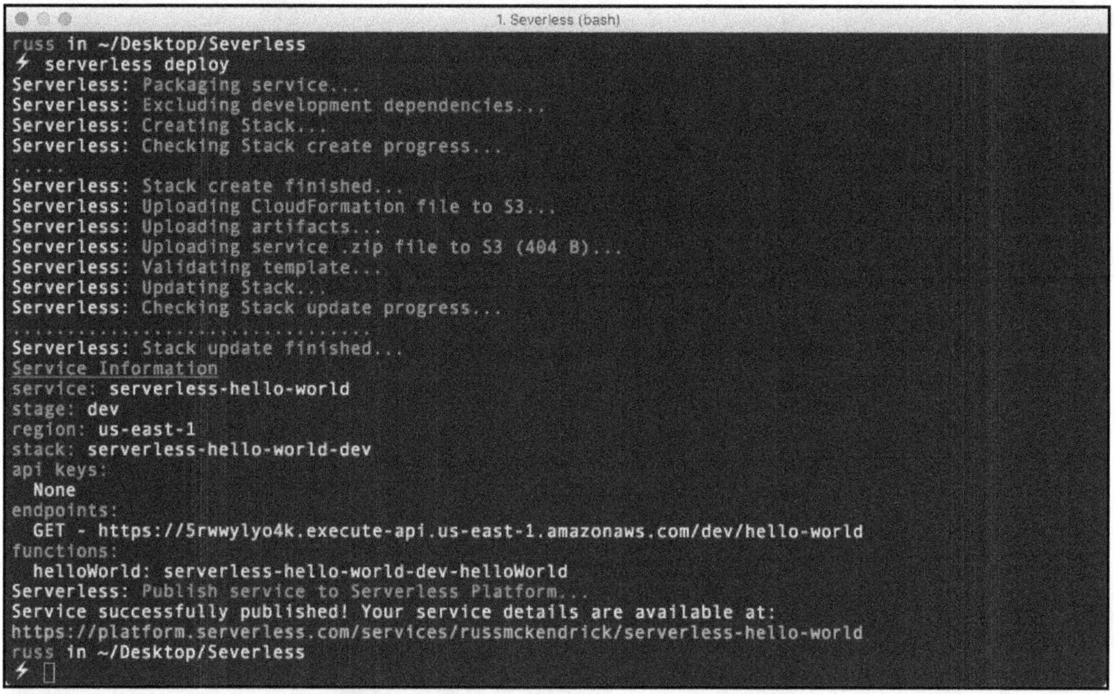

```
russ in ~/Desktop/Severless
⚡ serverless deploy
Serverless: Packaging service...
Serverless: Excluding development dependencies...
Serverless: Creating Stack...
Serverless: Checking Stack create progress...
.....
Serverless: Stack create finished...
Serverless: Uploading CloudFormation file to S3...
Serverless: Uploading artifacts...
Serverless: Uploading service .zip file to S3 (404 B)...
Serverless: Validating template...
Serverless: Updating Stack...
Serverless: Checking Stack update progress...
..............................
Serverless: Stack update finished...
Service Information
service: serverless-hello-world
stage: dev
region: us-east-1
stack: serverless-hello-world-dev
api keys:
  None
endpoints:
  GET - https://5rwwylyo4k.execute-api.us-east-1.amazonaws.com/dev/hello-world
functions:
  helloWorld: serverless-hello-world-dev-helloWorld
Serverless: Publish service to Serverless Platform...
Service successfully published! Your service details are available at:
https://platform.serverless.com/services/russmckendrick/serverless-hello-world
russ in ~/Desktop/Severless
⚡
```

Access the endpoint URL using HTTPie:

```
$ http --body
"https://5rwwylyo4k.execute-api.us-east-1.amazonaws.com/dev/hello-world"
```

This returns the following JSON:


```
{
    "input": {
        "body": null,
        "headers": {
            "Accept": "*/*",
            "Accept-Encoding": "gzip, deflate",
            "CloudFront-Forwarded-Proto": "https",
            "CloudFront-Is-Desktop-Viewer": "true",
            "CloudFront-Is-Mobile-Viewer": "false",
            "CloudFront-Is-SmartTV-Viewer": "false",
            "CloudFront-Is-Tablet-Viewer": "false",
            "CloudFront-Viewer-Country": "GB",
            "Host": "5rwwylyo4k.execute-api.us-east-1.amazonaws.com",
```

```
            "User-Agent": "HTTPie/0.9.9",
            "Via": "1.1 dd12e7e803f596deb3908675a4e017be.cloudfront.net
             (CloudFront)",
            "X-Amz-Cf-Id": "bBd_ChGfOA21EBz2YQDPPawOYlHQKYpA-
             XSsYvVonXzYAypQFuuBJw==",
            "X-Amzn-Trace-Id": "Root=1-59b417ff-5139be7f77b5b7a152750cc3",
            "X-Forwarded-For": "109.154.205.250, 54.240.147.50",
            "X-Forwarded-Port": "443",
            "X-Forwarded-Proto": "https"
        },
        "httpMethod": "GET",
        "isBase64Encoded": false,
        "path": "/hello-world",
        "pathParameters": null,
        "queryStringParameters": null,
        "requestContext": {
            "accountId": "687011238589",
            "apiId": "5rwwylyo4k",
            "httpMethod": "GET",
            "identity": {
                "accessKey": null,
                "accountId": null,
                "apiKey": "",
                "caller": null,
                "cognitoAuthenticationProvider": null,
                "cognitoAuthenticationType": null,
                "cognitoIdentityId": null,
                "cognitoIdentityPoolId": null,
                "sourceIp": "109.154.205.250",
                "user": null,
                "userAgent": "HTTPie/0.9.9",
                "userArn": null
            },
            "path": "/dev/hello-world",
            "requestId": "b3248e19-957c-11e7-b373-8baee2f1651c",
            "resourceId": "zusllt",
            "resourcePath": "/hello-world",
            "stage": "dev"
        },
        "resource": "/hello-world",
        "stageVariables": null
    },
    "message": "Go Serverless v1.0! Your function executed successfully!"
}
```

Entering the endpoint URL in your browser, (in my case as I am using Safari) shows you the RAW output:

Going to the URL mentioned at the very end of the `serverless deploy` command gives you an overview of the function you have deployed to Lambda using serverless:

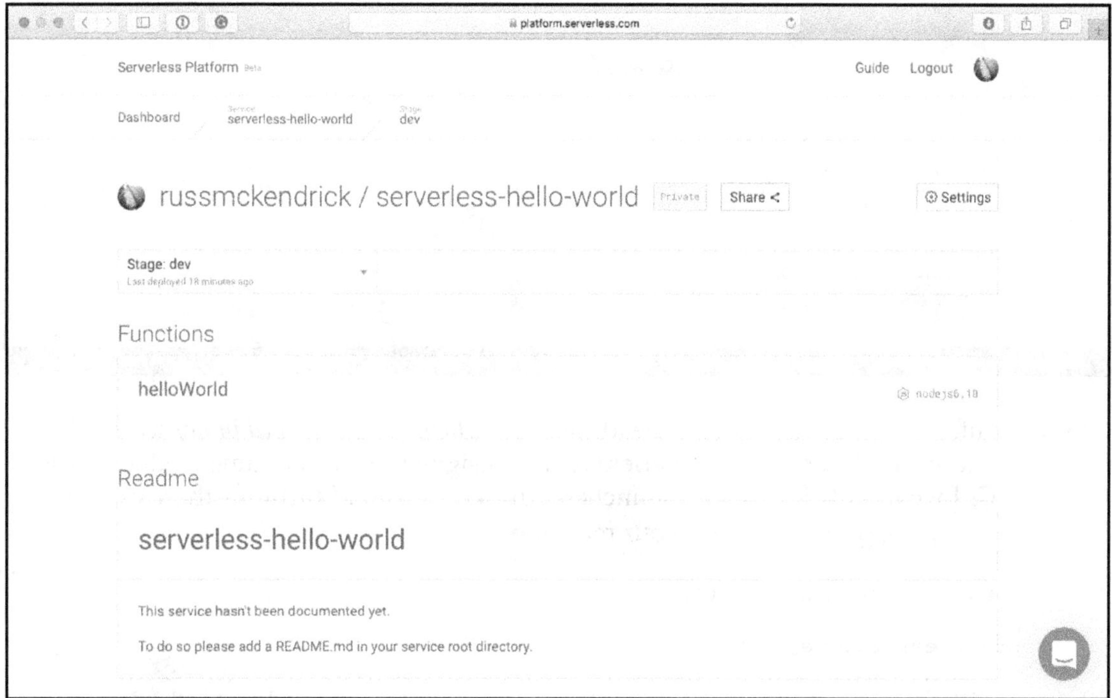

Open the AWS Console by going to `https://console.aws.amazon.com/`, select **Lambda** from the **Services** menu, and then change to the region your function was launching in; this should show you your function:

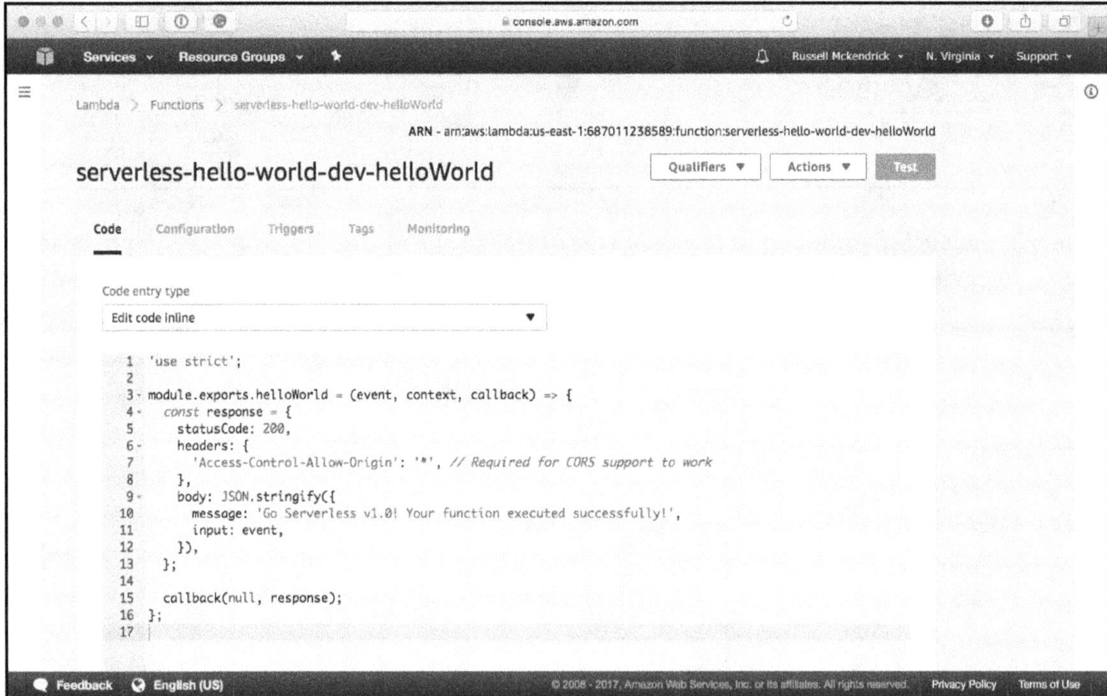

At this point, you might scratch your head thinking, *How was it launched in my account? I didn't provide any credentials!* The serverless tool is designed to use the same credentials as the AWS CLI we installed before we launched our first Lambda function—these can be found at `~/.aws/credentials` on your machine.

To remove the function, simply run:

```
$ serverless remove
```

And this will remove everything in your AWS account that the serverless toolkit has created.

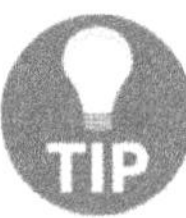

For more information on how to use the serverless toolkit to launch an Azure Function, please see the quick-start guide which can be found at `https://serverless.com/framework/docs/providers/azure/guide/quick-start/`.

Problems solved by serverless and Functions as a Service

Even though we have only been launching the most basic applications so far, I hope you are starting to see how using serverless could help with the development of your applications.

Imagine you have a JavaScript application which is being hosted in an object store such as Amazon's S3 service. Your application could be written in, say, React (`https://facebook.github.io/react/`) or Angular (`https://angular.io/`), and both of these technologies allow you to load external data using JSON. This data can be requested and delivered using a serverless function—combining these technologies allows you to create an application that not only has no single point of failure, but also, when using public cloud offerings, is a true *you only pay for what you use* application.

As the serverless function is being executed and then is immediately terminated, you should not have to worry about where or how it is executed, just that it is. This means that your application, in theory, should be scalable and also more fault-tolerant than a more traditional server-based application.

For example, if something goes wrong when one of your functions is called, for instance, if it crashes or there are resource issues and you know that when your function is next called it will be being launched afresh, you don't need to worry about your code being executed on a server which is having issues.

Summary

In this chapter, we have taken a very quick look at what is meant by serverless, and we have launched and interacted with serverless functions in AWS and also Microsoft Azure as well as used a third-party tool, which just happens to be called serverless, to create a serverless function in AWS.

You will have noticed that so far we haven't mentioned Kubernetes at all, which you may be thinking for a book entitled *Kubernetes for Serverless Applications* is a little strange. Don't worry though; in the next chapter we will be looking at Kubernetes in more detail and all will become clear.

2
An Introduction to Kubernetes

As mentioned at the end of the previous chapter, in this chapter we are going to look at Kubernetes. We will discuss:

- A brief history of Kubernetes—where did it come from?
- How does it operate?
- What are the use cases for Kubernetes and who is using it?
- Why would you run serverless on servers?

A brief history of Kubernetes

Before we discuss where Kubernetes came from, we should quickly discuss what Kubernetes is. It is pronounced **koo-ber-net-eez** and sometimes referred to as **K8s**. **Kubernetes** is the Greek name for a helmsman or pilot of a ship, which is apt when you consider what Kubernetes is designed to do. The project's website, which you can find at `https://kubernetes.io/`, describes it as:

> *"An open-source system for automating deployment, scaling, and management of containerized applications."*

The project has its roots in an internal project at Google called **Borg**. Google has been a longtime user of container technology, long before Docker made a splash.

Control groups

Google's own container journey started in 2006 when two of their engineers made a start on the **control groups** (**cgroups**) project. This is the Linux kernel feature which makes it possible to isolate resources such as RAM, CPU, networking, and disk I/O for a collection of processes. cgroups was initially released in 2007, and in early 2008 the functionality was merged into the Linux kernel mainline version 2.6.24.

You can find the release notes for version 2.6.24 of the Linux kernel at `https://kernelnewbies.org/Linux_2_6_24`. You can find information about the introduction of cgroups at *point 10* in the *Important things* list where it discusses the framework that allows cgroups to hook into the kernel.

lmctfy

A few years later, in October 2013, Google released an open source version of their own container system called **lmctfy**, which is actually short for **Let Me Contain That For You**. This tool is actually what they used on their own servers to enable them to run Linux application containers, and it was designed as an alternative to LXC.

lmctfy, LXC, and Docker all occupy the same space. To this end, Google actually stopped all development on lmctfy in 2015. The project's GitHub page has an announcement that states that Google has been collaborating with Docker and they are porting the core concepts of lmctfy to libcontainer.

Borg

This is where the Borg project comes in. Google uses containers a lot, and when I say a lot I mean *a lot*. In May 2014, Joe Beda from Google gave a presentation at Gluecon entitled *Containers At Scale*. There were a few takeaway quotes from the presentation such as:

> *"Everything at Google runs in a container."*

And the one that gets talked about the most is:

> *"We start over 2 billion containers per week."*

This works out at around 3,000 per second and, during the talk, it was mentioned that the number didn't include any long-running containers.

While Joe went into some detail about how Google was using containers at that time, he did not mention anything directly about the Borg project; instead, it was simply referred to as a cluster scheduler.

The final takeaway from the presentation was the slide entitled *Declarative Over Imperative*, which introduced the following concepts:

- **Imperative**: Start this container on that server
- **Declarative**: Run 100 copies of this container with a target of <= 2 tasks down at any time

This concept explains how Google was able to launch those 2 billion containers per week without having to really manage well over 2 billion containers.

It wasn't until Google published a paper entitled *Large-scale cluster management at Google with Borg* in 2015 that we really got an insight into the practices and design decisions that went into the cluster scheduler mentioned by Joe Beda the previous year.

The paper talks about how Google's internal tooling, called Borg, runs thousands of jobs, which go to make up pretty much all of Google's applications across clusters made up of tens of thousands of machines.

It then goes on to reveal that customer-facing services such as Google Mail, Google Docs, and Google Search are all served from Borg-managed clusters as well as their own internal tools. It details the job specification language that users can use to declare their desired state, making it easy for users to deploy their applications without having to worry about all of the steps needed to deploy their application in a highly available configuration across Google's infrastructure.

I would recommend reading through the paper as it gives an excellent overview of how Google approaches its own container services.

Also, in case you are wondering, Borg was named after the alien race from the *Star Trek: The Next Generation* TV show.

Project Seven

In 2014 Joe Beda, Brendan Burns, and Craig McLuckie were joined by Brian Grant and Tim Hockin on Project Seven.

This project, named after the *Star Trek* character *Seven of Nine*, aimed to make a friendlier version of Borg. By the time of the first commit, the project had an external name, Kubernetes.

You can see the first commit at `https://github.com/kubernetes/kubernetes/commit/2c4b3a562ce34cddc3f8218a2c4d11c7310e6d56` and the first really stable release, which came four months later, can be found at `https://github.com/kubernetes/kubernetes/releases/tag/v0.4`.

Initially, the aim of Kubernetes was to take everything Google had learned from Borg and running its large container clusters and open source it as a way of attracting customers to Google's own public Cloud Platform—which is why you may still find reference to the project's original GitHub page at `https://github.com/GoogleCloudPlatform/kubernetes/`.

However, by the time of its 1.0 release in July 2015, Google had seen that it had quickly become much more than that and they joined the Linux Foundation, Twitter, Intel, Docker, and VMware (to name a few) in forming the Cloud Native Computing Foundation. As part of this new partnership, Google donated the Kubernetes project as the foundation of the new group.

Since then, other projects have joined Kubernetes, such as:

- Prometheus (`https://prometheus.io/`), originally developed by SoundCloud, is a time series database that can be used to store metrics
- Fluentd (`https://www.fluentd.org/`) is a data collector that allows you to take data from many different sources, filter or normalize it, and then route it to a storage engine such as Elasticsearch, MongoDB or Hadoop (to name a few)
- containerd (`http://containerd.io/`) is an open-source container runtime originally developed by Docker to implement Open Container Initiative standards
- CoreDNS (`https://coredns.io/`) is a DNS service built entirely on plugins, meaning that you can create DNS services that traditionally would be extremely complex to configure

As well as this, new members such as AWS, Microsoft, Red Hat, and Oracle are all lending their support and resources to the foundation's projects.

An overview of Kubernetes

Now that we have an idea of how Kubernetes came to be, we should walk through all of the different components that go to make up a typical Kubernetes cluster.

Kubernetes itself is written in Go. While the project's GitHub page shows that the project is currently 84.9% Go, the rest, 5.8% HTML, 4.7% Python, and 3.3% Shell (with the remainder being configuration/spec files, and so on), are all documentation and helper scripts.

Go is a programming language developed and open sourced by Google who describes it as *A fast, statically typed, compiled language that feels like a dynamically typed, interpreted language.* For more information, see `https://golang.org/`.

Components

There are two main server roles with Kubernetes: masters and nodes; each of these roles is made up of several components.

Master servers are the brains of the cluster and they make decisions on where pods (more on those in the next section) are deployed within the cluster, as well as acting on and looking at the health of not only the cluster, but also the pods themselves.

The core components of a master server are:

- `kube-apiserver`: This is the frontend to your Kubernetes control panel; no matter what you use to manage your cluster it will be talking directly to this API service.
- `etcd`: `etcd` is a distributed key-value store that Kubernetes uses to store the state of your cluster.
- `kube-controller-manager`: This service does behind-the-scenes work to maintain your cluster. It looks for nodes joining and leaving the cluster, ensuring that the correct number of pods are running, and that they are healthy and so on.
- `cloud-controller-manager`: This service is new to Kubernetes. It works alongside `kube-controller-manager` and its purpose is to interact with the APIs of cloud providers such as AWS, Google Cloud, and Microsoft Azure. An example of the tasks it performs would be that, if a node was to be removed from the cluster, it would check your cloud services API to see if the node still exists. If it does then there could be a problem; if not, then more than likely the node has been removed because of a scaling event.

- `kube-scheduler`: This chooses where pods should be launched based on a series of rules, utilization, and availability.

Next up we have nodes. Once deployed, the master interacts with components which are installed on the nodes to effect change within the cluster; these are where your pods run.

The components that go to make up the nodes are:

- `kubelet`: This is the main component that runs on the node. It is responsible for accepting instructions from and reporting back to the master servers.
- `kube-proxy`: This service helps the cluster communicate. It acts as a basic proxy for all network traffic on the nodes, and is capable of configuring TCP/UDP forwarding or acting as a TCP/UDP round-robin load balancer to a number of backends.
- `docker` or `rkt`: These are the actual container engines on the nodes. The `kubelet` service interacts with these to launch and manage the containers running on each of your cluster nodes. Throughout the following chapters, we will look at launching nodes running both.
- `supervisord`: This process manager and monitor maintains the availability of other services such as `kubelet`, `docker`, and `rkt` on the nodes.
- `fluentd`: This service helps with cluster-level logging.

You may have noticed that the only mention of containers in these services was `docker` and `rkt`. Kubernetes does not actually directly interact with your containers; instead, it communicates with a pod.

Pods and services

As already mentioned, Kubernetes does not deploy containers; instead, it launches pods. In its most simple form, a pod can actually be a single container; however, typically a pod is made up of several containers, storage, and networking.

The following is meant to be illustrative and not a practical example; we will be working through a practical example in the next chapter.

Think of a pod as a complete application; for example, if you were running a simple web application it would probably be running a single NGINX container—the pod definition file for this would look something like the following:

```
apiVersion: v1
kind: Pod
metadata:
  name: nginx
spec:
  containers:
  - name: nginx
    image: nginx:latest
    ports:
    - containerPort: 8080
```

As you can see, we are providing some simple metadata about our pod, which in this case is just the name so we can identify it. We then have a single container defined, which is running the latest NGINX image from the Docker hub and port `8080` is exposed.

As it stands, this pod is quite useless as we are only going to display a **Welcome to nginx!** page. Next up, we need to add a volume to store our website data in. To do this, our pod definition file would look like this:

```
apiVersion: v1
kind: Pod
metadata:
  name: nginx
spec:
  containers:
  - name: nginx
    image: nginx:latest
    volumeMounts:
    - mountPath: /srv/www
      name: web-data
      readOnly: true
    ports:
    - containerPort: 8080
  volumes:
  - name: web-data
    emptyDir: {}
```

As you can see, we are now creating a volume called `web-data` and mounting it read-only at `/srv/www`, which is the default web root on our NGINX container. It is still a little pointless as our volume is empty, meaning that all our visitors will see is a 404 page.

Let's add a second container, which will sync our website's HTML from an Amazon S3 bucket:

```
apiVersion: v1
kind: Pod
metadata:
  name: nginx
spec:
  containers:
  - name: nginx
    image: nginx:latest
    volumeMounts:
    - mountPath: /srv/www
      name: web-data
      readOnly: true
    ports:
    - containerPort: 8080
  - name: sync
    image: ocasta/sync-s3:latest
    volumeMounts:
    - mountPath: /data
      name: web-data
      readOnly: false
    env:
    - ACCESS_KEY: "awskey"
      SECRET_KEY: "aws_secret"
      S3_PATH: "s3://my-awesome-website/"
      SYNC_FROM_S3: "true"
  volumes:
  - name: web-data
    emptyDir: {}
```

Now we have two containers: the NGINX one and now a container running the `s3 sync` command (`https://github.com/ocastastudios/docker-sync-s3/`). This will copy all of our website data from the Amazon S3 bucket called `my-awesome-website` to the volume that is also being shared with the NGINX container. This means we now have a website; note that this time, as we want to write to the volume, we are not mounting it read-only.

So far, so good, you might be thinking to yourself; we have a pod serving our website that is being deployed from an Amazon S3 bucket, which is all true. However, we have not quite finished. We have a pod running, but we need to expose that pod to the network to be able to access it in a browser.

To do this, we need to launch a service. For our example, the service file would look something like:

```
apiVersion: v1
kind: Service
metadata:
  name: nginx-service
spec:
  selector:
    app: nginx
  ports:
  - protocol: TCP
    port: 80
    targetPort: 8080
```

As you can see, the service definition looks similar to the pod one. We are setting a name using the metadata section. We are then selecting our NGINX pod and mapping port `80` to port `8080`, which is what our pod is listening on.

As already mentioned, we will look at this in more detail in the next chapter when we launch our first Kubernetes cluster, but for now, this should give you a good idea of how Kubernetes hangs together.

Workloads

In the previous section, we looked at pods and services. While these can be launched manually, you also can use controllers to manage your pods. These controllers allow for different types of workload to be executed. We are going to take a quick look at the different types of controller and also discuss when you would use them.

ReplicaSet

A ReplicaSet can be used to launch and maintain a number of copies of the the same pod. For example, using the NGINX pod we discussed in the previous section, we could create a ReplicaSet that launches three copies of the same pod. Traffic could then be load-balanced between the three pods.

Our three pods can be spread across multiple hosts, meaning that, if a host wants to disappear for any reason, taking one of our pods out of service, it will automatically be replaced on a healthy node. You can also use a ReplicaSet to both automatically and manually add and remove pods.

Deployments

One thing you may be thinking you will be able to do with a ReplicaSet is rolling upgrades and rollbacks. Unfortunately, ReplicaSets can only replicate the same version of a pod; luckily, this is where deployments come in.

A deployment controller is designed to update a ReplicaSet or pod. Lets use NGINX as an example. As you can see from the following definition, we have `3` replicas all running NGINX version `1.9.14`:

```
apiVersion: apps/v1beta1
kind: Deployment
metadata:
  name: nginx-deployment
spec:
  replicas: 3
  template:
    metadata:
      labels:
        app: nginx
    spec:
      containers:
      - name: nginx
        image: nginx:1.9.14
        ports:
        - containerPort: 80
```

`kubectl` is the command-line client for Kubernetes; we will be looking at this in more detail in our next chapter.

We could deploy this using the following command:

```
$ kubectl create -f nginx-deployment.yaml
```

Now say we want to update the version of the NGINX image used. We simply need to run the following command:

```
$ kubectl set image deployment/nginx-deployment nginx=nginx:1.13.5
deployment "nginx-deployment" image updated
```

This will update each pod in turn until all of the pods are running the new version of NGINX.

StatefulSets

This controller is new to Kubernetes and has been designed to replace PetSets. As you may have guessed by the name, pods maintain their state as part of a deployment. They are designed to have:

- Consistent unique network identifiers throughout the pod's life cycle
- Persistent storage
- Graceful deployment and scaling executed in the order you define
- User-defined and controlled automated rolling updates

So while there is a change in name, you should think of StatefulSets as pets and ReplicaSets as cattle.

Kubernetes use cases

As we have already touched upon in this chapter, Kubernetes can run pretty much anywhere, from just your local machine (which we will cover in our next chapter), from your on-premise hardware of virtual machine infrastructure to potential spanning hundreds of public cloud instances in AWS, Microsoft Azure, or Google Cloud. In fact, you could even span multiple environments with your Kubernetes cluster.

This means that you get a consistent experience no matter where you are running your application, but also get to take advantage of your underlying platform's features, such as load balancing, persistent storage, and auto scaling, without have to really design your application to be aware it is running on, say, AWS or Microsoft Azure.

One of the common threads you will notice when reading through success stories is that people are talking about not being locked into one particular vendor. As Kubernetes is open source, they are not locked into any licensing costs. If they have a problem or want to add functionality, they are able to dive straight into the source code and make changes; they can also contribute any changes they make back to the project via a pull request.

Also, as already discussed, using Kubernetes allows them to not get locked into any one particular platform vendor or architecture. This is because it is reasonable to assume Kubernetes will perform in exactly the same way when installed on other platforms. Because of this, all of a sudden you are able to take your application and move it between providers with relative ease.

Another common use case is operations teams using Kubernetes as an **Infrastructure as a Service** (**IaaS**) platform. This allows them to offer their developers resources they can consume via APIs, the web, and CLIs, meaning that they can easily hook into their own workflows. It also provides a consistent environment for local development, all the way from staging or **user acceptance testing** (**UAT**) to eventually running their applications in production.

This is part of the reason why using Kubernetes to execute your serverless workloads is a good idea. You are not locked in by any one provider, such as AWS or Microsoft Azure. In fact, you should think of Kubernetes as a cloud platform like the ones we looked at in `Chapter 1`, *The Serverless Landscape*; it has a web-based console, an API, and a command-line client.

References

There are several case studies about Kubernetes where users go into detail on their journey with using Kubernetes:

- **Wink**: `https://kubernetes.io/case-studies/wink/`
- **Buffer**: `https://kubernetes.io/case-studies/buffer/`
- **Ancestry**: `https://kubernetes.io/case-studies/ancestry/`
- **Wikimedia Foundation**: `https://kubernetes.io/case-studies/wikimedia/`

There are also talks, interviews, and presentations from the following:

- **The New Times**: `https://www.youtube.com/watch?v=P5qfyv_zGcU`
- **Monzo**: `https://www.youtube.com/watch?v=YkOY7DgXKyw`
- **Goldman Sachs**: `https://blogs.wsj.com/cio/2016/02/24/big-changes-in-goldmans-software-emerge-from-small-containers/`

Finally, you can read more about the Cloud Native Computing Foundation at `https://www.cncf.io/`.

Summary

In this chapter, we spoke a lot about where Kubernetes came from and we also covered some of its use cases. We also looked at some of the basic functionality.

In the next chapter, we are going to get hands-on with Kubernetes by installing Minikube locally. Once we have our local Kubernetes installation, we will be ready to proceed to `Chapter 4`, *Introducing Kubeless Functioning*, where we will start to deploy our first serverless functions on Kubernetes.

3
Installing Kubernetes Locally

In this chapter, we will look at how to get a local Kubernetes installation up and running using Minikube. Once we have our local Kubernetes installation running, we will work through some of the basic functionality and discuss the limitations of running Kubernetes locally. We will work through installing Kubernetes on:

- macOS 10.13 High Sierra
- Windows 10 Professional
- Ubuntu 17.04

Before we start the installation, let's quickly take a look at the tool we will be using to deploy our local Kubernetes cluster.

About Minikube

One of the things you may have been thinking to yourself when reading the previous chapter is that Kubernetes seems complex. There are a lot of moving parts, which not only need to be configured but also monitored and managed.

I remember when I originally looked at Kubernetes when it was first released before the stable version, and the installation instructions were very long and also things were a little delicate.

Misread a step at the beginning of the installation process and you could find yourself in a lot of trouble later in the installation—it reminded me of when magazines used to contain type in listings for games. If you made a typo anywhere then things would either flat-out not work or crash unexpectedly.

As Kubernetes matured, so did the installation process. Quite quickly a number of helper scripts were developed to aid in launching Kubernetes across various platforms; Minikube is one of these tools.

It has one job, to create a local Kubernetes node. Considering the breadth of features supported by Kubernetes, it has a surprising number of features, such as:

- DNS, NodePorts, and Ingress
- ConfigMaps and Secrets
- A choice of container runtimes; you can use either Docker or rkt
- Persistent Volumes via `hostPath`
- Dashboards

Kubernetes features that would typically require a public cloud provider, such as AWS, Microsoft Azure, or Google Cloud, or multiple hosts, are not supported. Some of these features are:

- LoadBalancers
- Advanced scheduling policies

This is because Minikube only launches a single node on a virtual machine on your local PC. This shouldn't limit you though; remember that you would only ever want to use Minikube for development and you should never build production services using it. There are a lot more tools, which will be covered in `Chapter 6`, *Installing Kubernetes in the Cloud,* more suited to launching production-ready Kubernetes clusters in public clouds or other vendors.

Minikube is made up of two core components:

- **libmachine**: This library from Docker is used to provision virtual machines on your host machine. It is a core component of Docker Machine as well as Docker for macOS and Docker for Windows.
- **localkube**: This library, developed and donated to the Minikube project by Redspread (which is now a part of CoreOS), is responsible for deploying and maintaining the Kubernetes node once the virtual machine has been launched.

Rather than talking about what Minikube can do any more, we should look at installing it and then discuss how we can interact with it.

Installing Minikube

We will be looking at installing Minikube on the three different operating systems mentioned in the introduction. Once installed, the process for interacting with Minikube is mostly consistent, meaning that, while I will be using macOS in the examples, the same commands will work on both Windows and Linux. Given the complexities of the early Kubernetes installation and configuration procedure, you will be pleasantly surprised how simple the process now is.

macOS 10.13 High Sierra

To install Minikube on macOS, you will first have to have Homebrew and Cask installed.

Homebrew is a command-line-based package manager for macOS. Homebrew is used to install both command-line tools and Cask, which is an add-on used to manage desktop applications. It is extremely useful for managing software that is not available in the macOS App Store, as well as saving you from having to manually compile software on your machine.

If you have not already got Homebrew installed, you can install it by running the following command:

```
$ /usr/bin/ruby -e "$(curl -fsSL
https://raw.githubusercontent.com/Homebrew/install/master/install)"
```

Once installed, you will need to install Cask by running:

```
$ brew install cask
```

If you have Homebrew and Cask installed, then you should ensure that everything is up-to-date and ready to run using the following commands:

```
$ brew update
$ brew doctor
```

Once Homebrew and Cask are ready, you can install Minikube by running the following command:

```
$ brew cask install minikube
```

This will first of all download the dependencies and then install Minikube:

```
1. russ (bash)
russ in ~
⚡ brew cask install minikube
==> Satisfying dependencies
==> Installing Formula dependencies: kubernetes-cli
==> Installing kubernetes-cli
==> Downloading https://homebrew.bintray.com/bottles/kubernetes-cli-1.8.0.high_sierra.bottle.tar.gz
==> Downloading from https://akamai.bintray.com/f3/f32e3efdf35b5585072762efe51ed47dd3d6cad9e7ad7be9c
######################################################################## 100.0%
==> Pouring kubernetes-cli-1.8.0.high_sierra.bottle.tar.gz
==> Caveats
Bash completion has been installed to:
  /usr/local/etc/bash_completion.d

zsh completions have been installed to:
  /usr/local/share/zsh/site-functions
==> Summary
🍺 /usr/local/Cellar/kubernetes-cli/1.8.0: 106 files, 50.5MB
==> Downloading https://storage.googleapis.com/minikube/releases/v0.22.2/minikube-darwin-amd64
######################################################################## 100.0%
==> Verifying checksum for Cask minikube
==> Installing Cask minikube
==> Linking Binary 'minikube-darwin-amd64' to '/usr/local/bin/minikube'.
🍺 minikube was successfully installed!
russ in ~
⚡
```

The process takes less than a minute and, once installed, you should be able to perform the following:

```
$ minikube version
```

This will display the current version; in my case, this was `v0.22.2`. We now have Minikube installed and ready to go.

Windows 10 Professional

Similarly to how we installed Minikube on macOS, we will be using a package manager; this time it is called Chocolatey.

Chocolatey is a package manager for Windows, similar to Homebrew on macOS. It enables you to install software from the command line, and supports both PowerShell and `cmd.exe`. We will be using PowerShell.

If you do not have Chocolatey installed, you can run the following command in a PowerShell console that has been launched with administrator privileges:

The following command is a single line and not multiple lines. Also, as we are running the install command using `Set-ExecutionPolicy Bypass`, you will be asked if you are sure. As we are running the script directly from the Chocolatey site over HTTPS, you should be able to trust the script and answer yes.

```
$ Set-ExecutionPolicy Bypass; iex ((New-Object
System.Net.WebClient).DownloadString('https://chocolatey.org/install.ps1'))
```

Once Chocolatey is installed, you can install Minikube by running:

```
$ choco install minikube
```

This will download and install the dependencies, and then install Minikube. When you are asked to confirm if you would like to run the script, respond with yes:

```
Administrator: Windows PowerShell
Windows PowerShell
Copyright (C) 2016 Microsoft Corporation. All rights reserved.

PS C:\WINDOWS\system32> choco install minikube
Chocolatey v0.10.8
Installing the following packages:
minikube
By installing you accept licenses for the packages.
Progress: Downloading kubernetes-cli 1.7.6... 100%
Progress: Downloading Minikube 0.22.2... 100%

kubernetes-cli v1.7.6 [Approved]
kubernetes-cli package files install completed. Performing other installation steps.
The package kubernetes-cli wants to run 'chocolateyInstall.ps1'.
Note: If you don't run this script, the installation will fail.
Note: To confirm automatically next time, use '-y' or consider:
choco feature enable -n allowGlobalConfirmation
Do you want to run the script?([Y]es/[N]o/[P]rint):
```

Once installed, you will be able to run the following command:

```
$ minikube version
```

This will return the version of Minikube installed; for me, this was `v0.22.2`.

Ubuntu 17.04

Unlike the macOS and Windows version, we will not be using a package manager to install Minikube on Ubuntu 17.04. Instead, we will just be downloading the binaries directly from the project page. To do this, simply run the following command:

```
$ curl -Lo minikube
https://storage.googleapis.com/minikube/releases/v0.22.2/minikube-linux-amd
64 && chmod +x minikube && sudo mv minikube /usr/local/bin/
```

Minikube will be downloaded, will have execute permissions set, and will be moved to `/usr/local/bin/` so it is in a system path.

Now that Minikube is installed, we need to download `kubectl`. During the macOS and Windows installation, this was taken care of by the package manager; luckily, the process is pretty much the same as the command we just ran to install Minikube:

```
$ curl -LO https://storage.googleapis.com/kubernetes-release/release/$(curl
-s
https://storage.googleapis.com/kubernetes-release/release/stable.txt)/bin/l
inux/amd64/kubectl && chmod +x ./kubectl && sudo mv ./kubectl
/usr/local/bin/kubectl
```

Once installed, you should again be able to run the following command to confirm the version of Minikube installed:

```
$ minikube version
```

When I ran the command, it returned `v0.22.2`, as seen in the following screenshot:

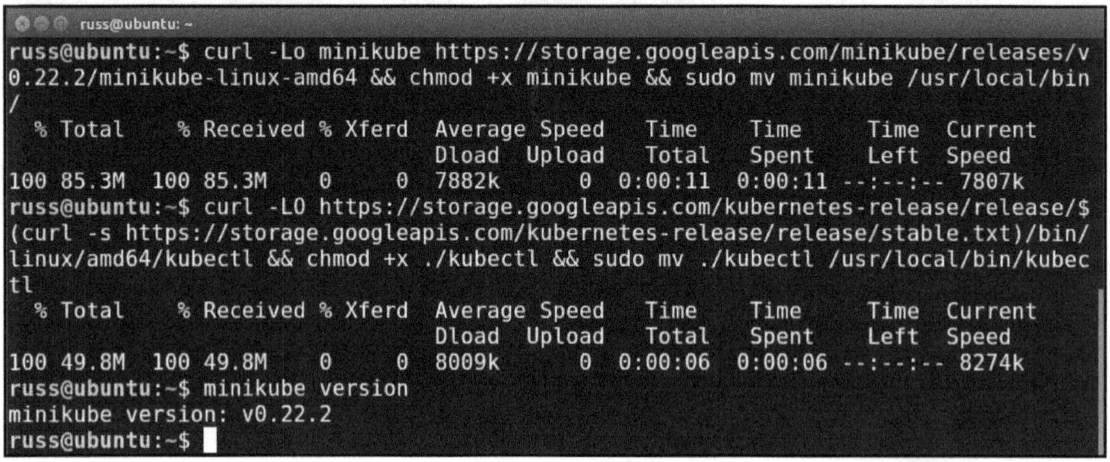

```
russ@ubuntu: ~
russ@ubuntu:~$ curl -Lo minikube https://storage.googleapis.com/minikube/releases/v
0.22.2/minikube-linux-amd64 && chmod +x minikube && sudo mv minikube /usr/local/bin
/
  % Total    % Received % Xferd  Average Speed   Time    Time     Time  Current
                                 Dload  Upload   Total   Spent    Left  Speed
100 85.3M  100 85.3M    0     0  7882k      0  0:00:11  0:00:11 --:--:-- 7807k
russ@ubuntu:~$ curl -LO https://storage.googleapis.com/kubernetes-release/release/$
(curl -s https://storage.googleapis.com/kubernetes-release/release/stable.txt)/bin/
linux/amd64/kubectl && chmod +x ./kubectl && sudo mv ./kubectl /usr/local/bin/kubec
tl
  % Total    % Received % Xferd  Average Speed   Time    Time     Time  Current
                                 Dload  Upload   Total   Spent    Left  Speed
100 49.8M  100 49.8M    0     0  8009k      0  0:00:06  0:00:06 --:--:-- 8274k
russ@ubuntu:~$ minikube version
minikube version: v0.22.2
russ@ubuntu:~$
```

Hypervisors

A number of different hypervisors are supported by Minikube. A hypervisor is a process that is used to launch the virtual machine; it isolates the virtual machine's operating system from your own while allowing it to share resources such as CPU, RAM, and drive space.

The following hypervisors are supported out-of-the-box by Minikube:

- **Hyper-V (Windows 10)**: This is the native hypervisor; it is available in Windows 10 Professional and Windows Servers
- **KVM (Ubuntu 17.04)**: This is the native Linux hypervisor, which operates inside the Linux kernel on most modern distributions
- **VirtualBox (macOS, Windows 10, and Ubuntu 17.04)**: Released by Oracle, VirtualBox is an open source x86 hypervisor which can be run on a large number of operating systems
- **VMware Fusion (macOS)**: Fusion provides a macOS-optimized hypervisor whose biggest strength is its ability to run and expose Windows applications on macOS
- **xhyve (macOS)**: This is the native hypervisor on macOS; like KVM on Linux, it is built into the kernel

As you can tell from the list, only VirtualBox is supported across all three of the operating systems we are covering in this chapter. Because of this, it is the default hypervisor supported by Minikube. If you have already got VirtualBox installed, you can run the following commands, which are relevant to your choice of operating system.

For macOS, we can use Homebrew and Cask to install VirtualBox by running:

```
$ brew cask install virtualbox
```

Likewise, for Windows 10 you can use Chocolatey to install VirtualBox:

You cannot use VirtualBox on Windows 10 if Hyper-V is enabled. If you wish to follow along, please disable Hyper-V before proceeding.

```
$ choco install virtualbox
```

Finally, for Ubuntu 17.04 you will need to run the following commands to add the repository and key:

```
$ wget -q http://download.virtualbox.org/virtualbox/debian/oracle_vbox.asc
-O- | sudo apt-key add -
$ sudo sh -c 'echo "deb http://download.virtualbox.org/virtualbox/debian
$(lsb_release -sc) contrib" >> /etc/apt/sources.list'
```

And then run the following commands to load the repository we added previously and install the package:

```
$ sudo apt-get update
$ sudo apt-get install virtualbox-5.1
```

You should now be able to see Virtualbox in your listed software programs.

Starting Minikube

To complete our installation, we need to start Minikube. To do this, run the following command:

```
$ minikube start
```

On macOS, you should see something like this:

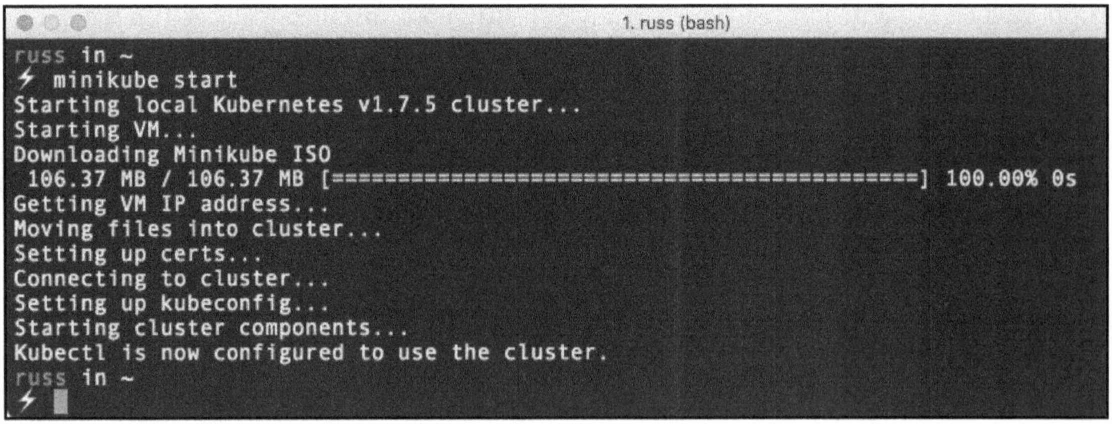

```
1. russ (bash)
russ in ~
⚡ minikube start
Starting local Kubernetes v1.7.5 cluster...
Starting VM...
Downloading Minikube ISO
 106.37 MB / 106.37 MB [============================================] 100.00% 0s
Getting VM IP address...
Moving files into cluster...
Setting up certs...
Connecting to cluster...
Setting up kubeconfig...
Starting cluster components...
Kubectl is now configured to use the cluster.
russ in ~
⚡
```

As you can see, the ISO used to create the virtual machine has been downloaded. The virtual machine starts, the certificates that we will be using to authenticate against our one node cluster are generated, and then finally `kubectl` is configured with the details of our local Kubernetes cluster.

Running the same command on Windows 10 results in exactly the same set of steps:

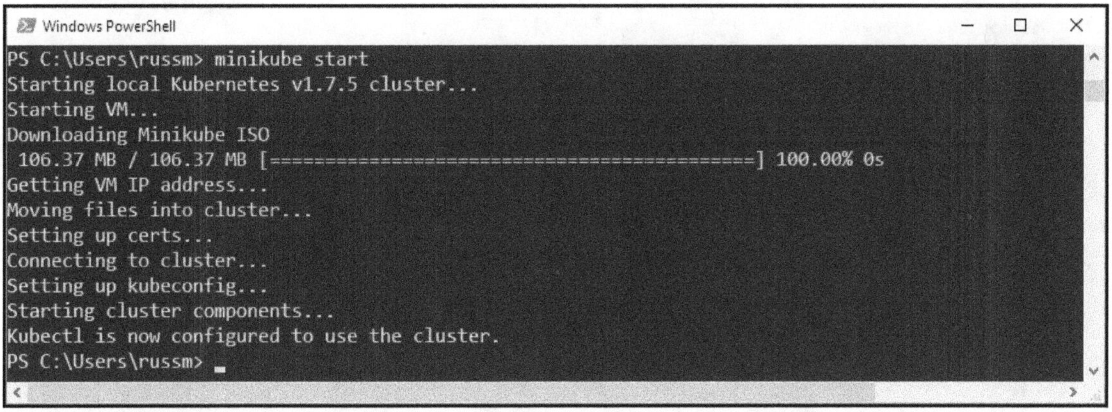

```
Windows PowerShell
PS C:\Users\russm> minikube start
Starting local Kubernetes v1.7.5 cluster...
Starting VM...
Downloading Minikube ISO
 106.37 MB / 106.37 MB [============================================] 100.00% 0s
Getting VM IP address...
Moving files into cluster...
Setting up certs...
Connecting to cluster...
Setting up kubeconfig...
Starting cluster components...
Kubectl is now configured to use the cluster.
PS C:\Users\russm>
```

Also, as you may have already guessed, running on Ubuntu 17.04 gives the same results. Run the following:

```
$ minikube status
```

You will receive a message confirming that everything is running and that `kubectl` has been correctly configured to communicate with your Kubernetes cluster:

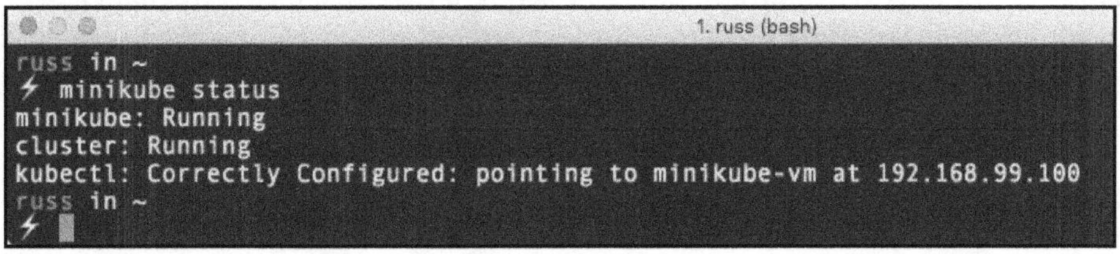

```
1. russ (bash)
russ in ~
⚡ minikube status
minikube: Running
cluster: Running
kubectl: Correctly Configured: pointing to minikube-vm at 192.168.99.100
russ in ~
⚡
```

If you were to open VirtualBox, you should see your Minikube virtual machine running; for example, this is what I see when opening VirtualBox on Windows 10:

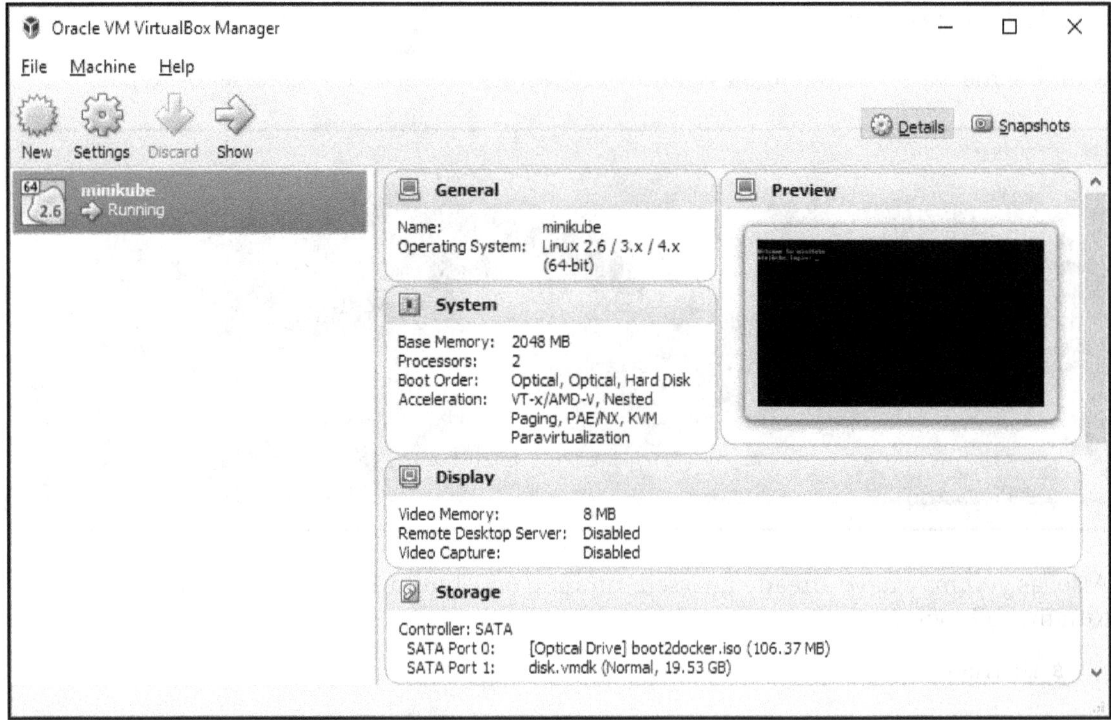

Even though we have launched Minikube on three different operating systems, other than the initial installation, you can already experience what we discussed in `Chapter 2`, *An Introduction to Kubernetes*: there is no vendor lock-in and a consistent experience, and this is before we have started to use our newly installed Kubernetes cluster.

Minikube commands

So far, we have used the `minikube start` and `minikube status` commands to launch our single-node Kubernetes cluster and check that everything is running as expected. Before we look at interacting with Kubernetes, there are a few more basic Minikube commands I would like to cover.

Stop and delete

As we are running our single-node Kubernetes cluster as a virtual machine on your host, you may not want it running all of the time, using resources.

There are two options to achieve this, the first of which is `minikube stop`. This command will stop your node and keep the virtual machine intact. You should use this command if you plan on picking up where you left off when you next start your node by running `minikube start`.

While the `minikube stop` command stops your virtual machine from using CPU and RAM resources on the host machine, the hard disk image used to host the virtual machine will still be present on your machine. While a freshly launched cluster does not take much space on the host hard drive, on my macOS installation it is around 650 MB; as soon as you start to use the cluster, you may find that this space will at least double.

This is where our next command comes in. The `minikube delete` command will remove the cluster completely, including all of the virtual machine files, freeing the space used on the host machine.

At the time of writing, running `minikube delete` will immediately remove your machine, running or not. There is no prompt asking if you are sure, or any way back from the command (unless you have backups), so please ensure that you use this command with caution.

When you run `minikube start` again, your cluster will be started from scratch again, as we first experienced in the previous section.

Environment

Next up, we have a few commands that display information about the virtual machine and also the environment that Minikube has configured on your device.

First, we have quite a simple command, `minikube ip`. All this command does is return the IP address of the virtual machine. This is useful if you want to interact with your cluster through a script. You can include the output of the command to reference your cluster's current IP address without having to hardcode the actual IP address into your scripts.

The next command we are going to look at is `minikube docker-env`. Running this command should print something like the following output to your screen:

```
$ minikube docker-env
export DOCKER_TLS_VERIFY="1"
export DOCKER_HOST="tcp://192.168.99.101:2376"
export DOCKER_CERT_PATH="/Users/russ/.minikube/certs"
export DOCKER_API_VERSION="1.23"
# Run this command to configure your shell:
# eval $(minikube docker-env)
```

What that output does is allow you (if you have it installed) to configure your local Docker client to communicate with the Docker installation on our Minikube virtual machine. There is, however, a downside to doing this. The version of Docker that is currently being distributed as part of the Minikube virtual machine image is a little behind the current release. You can see this by running `eval $(minikube docker-env)` and then `docker version`. When I ran the two commands, I got the following results:

```
$ eval $(minikube docker-env)
$ docker version
Client:
 Version: 17.06.2-ce
 API version: 1.23
 Go version: go1.8.3
 Git commit: cec0b72
 Built: Tue Sep 5 20:12:06 2017
 OS/Arch: darwin/amd64

Server:
 Version: 1.12.6
 API version: 1.24 (minimum version )
 Go version: go1.6.4
 Git commit: 78d1802
 Built: Wed Jan 11 00:23:16 2017
 OS/Arch: linux/amd64
 Experimental: false
```

As you can see from the output, at the time of writing the version of Docker that Minikube is using is presently two versions behind my local installation of Docker for macOS, which is running the latest stable release. In the context of what we are covering in this book, running an older version of Docker is not a problem and nothing to worry about, as we will not be interacting with it directly.

Virtual machine access and logs

You are able to SSH into the Minikube virtual machine. As part of the installation, an SSH key was generated and shared with the virtual machine when it launched. You can check the location of this key by running `minikube ssh-key`. This returns the path of the private part of the key. You can use this in combination with other commands to SSH into your virtual machine by running the following on macOS or Ubuntu:

```
$ ssh docker@$(minikube ip) -i $(minikube ssh-key)
```

This generates the IP address of the virtual machine and path to the private key on-the-fly:

```
2. russ (ssh)
⚡ ssh docker@$(minikube ip) -i $(minikube ssh-key)
The authenticity of host '192.168.99.101 (192.168.99.101)' can't be established.
ECDSA key fingerprint is SHA256:7gvcfA7P68S3VwV2VfYEP/ok9iv1B9MvM6A6Uf//jtk.
Are you sure you want to continue connecting (yes/no)? yes
Warning: Permanently added '192.168.99.101' (ECDSA) to the list of known hosts.
$
```

However, Minikube also has a command that will run this for you and it is also supported on all platforms. Running `minikube ssh` will log you straight in to the virtual machine as the Docker user, as is shown by the following Terminal output:

```
2. russ (minikube-darwin-)
russ in ~
⚡ minikube ssh
$ whoami
docker
$
```

The final command we are going to quickly look at is `minikube logs`. This displays all of the logs being generated by the `localkube` instance:

```
2. russ (minikube-darwin-)
-- Logs begin at Sat 2017-10-07 14:27:51 UTC, end at Sat 2017-10-07 16:42:57 UTC. --
Oct 07 14:28:07 minikube systemd[1]: Starting Localkube...
Oct 07 14:28:08 minikube localkube[3113]: proto: duplicate proto type registered: google.protobuf.An
y
Oct 07 14:28:08 minikube localkube[3113]: proto: duplicate proto type registered: google.protobuf.Du
ration
Oct 07 14:28:08 minikube localkube[3113]: proto: duplicate proto type registered: google.protobuf.Ti
mestamp
Oct 07 14:28:08 minikube localkube[3113]: listening for peers on http://localhost:2380
Oct 07 14:28:08 minikube localkube[3113]: listening for client requests on localhost:2379
Oct 07 14:28:08 minikube localkube[3113]: name = default
Oct 07 14:28:08 minikube localkube[3113]: data dir = /var/lib/localkube/etcd
Oct 07 14:28:08 minikube localkube[3113]: member dir = /var/lib/localkube/etcd/member
Oct 07 14:28:08 minikube localkube[3113]: heartbeat = 100ms
Oct 07 14:28:08 minikube localkube[3113]: election = 1000ms
Oct 07 14:28:08 minikube localkube[3113]: snapshot count = 10000
Oct 07 14:28:08 minikube localkube[3113]: advertise client URLs = http://localhost:2379
:
```

These logs are used to help debug problems with your Minikube installation. They do not contain any user data, meaning that you cannot use them to help track down any problems with the services or pods you have launched.

Hello world

Now we have our single node Kubernetes cluster up and running, using Minikube we can look at launching a service. We will start off using the dashboard before moving on to the command-line client.

The dashboard

Each installation of Minikube comes with a web-based dashboard. This can be accessed by running `minikube dashboard`, which immediately opens the dashboard in your default browser:

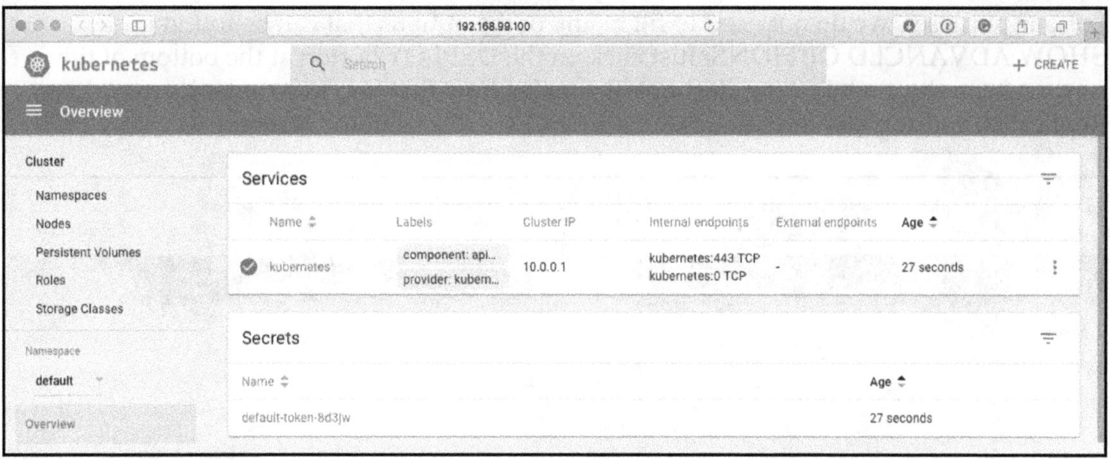

Clicking on the **+ CREATE** button, which can be found on the top-left of the page, will take you to a form that will let you deploy a containerized application.

On the **Deploy a Containerized App** page, you will find several options. Keeping the **Specify app details below** option enabled, fill them in as follows:

- **App name:** `dashboard-hello-world`
- **Container image:** `nginx:latest`
- **Number of pods:** `1`
- **Service: External**
- **Port:** `8080`
- **Target port:** `80`
- **Protocol: TCP**

For our purposes, we do not need to fill in any of the options that can be found under **SHOW ADVANCED OPTIONS**. Just click on the **DEPLOY** button at the bottom of the form. After a short while, your dashboard should show that you have a deployment, pod, ReplicaSet, and service, all with `dashboard-hello-world` in the **Name**:

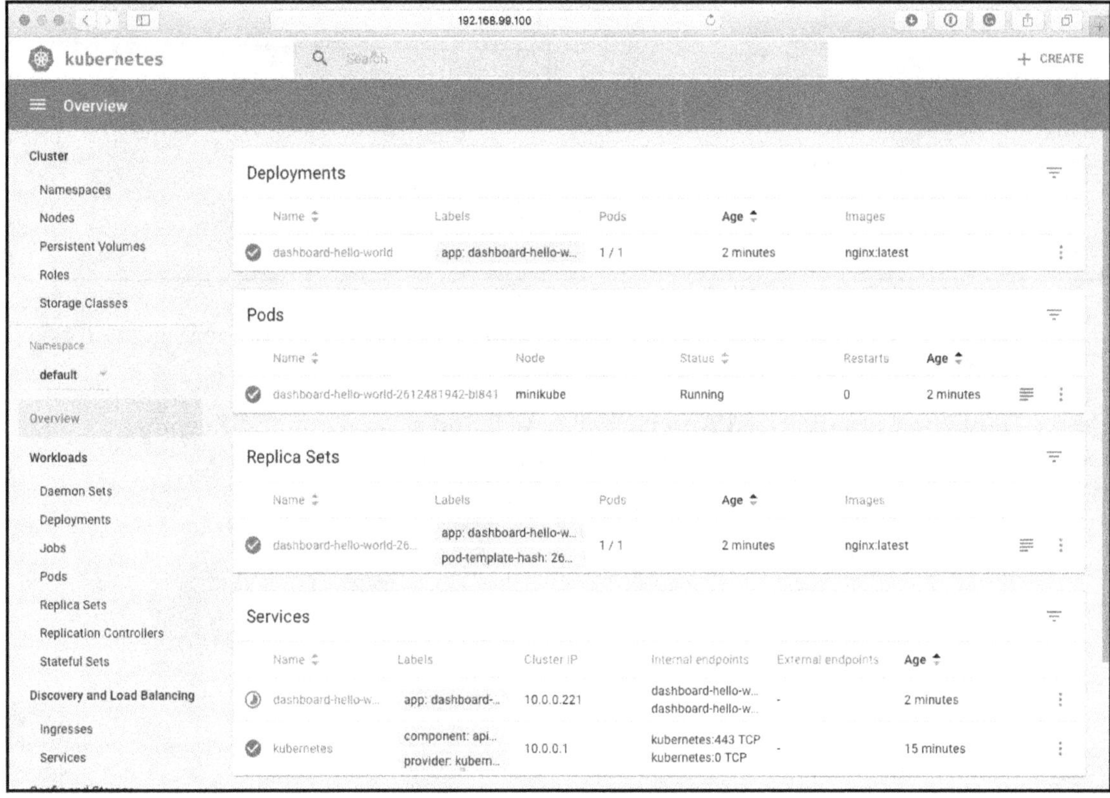

You can view the service by running the following command:

```
$ minikube service dashboard-hello-world
```

This will return the following message:

```
Opening kubernetes service default/dashboard-hello-world in default
browser...
```

Open your browser, where you should see the default NGINX page:

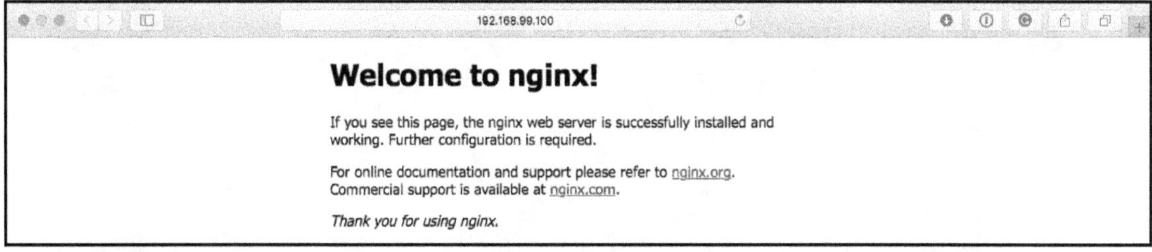

While this is a very basic example, it does show just how simple it is to launch a simple application using the dashboard. Now let's look at moving on to the command line.

The command line

In the previous chapter, we briefly touched upon how you can use YAML or JSON files to define your pods, ReplicaSets, and services. Let's use `kubectl` to launch to an application that is to the preceding one.

First of all, we need a file to launch; you can find a copy of the following one, which is called `cli-hello-world.yml`, in the `Chapter03` folder of the code bundle and GitHub repository that accompany this title:

```
apiVersion: v1
kind: Service
metadata:
  name: cli-hello-world
spec:
  selector:
    app: cli-hello-world
  type: NodePort
  ports:
  - protocol: TCP
    port: 8000
    targetPort: 80
---
apiVersion: apps/v1beta1
kind: Deployment
metadata:
  name: cli-hello-world
  labels:
    app: nginx
spec:
```

```
  replicas: 1
  selector:
    matchLabels:
      app: cli-hello-world
  template:
    metadata:
      labels:
        app: cli-hello-world
    spec:
      containers:
      - name: nginx
        image: nginx:latest
        ports:
        - containerPort: 80
```

As you may have noticed, while this is a single file we actually have two different sections. The first launches the external service, exposing it on port `8000` so that there isn't a clash with the external service we launched using the dashboard in the previous section. The second section defines the pod and replication set; this is pretty similar to what we launched using the dashboard.

To launch the application, we simply need to run the following command:

```
$ kubectl apply -f cli-hello-world.yml
```

You will almost immediately receive confirmation that a service and deployment have been created:

```
service "cli-hello-world" created
deployment "cli-hello-world" created
```

Once created, you should then be able to run the following command to open the application in the browser:

```
$ minikube service cli-hello-world
```

Again, you should be greeted by the default NGINX page.

I am sure that when we opened the dashboard you clicked around the menu items that can be found on the left of the page. All of this information can also be found on the command line, so let's briefly take a look at some of the commands we can use to find out more information about our cluster.

One of the more common commands you will be running is `kubectl get`. This fetches lists of the pods, ReplicaSets, and services, as well as much more. Running the following commands should give us a similar view to the dashboard overview:

```
$ kubectl get pods
$ kubectl get replicasets
$ kubectl get services
$ kubectl get secrets
```

As you can see from the following Terminal output, everything is listed along with its current status:

```
1. russ (bash)
⚡ kubectl get pods
NAME                                     READY     STATUS    RESTARTS   AGE
cli-hello-world-3678853705-f41d2         1/1       Running   0          24m
dashboard-hello-world-2612481942-3gcvz   1/1       Running   0          26m
russ in ~
⚡ kubectl get replicasets
NAME                               DESIRED   CURRENT   READY     AGE
cli-hello-world-3678853705         1         1         1         25m
dashboard-hello-world-2612481942   1         1         1         26m
russ in ~
⚡ kubectl get services
NAME                    TYPE           CLUSTER-IP    EXTERNAL-IP   PORT(S)          AGE
cli-hello-world         NodePort       10.0.0.22     <none>        8000:31327/TCP   25m
dashboard-hello-world   LoadBalancer   10.0.0.152    <pending>     8080:31376/TCP   26m
kubernetes              ClusterIP      10.0.0.1      <none>        443/TCP          38m
russ in ~
⚡ kubectl get secrets
NAME                  TYPE                                  DATA      AGE
default-token-v563p   kubernetes.io/service-account-token   3         38m
russ in ~
⚡
```

There are plenty of options you can get; for example, try running this:

```
$ kubectl get endpoints
$ kubectl get events
$ kubectl get storageclasses
```

Running just `kubectl get` will list all of the different parameters you can use. Now that have our full pod name, which in my case is `cli-hello-world-3678853705-f41d2`, we can find out more details about it by running the `kubectl describe` command. For example, I ran this:

```
$ kubectl describe pods/cli-hello-world-3678853705-f41d2
```

When you run the command locally, please update the pod name to reflect your own. Kubernetes adds a unique ID to each pod when launched to ensure that you can run multiples of the same pod on any given host.

I had the following information returned:

```
Name: cli-hello-world-3678853705-f41d2
Namespace: default
Node: minikube/192.168.99.100
Start Time: Sun, 08 Oct 2017 10:41:06 +0100
Labels: app=cli-hello-world
                pod-template-hash=3678853705
Annotations: kubernetes.io/created-
by={"kind":"SerializedReference","apiVersion":"v1","reference":{"kind":"Rep
licaSet","namespace":"default","name":"cli-hello-
world-3678853705","uid":"ce7b2030-ac0c-11e7-9136-08002...
Status: Running
IP: 172.17.0.5
Created By: ReplicaSet/cli-hello-world-3678853705
Controlled By: ReplicaSet/cli-hello-world-3678853705
Containers:
  nginx:
    Container ID:
docker://0eec13c8340b7c206bc900a6e783122cf6210561072b286bda10d225ffb3c658
    Image: nginx:latest
    Image ID: docker-
pullable://nginx@sha256:af32e714a9cc3157157374e68c818b05ebe9e0737aac06b55a0
9da374209a8f9
    Port: 80/TCP
    State: Running
      Started: Sun, 08 Oct 2017 10:41:09 +0100
    Ready: True
    Restart Count: 0
    Environment: <none>
    Mounts:
      /var/run/secrets/kubernetes.io/serviceaccount from default-token-
v563p (ro)
Conditions:
  Type Status
  Initialized True
  Ready True
  PodScheduled True
Volumes:
  default-token-v563p:
    Type: Secret (a volume populated by a Secret)
    SecretName: default-token-v563p
```

```
    Optional: false
QoS Class: BestEffort
Node-Selectors: <none>
Tolerations: <none>
Events:
  Type Reason Age From Message
  ---- ------ ---- ---- -------
  Normal Scheduled 31m default-scheduler Successfully assigned cli-hello-
world-3678853705-f41d2 to minikube
  Normal SuccessfulMountVolume 31m kubelet, minikube MountVolume.SetUp
succeeded for volume "default-token-v563p"
  Normal Pulling 31m kubelet, minikube pulling image "nginx:latest"
  Normal Pulled 31m kubelet, minikube Successfully pulled image
"nginx:latest"
  Normal Created 31m kubelet, minikube Created container
  Normal Started 31m kubelet, minikube Started container
```

You can use `kubectl describe` to find information on pretty much everything you can list using `kubectl get`, for example:

```
$ kubectl describe services/cli-hello-world
$ kubectl describe replicasets/cli-hello-world-3678853705
$ kubectl describe storageclasses/standard
```

Again, you can find out more by running just `kubectl describe` on its own. We will be introducing more commands throughout the following chapters so that, by the end of the book, you will be able to use `kubectl` to its fullest.

Before we finish this chapter, I want us to take a very quick look at how we can mount storage from our local machine inside the Minikube virtual machine and then inside our pods.

You will find a folder called `html` in the `Chapter03` folder. This contains a single file called `index.html`. Running the following command in the `Chapter03` folder will mount the HTML inside the virtual machine:

```
$ minikube mount ./html:/data/html
```

You can see this from the message that is displayed after the command has run:

```
1. chapter03 (minikube-darwin-)
russ in ~/Documents/Code/kubernetes-for-serverless-applications/Chapter03 on master*
⚡ minikube mount ./html:/data/html
Mounting ./html into /data/html on the minikube VM
This daemon process needs to stay alive for the mount to still be accessible...
ufs starting
```

At the time of writing there was a known bug using the `minikube mount` command on Windows 10 hosts, please see the following GitHub issues for more information `https://github.com/kubernetes/minikube/issues/1473` and `https://github.com/kubernetes/minikube/issues/2072`.

You will need to keep this process running, so open a new Terminal or PowerShell window for use in the remainder of this section.

Run the following commands:

```
$ minikube ssh
$ ls -lhat /data/html/
$ exit
```

These will log you in to the Minikube virtual machine, get a directory listing of `/data/html/`, and then `exit` out of the virtual machine:

```
2. russ (bash)
russ in ~
⚡ minikube ssh

$ ls -lhat /data/html
total 1.0K
-rw-r--r-- 1 501 20 690 Oct  8 11:10 index.html
$ exit
logout
russ in ~
⚡
```

As you can see, our `index.html` file is available on the cluster node in `/data/html/`. Moving back to the `Chapter03` folder, you should see a file called `cli-hello-world-storage.yml`. This contains the service and deployment information that uses this mounted folder.

The service section looks pretty similar to the one we used earlier in this section; however, there is an addition to the deployment section:

```
apiVersion: apps/v1beta1
kind: Deployment
metadata:
  name: cli-hello-world-storage
  labels:
```

```
      app: nginx
  spec:
    replicas: 1
    selector:
      matchLabels:
        app: cli-hello-world-storage
    template:
      metadata:
        labels:
          app: cli-hello-world-storage
      spec:
        volumes:
        - name: html
          hostPath:
            path: /data/html
        containers:
        - name: nginx
          image: nginx:latest
          ports:
          - containerPort: 80
          volumeMounts:
          - mountPath: /usr/share/nginx/html
            name: html
```

As you can see, in the `spec` part of the deployment we are now defining a `volume` named `html`, then in the container part we are taking the volume named `html` and using the `mountPath` option to tell Kubernetes that we want the volume to be mounted at `/usr/share/nginx/html`, which is the default web root for the NGINX container image we are using within the container.

Use the `kubectl apply` command to launch your application, and then the `minikube service` command to open the service in your browser:

```
$ kubectl apply -f cli-hello-world-storage.yml
$ minikube service cli-hello-world-storage
```

You should see the following page:

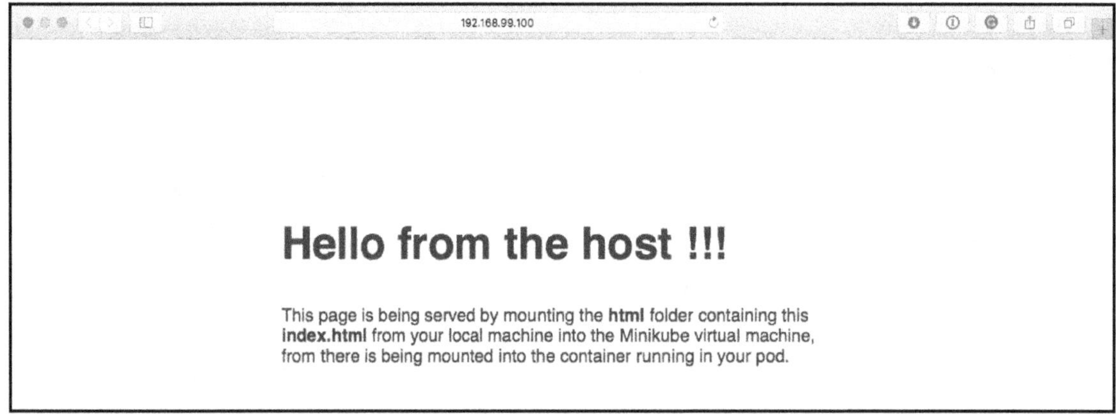

If you edit `index.html` in the `html` folder on your local machine, the changes will be immediately reflected when you refresh your browser window.

Before we move on to the next chapter, we should remove the Minikube machine we have used in this chapter so that we are starting with a clean slate. First of all, we have the process that is keeping the `html` folder from our host machine mounted. To terminate this process, go back to the Terminal or PowerShell and press *Ctrl* + *C*; this will send a termination signal to the process and return you to the command line. We can then run:

```
$ minikube delete
```

This will remove the current virtual machine, meaning that, when we next start Minikube, it will be from scratch.

References

More information on the tools we have used in this chapter can be found at their project pages:

- **Minikube**: `https://github.com/kubernetes/minikube`
- **kubectl**: `https://kubernetes.io/docs/user-guide/kubectl-overview/`
- **Homebrew**: `https://brew.sh/`

- **Cask**: `https://caskroom.github.io/`
- **Chocolatey**: `https://chocolatey.org/`
- **VirtualBox**: `https://www.virtualbox.org/`

Summary

In this chapter, we installed a single-node Kubernetes cluster on our local machine using Minikube; we looked at how to achieve this on macOS, Windows 10, and Ubuntu Linux. Once installed, we discovered that we can interact with our single-node Kubernetes cluster in exactly the same way, no matter which operating system our local machine is running.

We then took our first steps in launching pods, ReplicaSets, and services using both the Kubernetes dashboard and the Kubernetes command-line client called `kubectl`.

In the next chapter, we are going to be launching our first serverless tool, which is called Kubeless, on top of the single-node Kubernetes cluster we now have running locally.

4
Introducing Kubeless Functioning

Now that we have our Kubernetes installation up-and-running, we can look at running our first serverless applications; we are going to start by installing and running Kubeless by working through some examples. We will cover the following topics:

- Installing Kubeless
- Kubeless overview
- Running our first functions using Kubeless—the hello world examples
- A more advanced example—posting tweets
- The serverless plugin

Let's get started by installing Kubeless on our three target operating systems.

Installing Kubeless

There are two components to Kubeless; the first is the stack, which runs on Kubernetes, and the second part is the command-line client you use to interact with your Kubeless cluster.

We will first look at getting the Kubernetes side of Kubeless up-and-running. Once up we will then look at installing the command client on our three target operating systems.

The Kubeless Kubernetes cluster

We will be installing Kubeless on the single-node Minikube cluster we installed and configured in the previous chapter. The first thing we need to do is ensure that we are starting with a clean Kubernetes installation. To do this, we simply need to run the following two commands:

Please remember that running the `minikube delete` command will immediately remove your currently running virtual machine without warning, meaning everything that is currently active on your Minikube single-node cluster will be lost.

```
$ minikube delete
$ minikube start
```

Now that we have our fresh single-node Kubernetes cluster up-and-running, we need to create a namespace for Kubeless by running:

```
$ kubectl create ns kubeless
```

And then install Kubeless itself by running the following command:

At the time of writing, the current version of Kubeless was v0.2.3. You can check for the latest release at the projects, GitHub releases page, which is at `https://github.com/kubeless/kubeless/releases`. To install a later version simply use the newer releases version number in the following URL—however, please be warned that there may be differences in the output between versions.

```
$ kubectl create -f
https://github.com/kubeless/kubeless/releases/download/v0.2.3/kubeless-v0.2
.3.yaml
```

As you can see, this will create and launch all of the components needed to run Kubeless on your single-node Kubernetes cluster:

```
1. russ (bash)
⚡ minikube start
Starting local Kubernetes v1.7.5 cluster...
Starting VM...
Getting VM IP address...
Moving files into cluster...
Setting up certs...
Connecting to cluster...
Setting up kubeconfig...
Starting cluster components...
Kubectl is now configured to use the cluster.
russ in ~
⚡ kubectl create ns kubeless
namespace "kubeless" created
russ in ~
⚡ kubectl create -f https://github.com/kubeless/kubeless/releases/download/v0.2.3/kubeless-v0.2.3.y
aml
customresourcedefinition "functions.k8s.io" created
statefulset "kafka" created
service "zookeeper" created
service "kafka" created
service "zoo" created
statefulset "zoo" created
deployment "kubeless-controller" created
serviceaccount "controller-acct" created
service "broker" created
russ in ~
⚡
```

It will take a few minutes for everything to start up. You can check the status of each of the components launched by running the following commands:

```
$ kubectl get pods -n kubeless
$ kubectl get deployment -n kubeless
$ kubectl get statefulset -n kubeless
```

This should show you something like the following output:

```
1. russ (bash)
⚡ kubectl get pods -n kubeless
NAME                                  READY     STATUS    RESTARTS   AGE
kafka-0                               1/1       Running   0          7m
kubeless-controller-2704426935-pxnl1  1/1       Running   0          7m
zoo-0                                 1/1       Running   0          7m
russ in ~
⚡ kubectl get deployment -n kubeless
NAME                  DESIRED   CURRENT   UP-TO-DATE   AVAILABLE   AGE
kubeless-controller   1         1         1            1           8m
russ in ~
⚡ kubectl get statefulset -n kubeless
NAME     DESIRED   CURRENT   AGE
kafka    1         1         8m
zoo      1         1         8m
russ in ~
⚡
```

Alternatively, you can also check the status using the Kubernetes dashboard. To do this, open the dashboard by running the following command:

```
$ minikube dashboard
```

When the dashboard first opens, it is configured to display the default namespace, as the first command we executed created a new namespace called `kubeless`. We need to switch the `kubeless` namespace to see the **Pods**, **Deployments**, and **Stateful Sets** that have been deployed inside it.

Once you have changed namespaces you should see something on the following page:

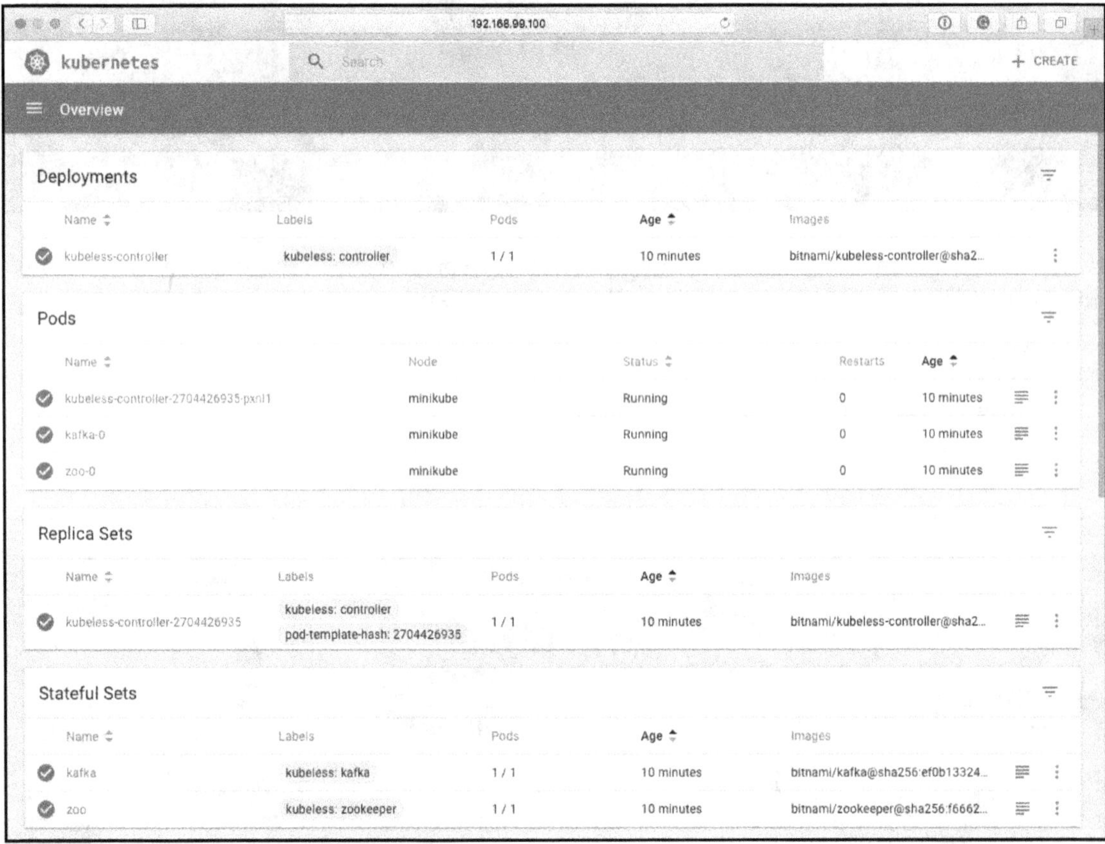

As you can see, we have deployed quite a complex set of services using just two commands. All of the heavy lifting and complexity has been completely abstracted away from us.

The command-line client

Now that Kubeless is installed on our single-node Kubernetes cluster we can look at getting the command-line client installed; this is how we will be interacting with our Kubeless cluster.

macOS 10.13 High Sierra

As we already have Homebrew installed from the previous chapter, we are going to use the `brew` command to install Kubeless. To do this, we need to add the Kubeless tap; a tap is a third-party repository that contains software installation instructions. Once the tap has been added, we can then install Kubeless in much the same way we did Minikube in `Chapter 2`, *An Introduction to Kubernetes*.

To install the tap and then install the Kubeless command-line client, run the following two commands:

```
$ brew tap kubeless/tap
$ brew install kubeless
```

Once installed you can check the version of the client that was installed by running the following command:

```
$ kubeless version
```

Do not worry too much if this returns a different version of the client than the software you installed; this should not be a problem.

Windows 10 Professional

Unfortunately, there is no Chocolatey installer available for Kubeless, so we will have to download and uncompress the executable file manually. To do this in PowerShell, run the following commands:

```
$ Invoke-WebRequest -Uri
https://github.com/kubeless/kubeless/releases/download/v0.2.3/kubeless_wind
ows-amd64.zip -Outfile C:\Temp\kubeless_windows-amd64.zip
$ expand-archive -path 'C:\Temp\kubeless_windows-amd64.zip' -
destinationpath 'C:\Temp\kubeless_windows-amd64'
$ Move-Item C:\Temp\kubeless_windows-amd64\bundles\kubeless_windows-
amd64\kubeless.exe .\
```

Alternatively, you can download the `kubeless_windows-amd64.zip` file from the Kubeless releases page. Once downloaded, extract the `.zip` file and put the `kubeless.exe` file where we can execute it. Run the following command from the folder that contains your `kubeless.exe` file:

```
$ ./kubeless version
```

This will return the version of the command-line client.

Ubuntu 17.04

Like the Windows 10 version of the command-line client for Kubeless, we have to download the release, uncompress it, and move the executable in place. To do this, run the following commands:

```
$ curl -Lo /tmp/kubeless.zip
https://github.com/kubeless/kubeless/releases/download/v0.2.3/kubeless_linu
x-amd64.zip
$ unzip /tmp/kubeless.zip -d /tmp
$ chmod +x /tmp/bundles/kubeless_linux-amd64/kubeless
$ sudo mv /tmp/bundles/kubeless_linux-amd64/kubeless /usr/local/bin/
```

Finally, to check that the executable is working as expected, run:

```
$ kubeless version
```

We are ready to use Kubeless on our Ubuntu Linux host.

The Kubeless web interface

Before we move on we can also install the web interface for Kubeless. This, like Kubeless itself, can easily be installed by running:

```
$ kubectl create -f
https://raw.githubusercontent.com/kubeless/kubeless-ui/master/k8s.yaml
```

You can then use Minikube to open the service in your browser by running:

```
$ minikube service ui --namespace kubeless
```

As you can see from the preceding command, as the `ui` service has been deployed in the `kubeless` namespace we need to let Minikube know that this is where the service is accessible by passing the `--namespace` flag. It may take up to several minutes for the Kubeless web interface to launch, but when it does you should be greeted by a page that looks like the following:

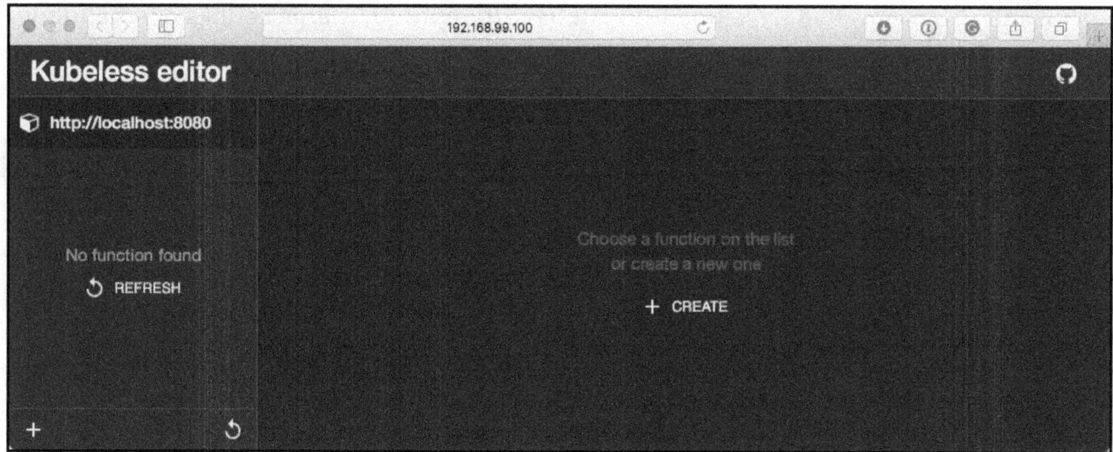

Kubeless overview

Before we start to deploy serverless functions using Kubeless we should take a little time to work through what it is we have just installed, and also take a look at the commands available when using the Kubeless command-line client.

As we have already mentioned, the installation process was extremely simple—while we were installing Kubeless on our single-node Kubernetes cluster the installation process would have remained pretty much the same if we were installing it on a Kubernetes made up of several nodes.

So what is Kubeless?

Kubeless is a framework that supports the deployment of serverless functions on your Kubernetes cluster, and it allows you to use both HTTP and event triggers to execute your Python, Node.js, or Ruby code. The framework is built using core Kubernetes functionality such as deployments, services, ConfigMaps, and so on. This keeps the Kubeless codebase small, and also means that developers do not have to reproduce large chunks of scheduling logic as it already exists within the Kubernetes core.

It works by taking advantage of Kubernetes controllers. Using controllers, the Kubeless developers have extended the Kubernetes API to add a function object within Kubernetes. The Kubeless controller runs within the Kubernetes cluster as a deployment, its primary job is to watch for the function endpoint being called. When the endpoint is called, runtimes containing the function code are executed; these are pre-built Docker images that wrap your functions, which are injected using ConfigMaps, in either an Apache Kafka consumer, which is used for events, or an HTTP server, which you can call like any other web page in your Kubernetes cluster.

Apache Kafka is a distributed streaming platform that lets you both publish and subscribe to a stream of information. In our case, this stream of information is an event being triggered to which the Kubeless controller is subscribed.

All of this means that we can get a similar experience of the serverless services we covered from AWS and Microsoft Azure in `Chapter 1`, *The Serverless Landscape*, on our Kubernetes cluster, including the single-node cluster we are running locally.

Who made Kubeless?

Kubeless was created by Bitnami (`https://bitnami.com/`) and it is one of several projects they have written and open-sourced to support the easy deployment of applications into a Kubernetes cluster.

Bitnami has for many years been a leader in distributing pre-packaged open source and commercially supported licensed applications—there are over 140 at the time of writing—in a predictable and consistent way across many different platforms and public clouds, so the jump to supporting and developing for Kubernetes was a natural fit for them.

They are a core contributor, alongside Microsoft and Google, to Helm, which is a package manager for Kubernetes maintained by the Cloud Native Computing Foundation forum, who as we know from Chapter 2, *An Introduction to Kubernetes*, also maintain Kubernetes itself.

You can find the Kubeless website at `http://kubeless.io/`.

Kubeless commands

The Kubeless command-line client has several commands. Before we look at launching our first serverless function on Kubernetes using Kubeless we should quickly discuss some of the commands we are going to be using.

The most common command we are going to be using is `kubeless function`. This allows us to `deploy`, `delete`, `edit`, and `list` functions. Also, we can execute our functions by using `call` and check the `logs`.

Next up, we have `kubeless ingress`; with this command we can `create`, `delete`, and `list` routes to our functions.

Finally, we will also be looking at `kubeless topic`; like `ingress`, it allows us to `create`, `delete`, and `list` topics as well as `publish` a message to a topic.

Hello world

To start off with we are going to look at deploying two very simple hello world functions. The first simply prints `Hello World!` and the second takes an input and then displays it back to you.

The basic example

First of all, we need our function. The static hello-world function requires the following three lines of Python code:

```
import json
def handler():
    return "Hello World!"
```

Place the preceding code, which is also available in the `Chapter04/hello-world` folder of the GitHub repository that accompanies this book, in a file called `hello.py`.

Now we have our function we can deploy it into the default namespace by running the following command:

```
$ kubeless function deploy hello \
  --from-file hello.py
  --handler hello.handler \
  --runtime python2.7 \
  --trigger-http
```

This command creates a function called `hello`, using the file `hello.py`. Whenever the function called `hello.handler` is executed, we are using the `python2.7` runtime, and our function is set to be triggered by an `http` request.

You may have noticed that, when you ran the command, there was no feedback, so to check that the function was created you can run the following command:

```
$ kubeless function ls
```

There are several columns in the preceding command:

- `NAME`: This is the name of the function
- `NAMESPACE`: The name of the namespace the function has been deployed into
- `HANDLER`: The name of the handler to run—in our case the handler is simply handler, so it is calling `hello-world.handler`
- `RUNTIME`: There is a separate runtime for each of the languages supported by Kubeless
- `TYPE`: This is how the function is being called, in our case this is HTTP
- `TOPIC`: If we were subscribing to a message queue this would be the topic we would be watching for messages in

Also, as mentioned in the previous section, Kubeless adds functions objects to Kubernetes. You can run the following command to check our function is being listed in the functions object:

```
$ kubectl get functions
```

Running through these commands should give you something like the following results:

```
2. hello-world (bash)
russ in ~/Documents/Code/kubernetes-for-serverless-applications/Chapter04/hello-world on master*
⚡ kubeless function deploy hello --from-file hello.py --handler hello.handler --runtime python2.7 -
-trigger-http
russ in ~/Documents/Code/kubernetes-for-serverless-applications/Chapter04/hello-world on master*
⚡ kubeless function ls
NAME    NAMESPACE       HANDLER         RUNTIME         TYPE    TOPIC   DEPENDENCIES
hello   default         hello.handler   python2.7       HTTP
russ in ~/Documents/Code/kubernetes-for-serverless-applications/Chapter04/hello-world on master*
⚡ kubectl get functions
NAME      AGE
hello     1m
russ in ~/Documents/Code/kubernetes-for-serverless-applications/Chapter04/hello-world on master*
⚡
```

Now that we have our function deployed, we can execute it. To do this run:

```
$ kubeless function call hello
```

This will give the following results:

```
2. hello-world (bash)
russ in ~/Documents/Code/kubernetes-for-serverless-applications/Chapter04/hello-world on master*
⚡ kubeless function call hello
Forwarding from 127.0.0.1:30000 -> 8080
Forwarding from [::1]:30000 -> 8080
Handling connection for 30000
Hello World!
russ in ~/Documents/Code/kubernetes-for-serverless-applications/Chapter04/hello-world on master*
⚡
```

Another way we can call the function is using the Kubeless web interface. Open it by running the following command:

```
$ minikube service ui --namespace kubeless
```

Once open, you should see the function `hello` listed on the left-hand side. Clicking on `hello` will show you the code in the function, and there is a button labelled **RUN FUNCTION** on the right-hand side; clicking this will execute the `hello` function and return `Hello World!`:

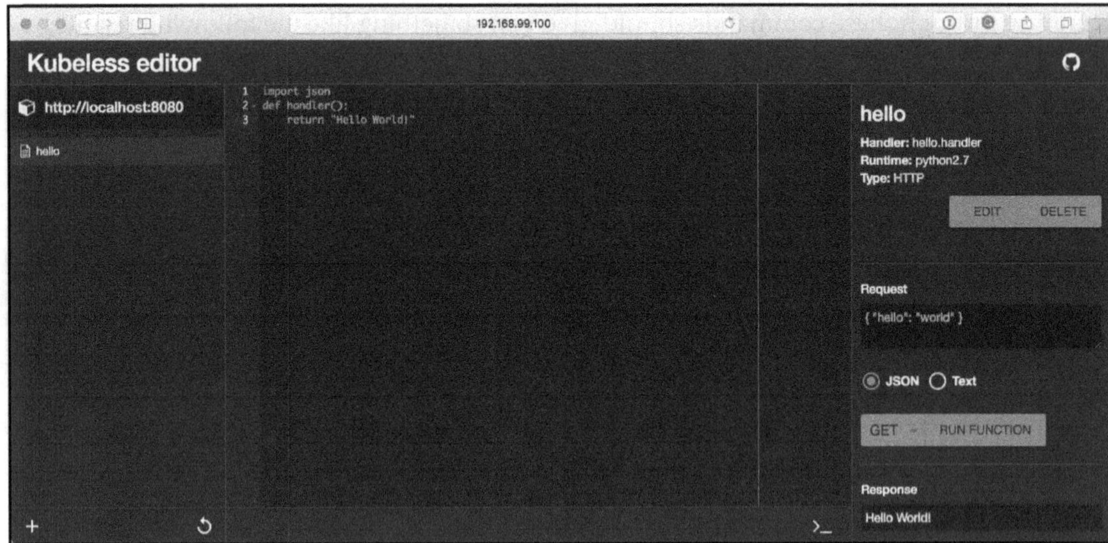

The final way we can interact with our function is to create an Ingress rule; however, before we do that we must enable the Ingress add-on in Minikube. To do that, run the following command:

```
$ minikube addons enable ingress
```

Now that the Ingress add-on is enabled we need to create the Ingress route using Kubeless. To do this we simply need to run the following command:

```
$ kubeless ingress create --function hello hello-ingress
```

We need to know the host that Kubeless created so that we can access our service. To do this, run the following:

```
$ kubeless ingress ls
```

This will give information on the Ingress route we created, including the host we will be able to use to access the service. For me, this was `http://hello.192.168.99.100.nip.io/`.

nip.io is a simple and free DNS service that allows you to create a DNS record to map your host to an IP address. Kubeless uses this service to create a valid host to route to your service.

Opening this URL in my browser returned `Hello World!`, as did running it through HTTPie, which we covered in `Chapter 1`, *The Serverless Landscape*, as you can see from the following Terminal output:

```
1. russ (bash)
⚡ minikube addons enable ingress
ingress was successfully enabled
russ in ~
⚡ kubeless ingress create --function hello hello-ingress
russ in ~
⚡ kubeless ingress ls
+---------------+-----------+----------------------------+------+--------------+--------------+
|     NAME      | NAMESPACE |            HOST            | PATH | SERVICE NAME | SERVICE PORT |
+---------------+-----------+----------------------------+------+--------------+--------------+
| hello-ingress | default   | hello.192.168.99.100.nip.io | /    | hello        |         8080 |
+---------------+-----------+----------------------------+------+--------------+--------------+
russ in ~
⚡ http http://hello.192.168.99.100.nip.io/
HTTP/1.1 200 OK
Connection: keep-alive
Content-Length: 12
Content-Type: text/html; charset=UTF-8
Date: Sat, 21 Oct 2017 16:56:16 GMT
Server: nginx/1.13.5

Hello World!

russ in ~
⚡
```

Now that we have our first function up-and-running, let's look at creating one that can be passed and print data.

An example of reading data

The code for our new function is still quite simple:

```
import json

def handler(context):
    print context.json
    return context.json
```

All this code does is take the JSON we post and display it back to us. Place it in a file called `hello-name.py` or use the one in the `Chapter04/hello-world/` folder in the GitHub repository. Once you have the file you can create the function by running:

```
$ kubeless function deploy hello-name \
   --from-file hello-name.py \
   --handler hello-name.handler \
   --runtime python2.7 \
   --trigger-http
```

Once you have deployed the function, you check it has been created by running:

```
$ kubeless function ls
```

You should see two functions listed, `hello` and `hello-name`. Now that we have created our new function you can call it by running:

```
$ kubeless function call hello-name --data '{ "name": "Russ" }'
```

Notice that this time we are using the `--data` flag to pass data to the function. Running all of the commands, you should see something like the following terminal output:

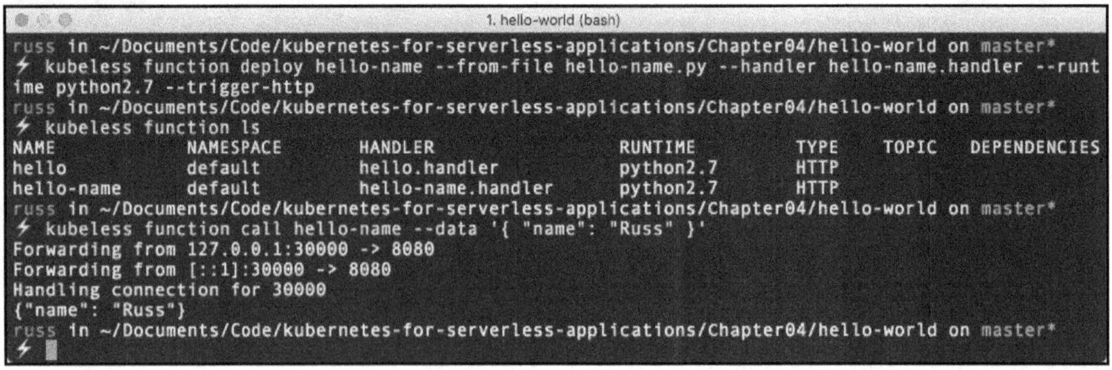

```
1. hello-world (bash)
russ in ~/Documents/Code/kubernetes-for-serverless-applications/Chapter04/hello-world on master*
⚡ kubeless function deploy hello-name --from-file hello-name.py --handler hello-name.handler --runt
ime python2.7 --trigger-http
russ in ~/Documents/Code/kubernetes-for-serverless-applications/Chapter04/hello-world on master*
⚡ kubeless function ls
NAME            NAMESPACE       HANDLER                 RUNTIME         TYPE    TOPIC   DEPENDENCIES
hello           default         hello.handler           python2.7       HTTP
hello-name      default         hello-name.handler      python2.7       HTTP
russ in ~/Documents/Code/kubernetes-for-serverless-applications/Chapter04/hello-world on master*
⚡ kubeless function call hello-name --data '{ "name": "Russ" }'
Forwarding from 127.0.0.1:30000 -> 8080
Forwarding from [::1]:30000 -> 8080
Handling connection for 30000
{"name": "Russ"}
russ in ~/Documents/Code/kubernetes-for-serverless-applications/Chapter04/hello-world on master*
⚡ █
```

When calling the function using the web interface, we also need to pass data. To do this, open the interface again by running:

```
$ minikube service ui --namespace kubeless
```

Once open, click on the `hello-name` function. Before clicking the **RUN FUNCTION** button change **GET** to **POST** using the drop-down menu, and in the **Request** form enter the following:

```
{ "name": "Russ" }
```

Now, press the **RUN FUNCTION** button. This will return the same result as the `kubeless function call` command:

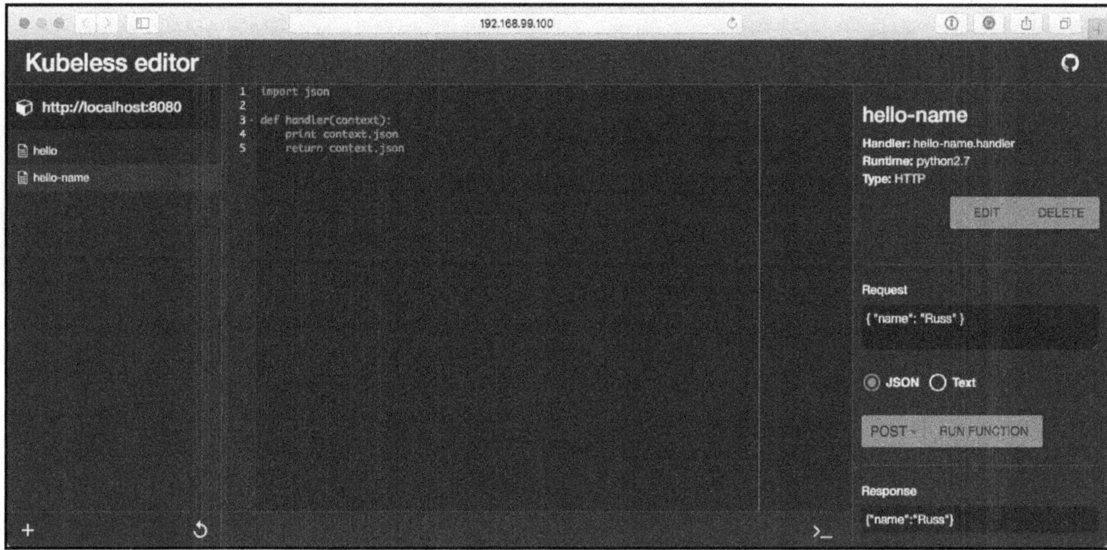

We can also interact with the service directly by configuring an Ingress route:

```
$ kubeless ingress create --function hello-name hello-name-ingress
$ kubeless ingress list
```

This will give you URLs for both of our functions:

```
1. hello-world (bash)
russ in ~/Documents/Code/kubernetes-for-serverless-applications/Chapter04/hello-world on master*
⚡ kubeless ingress create --function hello-name hello-name-ingress
russ in ~/Documents/Code/kubernetes-for-serverless-applications/Chapter04/hello-world on master*
⚡ kubeless ingress list
+--------------------+-----------+-----------------------------------+------+--------------+---------
-----+
|        NAME        | NAMESPACE |               HOST                | PATH | SERVICE NAME | SERVICE
PORT |
+--------------------+-----------+-----------------------------------+------+--------------+---------
-----+
| hello-ingress      | default   | hello.192.168.99.100.nip.io       | /    | hello        |
8080 |
| hello-name-ingress | default   | hello-name.192.168.99.100.nip.io | /    | hello-name   |
8080 |
+--------------------+-----------+-----------------------------------+------+--------------+---------
-----+
russ in ~/Documents/Code/kubernetes-for-serverless-applications/Chapter04/hello-world on master*
⚡
```

Unlike our first example, going to the URL for `hello-name`, which for me was `http://hello-name.192.168.99.100.nip.io/`, will give **Error: 500 Internal Server Error** (or on later versions of Kubeless, a 504 Gateway timeout):

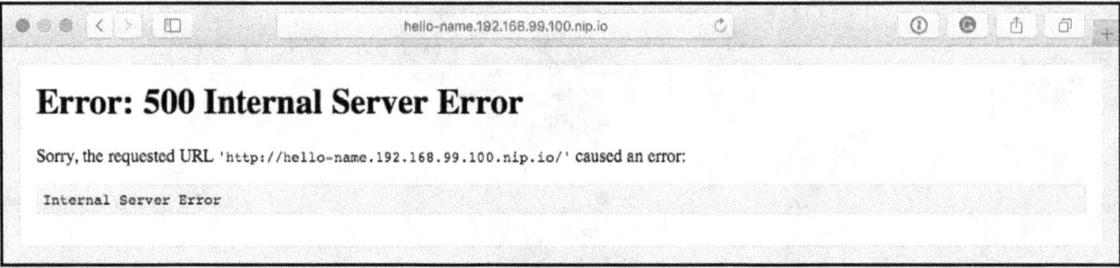

Why is that, given that it worked without error when we called it using the `kubeless function call` command and also using the Kubeless web interface?

Well, by simply entering the URL into a browser we have not posted any data for the function to return; this is why the error is being generated. We can confirm this by checking the logs. To do this, refresh the page in your browser a few times and then run the following command:

```
$ kubeless function logs hello-name
```

You should see something like the following:

```
1. hello-world (bash)
172.17.0.1 - - [21/Oct/2017:19:02:30 +0000] "GET /healthz HTTP/1.1" 200 2 "" "Go-http-client/1.1" 0/
78
Traceback (most recent call last):
  File "/usr/local/lib/python2.7/site-packages/bottle.py", line 862, in _handle
    return route.call(**args)
  File "/usr/local/lib/python2.7/site-packages/bottle.py", line 1740, in wrapper
    rv = callback(*a, **ka)
  File "/kubeless.py", line 33, in handler
    return func()
TypeError: handler() takes exactly 1 argument (0 given)
172.17.0.10 - - [21/Oct/2017:19:02:54 +0000] "GET / HTTP/1.1" 500 759 "" "Mozilla/5.0 (Macintosh; In
tel Mac OS X 10_13) AppleWebKit/604.1.38 (KHTML, like Gecko) Version/11.0 Safari/604.1.38" 0/582
russ in ~/Documents/Code/kubernetes-for-serverless-applications/Chapter04/hello-world on master*
⚡
```

The first line of the preceding log output is the internal health check, which was successful, as a `200` status was generated, which you can see after the `GET`. The next several lines contain the error we are after; as you can see, we get a `Traceback` and then the following: `TypeError: handler() takes exactly 1 argument (0 given)`. This means that the function was expecting data to be passed and none was. The next line is the request from our browser; as you can see after the `GET`, there is a status of `500`.

So how can we interact with our function that requires us to POST data rather than GET? There are a few ways you can achieve this on the macOS and Linux command line, but you will have to run something else on Windows. Rather than working through different examples I am going to install a piece of software called Postman. This desktop software works on all three of the operating systems we are covering in the book and it will provide a great graphical interface for us to interact with both the `hello-name` function and any other functions we launch.

To install Postman on macOS 10.13 High Sierra using Homebrew, simply run:

```
$ brew cask install postman
```

There is a Chocolatey package for Postman, so if you are using Windows 10 Professional, you can run:

```
$ choco install postman
```

To install Postman on Ubuntu 17.04 we need to run a few more additional steps. First of all, we need to download, uncompress, and move the file into place, making sure to clean up and move the files we need. To do this, run the following commands:

```
$ wget https://dl.pstmn.io/download/latest/linux64 -O postman.tar.gz
$ sudo tar -xzf postman.tar.gz -C /opt
$ rm postman.tar.gz
$ sudo ln -s /opt/Postman/Postman /usr/bin/postman
```

Now we have the files in the correct place, we can create a desktop launcher for them by running:

```
$ cat > ~/.local/share/applications/postman.desktop <<EOL
[Desktop Entry]
Encoding=UTF-8
Name=Postman
Exec=postman
Icon=/opt/Postman/resources/app/assets/icon.png
Terminal=false
Type=Application
```

```
Categories=Development;
EOL
```

Once you have created the launcher you should see a Postman icon appear in the list of installed software.

Now that we have installed Postman, open it and you will be greeted by a screen asking you to sign-up. It is up to you if you wish to sign-up or not; the service is free and you will find it of great use if you ever need to test posting data to APIs. Once you have passed the **Sign up** or **Sign in** option you will be presented with a screen that looks like the following:

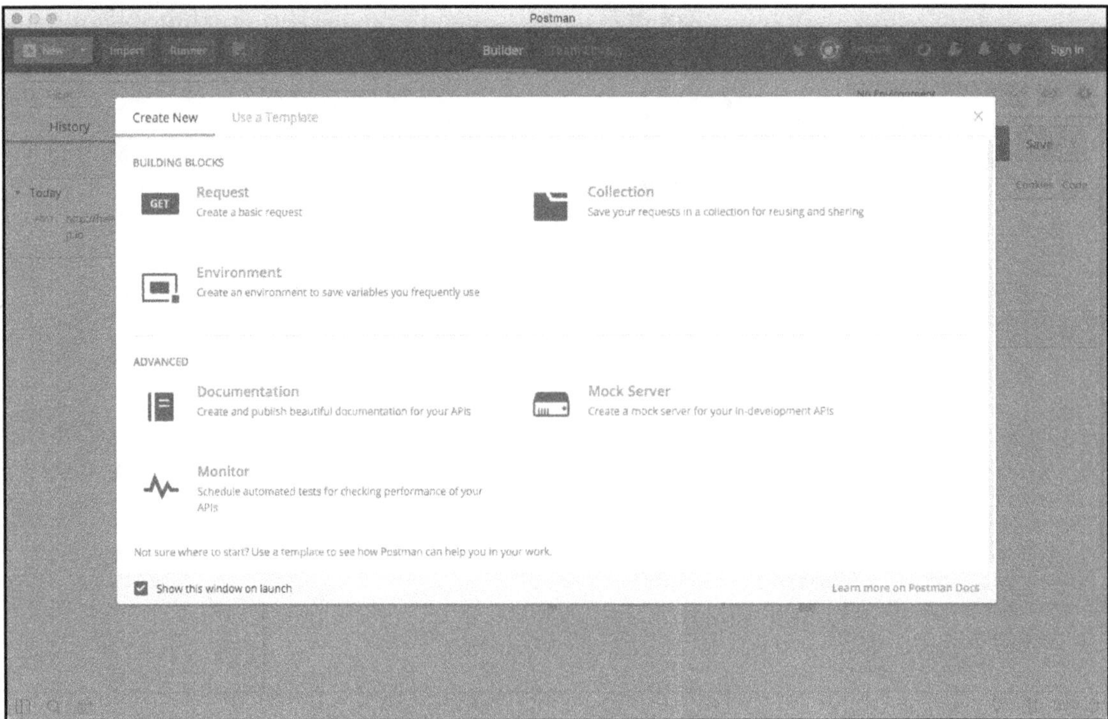

Click on the **Request** option under **BUILDING BLOCKS**; this will take you to a save dialog. Here, enter the **Request name** of `hello-name` and then click on **+Create Collection**. Here, create a collection called `Kubeless` and then click on the **Save to Kubeless** button.

First of all, change **GET** to **POST** using the drop-down menu, then in the space that is labelled **Enter request URL** enter `http://hello-name.192.168.99.100.nip.io` (or your URL if different). Now that we have defined that we are going to be posting our data, to we need to actually give Postman the data that needs to be passed to our function.

To enter the data click on **Body**, and then select the **raw** option. When you select **raw** the input field will change, and you should see the word **Text** with a drop-down icon next to it. Click on this and check the option for **JSON (application/json)**. Once changed, enter the following in the main field:

```
{
  "name": "Russ"
}
```

Now that Postman is configured to POST JSON data to our function you can click on **Send**. This will post the data we defined and then display the results in the bottom part of the screen, along with the HTTP status and the time the request took to be executed, just like the following screenshot:

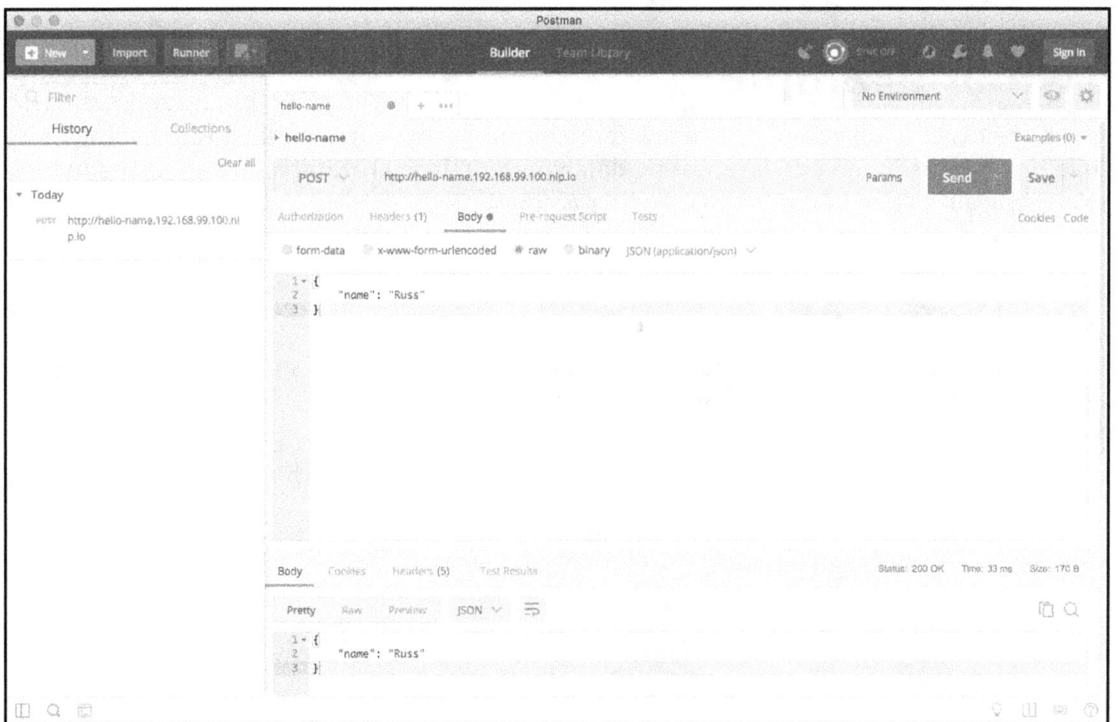

Clicking on the **Save** button will store the settings, should you want to re-run them.

Before we move on to the next section we should tidy up our functions. To do this, we simply need to run:

```
$ kubeless ingress delete hello
$ kubeless function delete hello
$ kubeless ingress delete hello-name
$ kubeless function delete hello-name
```

This will remove our two hello world functions and Ingress routes. You can also double-check that everything has been removed in the Kubeless web interface and Kubernetes dashboard; again, you can open these by running:

```
$ minikube service ui --namespace kubeless
$ minikube dashboard
```

If you spot anything left over for either `hello` or `hello-name` you can remove the services, pods, and even Ingress routes from the dashboard.

Twitter example

The Kubeless GitHub account has a few more example applications that do something more than printing static content or reposting data you sent. In this example, we are going to look at creating a function that posts to a Twitter account.

The Twitter API

Before we look at launching the function we need to generate keys for our function to be able to authenticate against Twitter and then post to your account. To do this, you need the following:

- A Twitter account
- A mobile number registered with the account

If you have them then going to the Twitter application page at `https://apps.twitter.com/` will present you with a form to fill in (**Application Details**)—I used the following information. However, a few of the fields need to be unique to you; these are marked with *:

- **Name***: `MedialGlassesKubeless`
- **Description:** `Testing posting to Twitter using Kubeless`
- **Website***: `https://media-glass.es/`
- **Callback URL**: Leave blank
- **Developer Agreement**: Agree to the agreement

Once you have filled in the preceding information, click on the **Create your Twitter application** button. Once the application has been created you will be taken to a page that allows you to manage your application. One of the tabs on the page is **Keys and Access Tokens**; clicking on this will reveal your **Consumer Key (API Key)** and **Consumer Secret (API Secret)**—make a note of these.

At the bottom of the page, you will have a button that allows you to create an **Access Token** and **Access Token Secret** for your account; clicking on the button will generate the tokens—again, make a note of these.

While the following examples will contain the keys I have generated, they have been revoked, and you should use your own. Also, as they allow both read and write access to your Twitter account, storing them in a publicly accessible place such as GitHub, Gists, or other version control software may result in third-parties having full access to your Twitter account without your permission.

Adding secrets to Kubernetes

Now that we have our Twitter application configured and all of the tokens we need to be able to post a tweet, we need to add them to Kubernetes. Kubernetes allows you to define secrets; these are variables such as API keys and tokens that your applications need to use to function. However, you might not want to put them under source control or embed them in your application because various deployments of the same code interact with the APIs using different keys—for example, the development version of the code uses a different set of API credentials from the production version.

To add the tokens you made a note of in the previous section you just need to run the following command, replacing the placeholders, which are in uppercase, with your tokens and keys:

```
$ kubectl create secret generic twitter \
  --from-literal=consumer_key=YOUR_CONSUMER_KEY \
  --from-literal=consumer_secret=YOUR_CONSUMER_SECRET \
  --from-literal=token_key=YOUR_TOKEN_KEY \
  --from-literal=token_secret=YOUR_TOKEN_SECRET
```

For me, the command looked like the following:

```
1. russ (bash)
⚡ kubectl create secret generic twitter --from-literal=consumer_key=TmMtCmNzgBee2Rr2W6qO8glD0 --fro
m-literal=consumer_secret=x0sGDLE6zrVbuDq1ZFKErvY6gbnoyi7bVWZqQr0IPcssqfT5dc --from-literal=token_ke
y=2213091858-8B8mhuTTBBrhJ3DhnhBXSxjR3xoaMpF6fkDz0HC --from-literal=token_secret=hhdDwRX8ZIRi75RjhAq
2VUH64DS8NuNm3Kzdb79Up7yAH
secret "twitter" created
russ in ~
⚡
```

This has created a secret called `twitter` that contains the four different keys and tokens we passed to the command. You can list the secrets by running:

```
$ kubectl get secret
```

This will list all of the secrets within your Kubernetes cluster, as you can see from the following Terminal output:

```
1. russ (bash)
russ in ~
⚡ kubectl get secret
NAME                  TYPE                                  DATA      AGE
default-token-0rzh4   kubernetes.io/service-account-token   3         18m
twitter               Opaque                                4         2m
russ in ~
⚡
```

There are the default Kubernetes service account tokens, which contain three items, and our `twitter` secret containing the four keys and tokens. You can also view secrets in the Kubernetes dashboard:

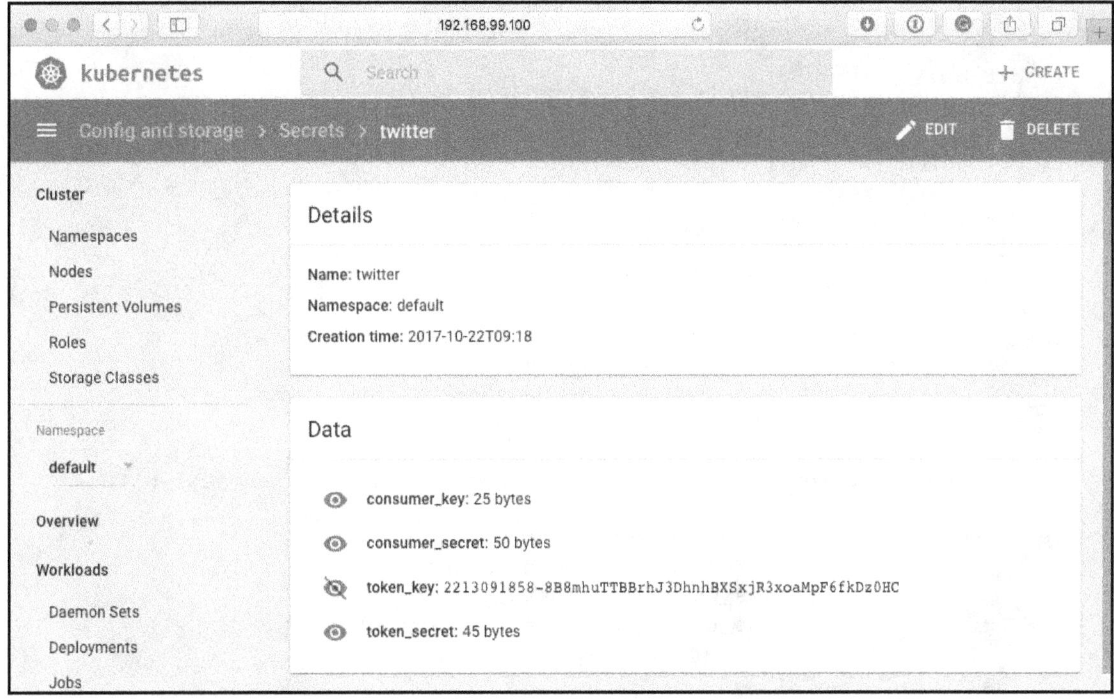

As you can see from the preceding screenshot, you also have the option of revealing the secret by clicking on the eye icon.

The Twitter function

Now that we have our environment prepared we can deploy the function. To do this we need two files; the first is the `requirements.txt` file, this contains just two lines:

```
python-twitter
kubernetes==2.0.0
```

The `requirements.txt` file lets Python know which external libraries to deploy alongside our code. In our file we are using the `twitter` library so that we can post the tweet easily, and also the `kubernetes` library to decode the secrets we created in the previous section. Using the libraries means that our code is quite streamlined, as all of the hard work takes place outside our core function. The code for the function is as follows:

```
import base64
import twitter

from kubernetes import client, config

config.load_incluster_config()

v1=client.CoreV1Api()

for secrets in v1.list_secret_for_all_namespaces().items:
    if secrets.metadata.name == 'twitter':
        consumer_key = base64.b64decode(secrets.data['consumer_key'])
        consumer_secret = base64.b64decode(secrets.data['consumer_secret'])
        token_key = base64.b64decode(secrets.data['token_key'])
        token_secret = base64.b64decode(secrets.data['token_secret'])

api = twitter.Api(consumer_key=consumer_key,
                  consumer_secret=consumer_secret,
                  access_token_key=token_key,
                  access_token_secret=token_secret)

def handler(context):
    msg = context.json
    status = api.PostUpdate(msg['tweet'])
```

Place this in a file called `tweet.py`. As before, both the `requirements.txt` and `tweet.py` files can be found in the GitHub repository at `Chapter04/twitter/`.

The command to deploy the function has one addition to the deployment command. As we are now loading external libraries, we need to let Kubeless know that we want to use a `requirements.txt` file by adding the `--dependencies` flag:

```
$ kubeless function deploy twitter \
  --from-file tweet.py \
  --handler tweet.handler \
  --runtime python2.7 \
  --trigger-http \
  --dependencies requirements.txt
```

As you can see from the following Terminal output, the dependencies are now listed when running the `kubeless function list` command:

```
1. twitter (bash)
russ in ~/Documents/Code/kubernetes-for-serverless-applications/Chapter04/twitter on master*
⚡ kubeless function deploy twitter --from-file tweet.py --handler tweet.handler --runtime python2.7
 --trigger-http --dependencies requirements.txt
russ in ~/Documents/Code/kubernetes-for-serverless-applications/Chapter04/twitter on master*
⚡ kubeless function list
NAME     NAMESPACE        HANDLER          RUNTIME          TYPE     TOPIC    DEPENDENCIES
twitter  default          tweet.handler    python2.7        HTTP              python-twitter
                                                                              kubernetes==2.0.0
russ in ~/Documents/Code/kubernetes-for-serverless-applications/Chapter04/twitter on master*
⚡
```

Now that our function has been deployed, we can start tweeting. To send our first tweet you simply need to run the following command:

```
$ kubeless function call twitter --data '{"tweet": "Testing twitter
function from Kubeless!"}'
```

You will not receive any feedback, but if you go to your Twitter account you should see the tweet:

You can also use Postman to send a tweet. First of all, create an Ingress route by running the following commands:

```
$ kubeless ingress create --function twitter twitter-ingress
$ kubeless ingress list
```

This will create the route and give us the host we need to use to access the function:

```
1. twitter (bash)
⚡ kubeless ingress create --function twitter twitter-ingress
russ in ~/Documents/Code/kubernetes-for-serverless-applications/Chapter04/twitter on master*
⚡ kubeless ingress list
+-----------------+-----------+--------------------------------+------+--------------+--------------+
|      NAME       | NAMESPACE |              HOST              | PATH | SERVICE NAME | SERVICE PORT |
+-----------------+-----------+--------------------------------+------+--------------+--------------+
| twitter-ingress | default   | twitter.192.168.99.100.nip.io  | /    | twitter      |         8080 |
+-----------------+-----------+--------------------------------+------+--------------+--------------+
russ in ~/Documents/Code/kubernetes-for-serverless-applications/Chapter04/twitter on master*
⚡
```

Now we can open Postman, and as before configure it in pretty much the same way, but this file uses the following as the post content:

```
{
  "tweet": "Testing twitter function from Kubeless using @postmanclient!"
}
```

Clicking on **Send** will post the tweet and, like when calling the function using the `kubeless function call` command, will not give us any feedback:

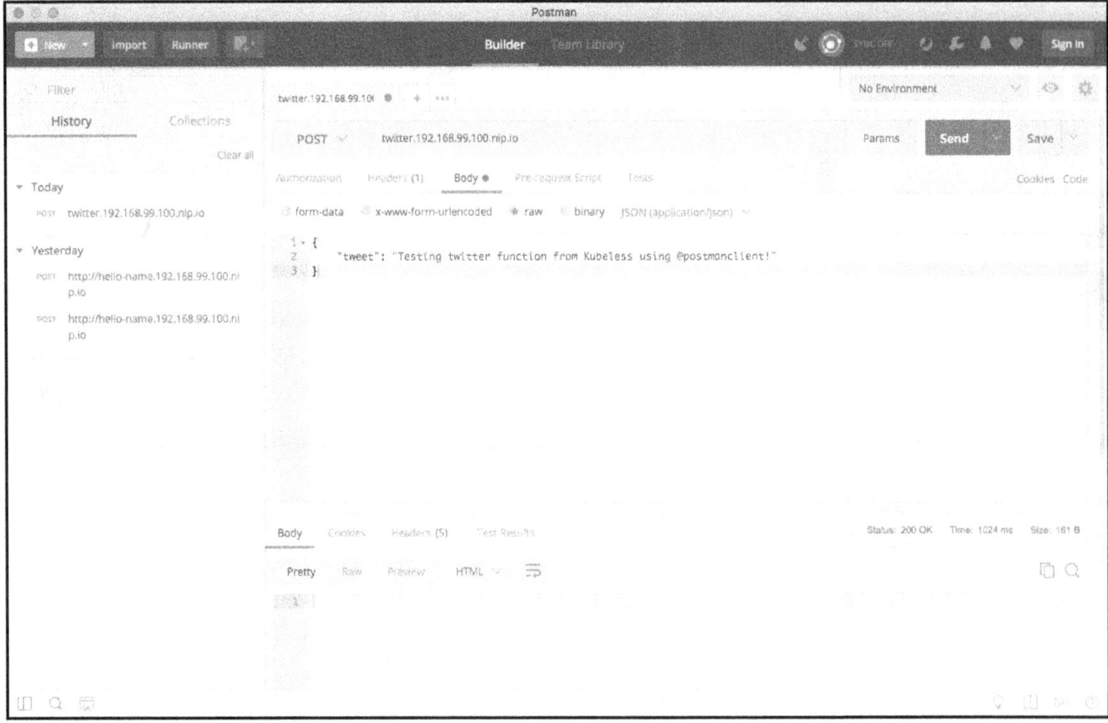

Checking Twitter should show you a second tweet, this time mentioning `@postmanclient`. You can view both of my test tweets at the following URLs:

- Command line tweet: `https://twitter.com/mediaglasses/status/922036070954536960`
- Postman tweet: `https://twitter.com/mediaglasses/status/922038490883346432`

Again, before moving on to the next section we should remove our function and tidy up:

```
$ kubeless function delete twitter
$ kubeless ingress delete twitter-ingress
$ kubectl delete secret twitter
```

Also, if you need to you should return to `https://apps.twitter.com/` and either remove or revoke your application or tokens.

The Kubeless serverless plugin

Back in `Chapter 1`, *The Serverless Landscape,* we installed the Serverless framework to deploy an AWS Lambda function; serverless also works with Kubeless.

If you didn't install serverless yet, here is a quick recap on how to install it on the three operating systems we are covering.

While every effort has been made to ensure that the following instructions work on all supported platforms there has been varying degrees of success of running the Kubeless serverless plugin on *Windows-based* operating systems due to compatibility issues with some of the dependencies required by the plugin.

For macOS 10.13 High Sierra, run the following command to install Node.js using Homebrew:

```
$ brew install node
```

If you are following along using Windows 10 Professional then you can install Node.js using Chocolatey by running:

```
$ choco install nodejs
```

Finally, if you are using Ubuntu 17.04, you can install Node.js using the following commands:

```
$ curl -sL https://deb.nodesource.com/setup_8.x | sudo -E bash -
$ sudo apt-get install -y nodejs
```

Now that the latest version of Node.js is installed we can use **Node Package Manager** (**NPM**) to install serverless by running:

```
$ npm install -g serverless
```

Once serverless is installed you can log in using the following command:

```
$ serverless login
```

Now that serverless is installed we can launch the demo Kubeless function by running the following commands:

```
$ serverless create --template kubeless-python --path new-project
$ cd new-project
$ npm install
```

If you are not following along, running these commands gives the following output:

```
russ in ~/Desktop
⚡ serverless create --template kubeless-python --path new-project
Serverless: Generating boilerplate...
Serverless: Generating boilerplate in "/Users/russ/Desktop/new-project"

                          The Serverless Application Framework
                                 serverless.com, v1.23.0

Serverless: Successfully generated boilerplate for template: "kubeless-python"
russ in ~/Desktop
⚡ cd new-project/
russ in ~/Desktop/new-project
⚡ npm install
npm notice created a lockfile as package-lock.json. You should commit this file.
npm WARN kubeless-python@1.0.0 No repository field.

added 99 packages in 5.482s
russ in ~/Desktop/new-project
⚡
```

This has installed the Kubeless serverless plugin and created the `serverless.yml` file that defines our function. This contains the following:

```
service: new-project

provider:
  name: kubeless
  runtime: python2.7

plugins:
  - serverless-kubeless

functions:
  hello:
    handler: handler.hello
```

As you can see, the code tells serverless that we are using Kubeless and that it should use the Kubeless plugin. It also defines a function and handler called `hello`. The function can be found in the `handler.py` file. This contains the following code and is pretty similar to the hello-world examples we looked at earlier in the chapter:

```
import json


def hello(request):
    body = {
        "message": "Go Serverless v1.0! Your function executed
successfully!",
        "input": request.json
    }

    response = {
        "statusCode": 200,
        "body": json.dumps(body)
    }

    return response
```

Now that we have our example function, we can deploy the service by running:

```
$ serverless deploy -v
```

Once the service has been deployed, the final step is to deploy the function itself. To do this, run:

```
$ serverless deploy function -f hello
```

Using serverless itself to invoke the function might result in an error like the following one—if it does, do not worry:

```
$ serverless invoke --function hello --data '{"Kubeless": "Welcome!"}' -l
```

```
1. new-project (bash)
⚡ serverless invoke --function hello --data '{"Kubeless": "Welcome!"}' -l
Serverless: Calling function: hello...

  Error --------------------------------------------------

  Service Unavailable

     For debugging logs, run again after setting the "SLS_DEBUG=*" environment variable.

  Get Support --------------------------------------------
     Docs:          docs.serverless.com
     Bugs:          github.com/serverless/serverless/issues
     Forums:        forum.serverless.com
     Chat:          gitter.im/serverless/serverless

  Your Environment Information -----------------------------
     OS:                     darwin
     Node Version:           8.7.0
     Serverless Version:     1.23.0

russ in ~/Desktop/new-project
⚡
```

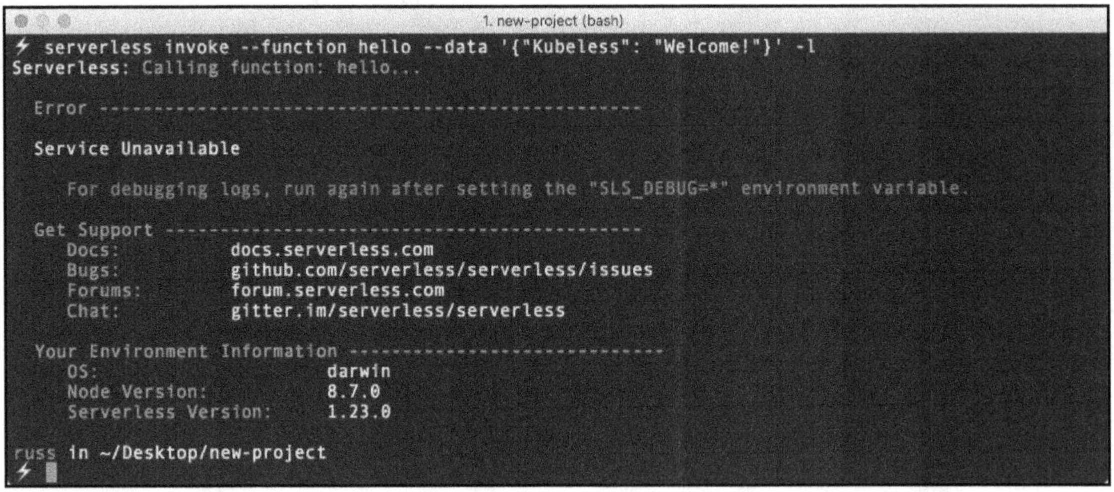

You can still access the function using Kubeless:

```
$ kubeless function list
$ kubeless function call hello --data '{"Kubeless": "Welcome!"}'
```

This will return the expected results:

```
1. new-project (bash)
russ in ~/Desktop/new-project
⚡ kubeless function list
NAME    NAMESPACE       HANDLER         RUNTIME         TYPE    TOPIC   DEPENDENCIES
hello   default         handler.hello   python2.7       HTTP
russ in ~/Desktop/new-project
⚡ kubeless function call hello --data '{"Kubeless": "Welcome!"}'
Forwarding from 127.0.0.1:30000 -> 8080
Forwarding from [::1]:30000 -> 8080
Handling connection for 30000
{"body": "{\"input\": {\"Kubeless\": \"Welcome!\"}, \"message\": \"Go Serverless v1.0! Your function
 executed successfully!\"}", "statusCode": 200}
russ in ~/Desktop/new-project
⚡
```

To remove the example function, run the following command:

```
$ serverless remove
```

Before we finish this chapter, let's look at an example that uses events rather than HTTP. In the `Chapter04/serverless-event/` folder in the GitHub repository, there is a sample application that listens for events.

The `serverless.yml` file differs from the previous HTTP example in that as well as a handler it adds an events section that contains the trigger/topic:

```
service: events

provider:
  name: kubeless
  runtime: python2.7

plugins:
  - serverless-kubeless

functions:
  events:
    handler: handler.events
    events:
      - trigger: 'hello_topic'
```

The `handler.py` file contains probably the most simplistic code we have looked at so far:

```
def events(context):
    return context
```

To launch the example, simply run the following commands from within the `Chapter04/serverless-event/` folder:

```
$ npm install
$ serverless deploy -v
$ kubeless function list
```

```
1. serverless-event (bash)
⚡ serverless deploy -v
Serverless: Packaging service...
Serverless: Excluding development dependencies...
Serverless: Deploying function events...
Serverless: Function events successfully deployed
Serverless: Skipping ingress rule generation
russ in ~/Documents/Code/kubernetes-for-serverless-applications/Chapter04/serverless-event on master*
⚡ kubeless function list
NAME    NAMESPACE       HANDLER         RUNTIME         TYPE    TOPIC           DEPENDENCIES
events  default         handler.events  python2.7       PubSub  hello_topic
```

As you can see from the preceding Terminal output, we have a type of `PubSub` and a topic of `hello_topic`. We can now publish an event in the `hello_topic` topic by running:

```
$ kubeless topic publish --topic hello_topic --data 'testing an event!'
$ kubeless topic publish --topic hello_topic --data 'and another event!'
```

Finally, we can check the logs to see the that the two events have been processed by running:

```
$ serverless logs -f events
```

As you can see from the following output, the events have successfully been published and processed by our test function:

```
1. serverless-event (bash)
russ in ~/Documents/Code/kubernetes-for-serverless-applications/Chapter04/serverless-event on master*
⚡ kubeless topic publish --topic hello_topic --data 'testing an event!'
russ in ~/Documents/Code/kubernetes-for-serverless-applications/Chapter04/serverless-event on master*
⚡ kubeless topic publish --topic hello_topic --data 'and another event!'
russ in ~/Documents/Code/kubernetes-for-serverless-applications/Chapter04/serverless-event on master*
⚡ serverless logs -f events
testing an event!
and another event!
russ in ~/Documents/Code/kubernetes-for-serverless-applications/Chapter04/serverless-event on master*
⚡
```

Before moving on to the next chapter, we can remove our Kubeless Kubernetes single-node cluster by running the following command:

```
$ minikube delete
```

Summary

In this chapter we have deployed Kubeless onto our single-node Kubernetes, which we launched with Minikube. We installed the Kubernetes command-line client and web-based interface. Once the cluster was deployed and tools installed, we deployed and executed functions on our Kubeless installation.

We worked through installing two basic test functions before installing a more useful function that posts tweets. We then looked at how we can interact with Kubeless using the Serverless framework.

In the next chapter, we are going to be looking at an event-based framework called **Funktion**.

5
Using Funktion for Serverless Applications

Before we move on to launching a Kubernetes cluster in a public cloud, we are going to take a look at one more local example; this time we will be looking at Funktion. We will be covering the following subjects:

- Introducing Funktion
- Installing and configuring Funktion
- Running our first function using Funktion
- A Twitter flow

Before we walk through installing and configuring Funktion, we should take a moment to discuss what it does, as it is a little different from the other frameworks covered in this book.

Introducing Funktion

Funktion's tagline describes it as event-based Lambda programming for Kubernetes. On the face of it, Funktion seems pretty close to Kubeless and the other Serverless frameworks we have discussed in previous chapters. However, it has its own twist which sets it apart from the other frameworks we are looking at.

Most of the serverless functions we are looking at support two basic event types:

- **HTTP**: This is where data is passed to the framework using a standard HTTP request; typically the data will be posted as a JSON object
- **Subscription**: This is where the framework listens for topics in an event stream, for example, Kubeless uses Apache Kafka (`https://kafka.apache.org/`)

Funktion expands on the number of event types—in fact, it supports around 200 different types of event. That is a quite a jump! It achieves this using Apache Camel (`https://camel.apache.org/`). Apache Camel is an open source Java framework that acts as plumbing for developers, allowing them to both ingest and publish data.

To give you an idea of some of the event streams that are supported by Apache Camel, and therefore Funktion, here are some of the highlights:

- AWS-SNS support for working with Amazon's **Simple Notification Service (SNS)**
- Braintree allows for interaction with the Braintree payment gateway service
- etcd allows you to interact with the etcd key value store
- Facebook opens up the full Facebook API
- GitHub allows you to listen for events from GitHub
- Kafka—like Kubeless, you can subscribe to Kafka streams
- Twitter gives you the ability to listen out for hashtags, posts, and more

There are numerous others such as LinkedIn, Slack, various SQL and NoSQL databases, file services such as S3 from AWS, Dropbox, and Box, to name but a few.

All of this choice makes it a very good proposition compared to the other frameworks we have been and will be looking at.

There are several different components that make up a Funktion deployment. To start with we have a **function**; this is the code itself, which is managed by Kubernetes ConfigMap.

A function by itself is not very useful as it only exists as data within a ConfigMap. Because of this, we need a **runtime**, a Kubernetes deployment that takes the function and executes it when called. Runtimes are automatically created when the Funktion operator (more on that in a little while) detects that a new function is added.

Next, we have a **connector**; this is a representation of an event source such as the ones we discussed earlier in this section—it contains information on the event type, the configuration (such as API credentials), and also data search parameters.

Then we have **flow**; this is a sequence of steps that could be consuming events from a connector that invokes a function.

Finally, we have the **Funktion** operator. This is a pod running in Kubernetes that monitors all of the components that make up our Funktion deployments, such as function, runtime, connector, and flow. It is responsible for creating the Kubernetes services that provide the Funktion functionality.

Funktion is open source and is released under Apache License 2.0; it was developed by fabric8, which is an upstream project for Red Hat's JBoss Middleware platform. fabric8 itself is a Java-focused microservice platform based on Docker, Kubernetes, and Jenkins. It also works well with Red Hat's own OpenShift platform.

Now that we have a little bit of background about how Funktion differs from the other frameworks, we can look at installing it on our single-node Kubernetes cluster.

Installing and configuring Funktion

There are three steps to get up-and-running with Funktion. First, we need to install the command line. This is where the bulk of the commands that deploy and manage our Funktion deployments will be entered. Once the command-line client is installed we can launch our single-node Kubernetes cluster using Minikube, before then using the Funktion CLI to bootstrap our environment.

The command-line client

Like a lot of the frameworks we are covering, Funktion is written in Go. This means that there are standalone executables for our three platforms.

However, at the time of writing, there is no installer available using either Homebrew on macOS or Chocolatey on Windows 10 Professional, meaning that we will be doing a manual installation on all three platforms.

The executables are available from the project's releases page on GitHub, which you can find at `https://github.com/funktionio/funktion/releases/`. At the time of writing, the current version is 1.0.14 so the following instructions will cover the installation of that version; if you need to install a later version then please replace the version number in the following commands.

Let's start by working through how to install on macOS.

macOS 10.13 High Sierra

Installing on macOS is simple, as the project has published uncompressed standalone executables. All we need to do is download the right package and make it executable. To do this, run the following commands:

```
$ curl -L
https://github.com/funktionio/funktion/releases/download/v1.0.14/funktion-d
arwin-amd64 > /usr/local/bin/funktion
$ chmod +x /usr/local/bin/funktion
```

Now that the command-line tool is installed we can test it by running the following command:

```
$ funktion version
```

The Funktion version will be returned as follows:

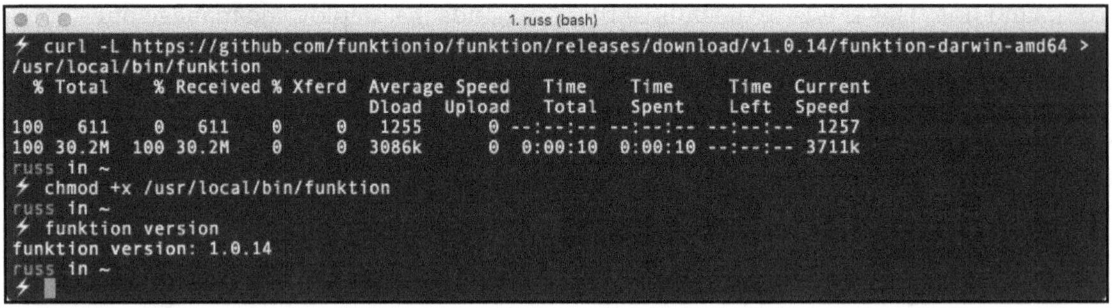

```
1. russ (bash)
⚡ curl -L https://github.com/funktionio/funktion/releases/download/v1.0.14/funktion-darwin-amd64 >
/usr/local/bin/funktion
  % Total    % Received % Xferd  Average Speed   Time    Time     Time  Current
                                 Dload  Upload   Total   Spent    Left  Speed
100   611    0   611    0     0   1255      0 --:--:-- --:--:-- --:--:--  1257
100 30.2M  100 30.2M    0     0  3086k      0  0:00:10  0:00:10 --:--:-- 3711k
russ in ~
⚡ chmod +x /usr/local/bin/funktion
russ in ~
⚡ funktion version
funktion version: 1.0.14
russ in ~
⚡
```

As you can see, while the installation process is quite simple there is a downside to the package not being available within Homebrew. If it was, then it would be easier to update to later versions as Homebrew takes care of checking for and installing upgrades whenever you run:

```
$ brew update
$ brew upgrade
```

As it stands, you would have to remove the current version and download the new version in its place if you needed to upgrade.

Windows 10 Professional

The process for installing the Funktion command-line client on Windows is similar to that of macOS. First of all, open a PowerShell window as the admin user by selecting **Run as Administrator** from the PowerShell menu in the taskbar. Once open, you should see that you are in the folder `C:\WINDOWS\system32`; if you aren't, then run:

```
$ cd C:\WINDOWS\system32
```

Once you are in the in the `C:\WINDOWS\system32` folder run the following command:

```
$ Invoke-WebRequest -Uri
https://github.com/funktionio/funktion/releases/download/v1.0.14/funktion-w
indows-amd64.exe -UseBasicParsing -OutFile funktion.exe
```

You should be able to then run the following command to check the version of the Funktion command-line client installed by running:

```
$ funktion version
```

The Funktion version will be returned as follows:

```
Select Administrator: Windows PowerShell
PS C:\WINDOWS\system32> Invoke-WebRequest -Uri https://github.com/funktionio/funktion/releases/download/v1.0.14/funktion
-windows-amd64.exe -UseBasicParsing -OutFile funktion.exe
PS C:\WINDOWS\system32> funktion version
funktion version: 1.0.14
PS C:\WINDOWS\system32>
```

Again, as we have not used a package manager to install Funktion upgrading, to do so you will have to remove the old executable and then repeat the installation process, making sure to update the version number in the URL to reflect your desired version.

Ubuntu 17.04

Lastly, we have Ubuntu 17.04. The installation process is pretty much the same as the commands we executed for macOS. However, making sure that we download the correct executable and also that we use the `sudo` command as the permissions on the `/usr/local/bin` folder is slightly different between the operating systems:

```
$ sudo sh -c "curl -L
https://github.com/funktionio/funktion/releases/download/v1.0.14/funktion-l
inux-amd64 > /usr/local/bin/funktion"
$ sudo chmod +x /usr/local/bin/funktion
```

Once downloaded and made executable you should be able to run:

```
$ funktion version
```

You should see something like the following:

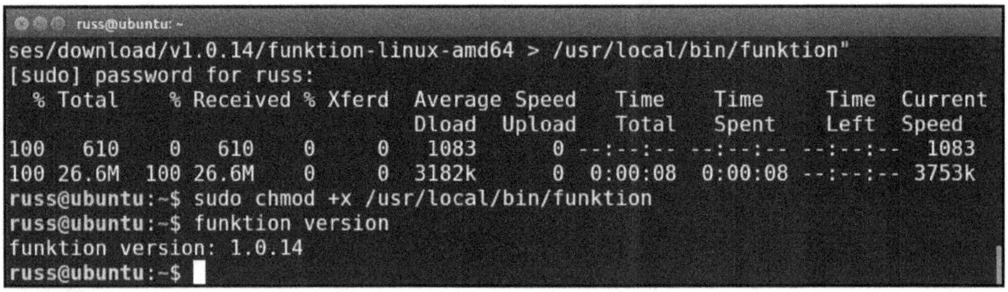

```
russ@ubuntu: ~
ses/download/v1.0.14/funktion-linux-amd64 > /usr/local/bin/funktion"
[sudo] password for russ:
  % Total    % Received % Xferd  Average Speed   Time    Time     Time  Current
                                 Dload  Upload   Total   Spent    Left  Speed
100   610    0   610    0     0   1083      0 --:--:-- --:--:-- --:--:--  1083
100 26.6M  100 26.6M    0     0  3182k      0  0:00:08  0:00:08 --:--:-- 3753k
russ@ubuntu:~$ sudo chmod +x /usr/local/bin/funktion
russ@ubuntu:~$ funktion version
funktion version: 1.0.14
russ@ubuntu:~$
```

Now that we have the command-line client installed on our three operating systems we can progress with the deployment.

Launching a single-node Kubernetes cluster

You may have noticed that we have again found ourselves in a position where we can now use the same command on whichever operating system you have used. This means that the remainder of the commands in the chapter will be able to run on all three of our target operating systems.

Before we launch our single-node Kubernetes cluster using Minikube, you can check to see if there are any updates by running the following commands. macOS 10.13 High Sierra users can run:

```
$ brew update
$ brew upgrade
```

Then to check and update Minikube, run the following commands, starting with:

```
$ brew cask outdated
```

This will present you with a list of the packages that can be updated. If Minikube is listed, run the following:

```
$ brew cask reinstall minikube
```

Windows 10 Professional users can run:

```
$ choco upgrade all
```

Ubuntu 17.04 users will need to check the release page details in `Chapter 3`, *Installing Kubernetes Locally*, remove the old binaries, and repeat the installation process using the newer releases.

Once you have checked for updates to Minikube you can launch your cluster by running:

```
$ minikube start
```

As per `Chapter 3`, *Installing Kubernetes Locally* and `Chapter 4`, *Introducing Kubeless Functioning*, this will launch the single-node Kubernetes cluster and configure your local Kubernetes client to interact with it. If you have updated Minikube, you may also notice that a more recent version of Kubernetes is downloaded and installed:

```
1. russ (bash)
⚡ minikube start
Starting local Kubernetes v1.8.0 cluster...
Starting VM...
Downloading Minikube ISO
 140.01 MB / 140.01 MB [============================================] 100.00% 0s
Getting VM IP address...
Moving files into cluster...
Downloading localkube binary
 148.56 MB / 148.56 MB [============================================] 100.00% 0s
Setting up certs...
Connecting to cluster...
Setting up kubeconfig...
Starting cluster components...
Kubectl is now configured to use the cluster.
russ in ~
⚡
```

If you have upgraded Minikube, you can check everything is running using the following commands:

```
$ minikube status
$ kubectl get all
$ minikube dashboard
```

Now we have our single-node Kubernetes cluster back up-and-running, the final stage in the Funktion installation is to bootstrap the deployment.

Bootstrapping Funktion

Installing Funktion is really straightforward—in fact, it is a single command:

```
$ funktion install platform
```

This will give the following output:

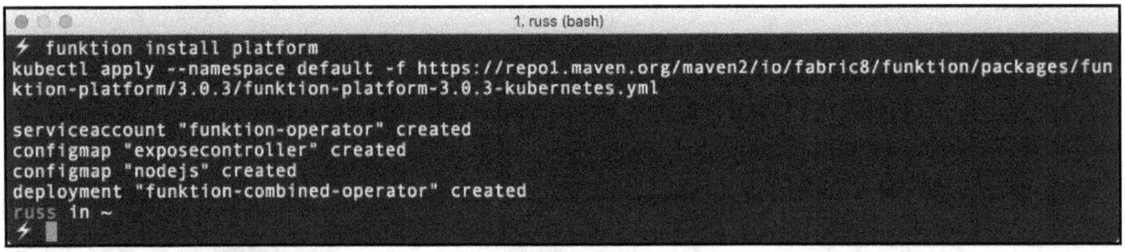

```
1. russ (bash)
⚡ funktion install platform
kubectl apply --namespace default -f https://repo1.maven.org/maven2/io/fabric8/funktion/packages/fun
ktion-platform/3.0.3/funktion-platform-3.0.3-kubernetes.yml

serviceaccount "funktion-operator" created
configmap "exposecontroller" created
configmap "nodejs" created
deployment "funktion-combined-operator" created
russ in ~
⚡
```

After a minute or two you should be able to run:

```
$ kubectl get pods
$ kubectl get deployments
```

The preceding commands will check the status of the deployment:

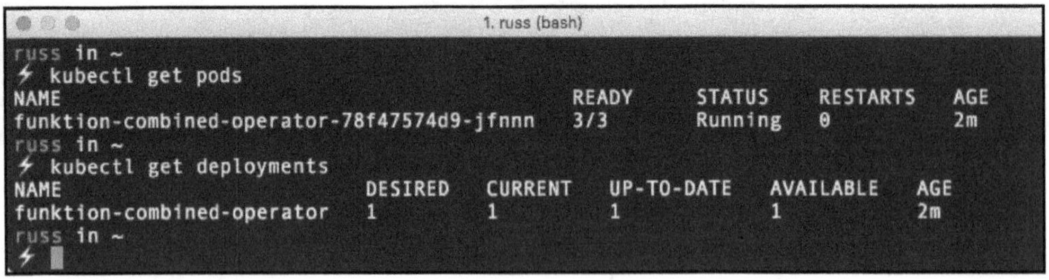

```
1. russ (bash)
russ in ~
⚡ kubectl get pods
NAME                                          READY     STATUS    RESTARTS   AGE
funktion-combined-operator-78f47574d9-jfnnn   3/3       Running   0          2m
russ in ~
⚡ kubectl get deployments
NAME                         DESIRED   CURRENT   UP-TO-DATE   AVAILABLE   AGE
funktion-combined-operator   1         1         1            1           2m
russ in ~
⚡
```

You should also be able to see the **Pods** and **Deployments** in the Kubernetes dashboard:

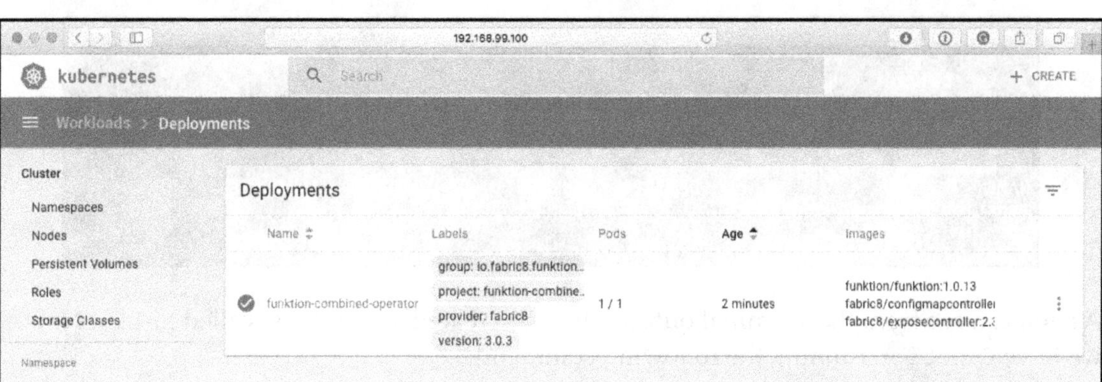

Running the following command should return an empty list:

```
$ funktion get function
```

This proves that the Funktion command-line client can connect to your newly installed Funktion deployment and interact with it.

Deploying a simple function

Now that we have our Funktion deployment up-and-running, we can look at deploying a really simple hello world example. In the `/Chapter05/hello-world/src` folder in the GitHub repository that supports this book, you will find a file called `hello.js`. This file contains the following code:

```
module.exports = function(context, callback) {
  var name = context.request.query.name || context.request.body || "World";
  callback(200, "Hello " + name + "!!");
};
```

Running the following command in the `/Chapter05/hello-world/` folder will create our first function using the preceding code:

```
$ funktion create fn -f src/hello.js
```

The output should look like this:

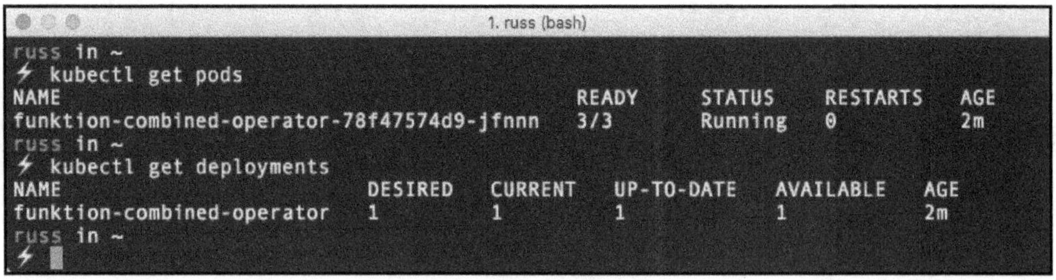

```
russ in ~
⚡ kubectl get pods
NAME                                        READY     STATUS    RESTARTS   AGE
funktion-combined-operator-78f47574d9-jfnnn   3/3       Running   0          2m
russ in ~
⚡ kubectl get deployments
NAME                         DESIRED   CURRENT   UP-TO-DATE   AVAILABLE   AGE
funktion-combined-operator   1         1         1            1           2m
russ in ~
⚡
```

As you can see from the Terminal output, this has created a `function` called `hello`. Now, we have `function` running the following command:

```
$ funktion get function
```

This should return some results. As you can see from the following output, we can now see the `NAME`, `PODS`, and `URL` listed:

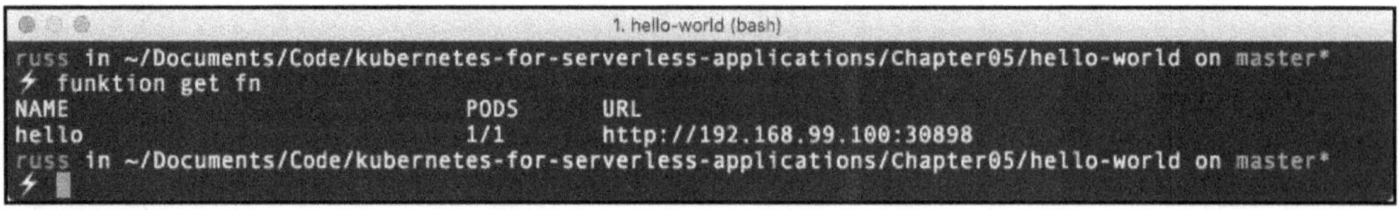

```
russ in ~/Documents/Code/kubernetes-for-serverless-applications/Chapter05/hello-world on master*
⚡ funktion get fn
NAME                                PODS      URL
hello                               1/1       http://192.168.99.100:30898
russ in ~/Documents/Code/kubernetes-for-serverless-applications/Chapter05/hello-world on master*
⚡
```

We can run the following commands to return just the `URL` of the function, or open it in our browser:

```
$ funktion url fn hello
$ funktion url fn hello -o
```

You should see the following results:

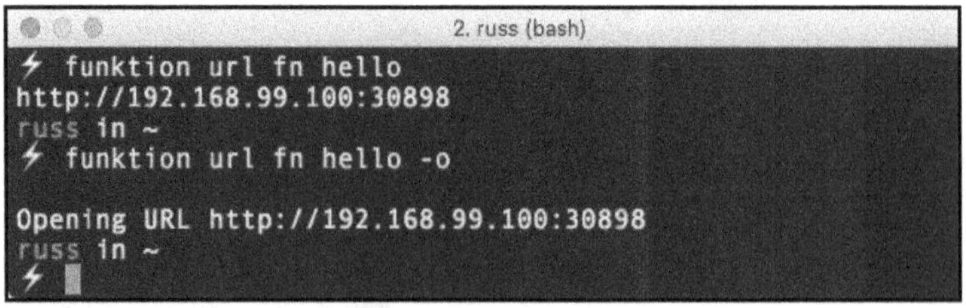

```
⚡ funktion url fn hello
http://192.168.99.100:30898
russ in ~
⚡ funktion url fn hello -o

Opening URL http://192.168.99.100:30898
russ in ~
⚡
```

The browser window that opens displays the following. I am sure you will agree it is not the most exciting of pages:

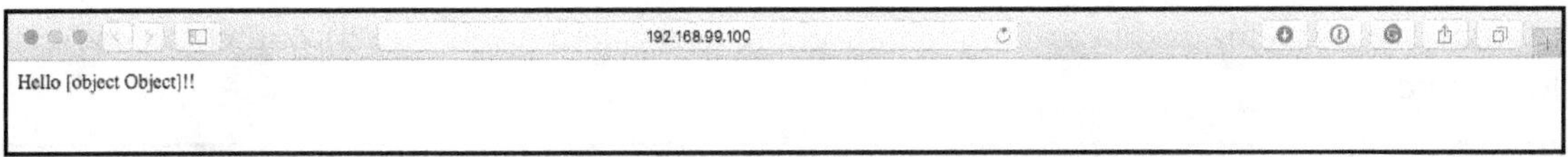

But it does demonstrate that our function is working and displaying content. You can display the logs for the function by running the following:

```
$ funktion logs function hello
```

This will stream the log content in real-time to your Terminal window. You can see this by refreshing your browser a few times—you should see your page requests being logged alongside the internal health check requests.

Now that we have our first function created, we can install some connectors. To do so, run the following command:

```
$ funktion install connector http4 timer twitter
```

Now that we have some connectors installed, we can create a flow. Our first flow will use the timer connector:

```
$ funktion create flow timer://foo?period=5000 http://hello/
```

This will create a flow called `foo` that will execute every `5000` milliseconds, targeting our function called `hello`. To get information on the flow you can run the following command:

```
$ funktion get flow
```

You should see the following:

```
2. russ (bash)
⚡ funktion create flow timer://foo?period=5000 http://hello/
2017/10/29 13:41:13 Flow timer-foo1 created timer://foo?period=5000 => http://hello/
russ in ~
⚡ funktion get flow
NAME                              PODS      STEPS
timer-foo1                        1/1       timer://foo?period=5000 => http://hello/
russ in ~
⚡
```

As you can see, the flow is called `timer-foo1`; we will need to use this name when interacting with it. For example, you can check the logs for the flow by running the following command:

```
$ funktion logs flow timer-foo1
```

Or in the Kubernetes dashboard you can find the pod called `timer-foo1` and check the logs there:

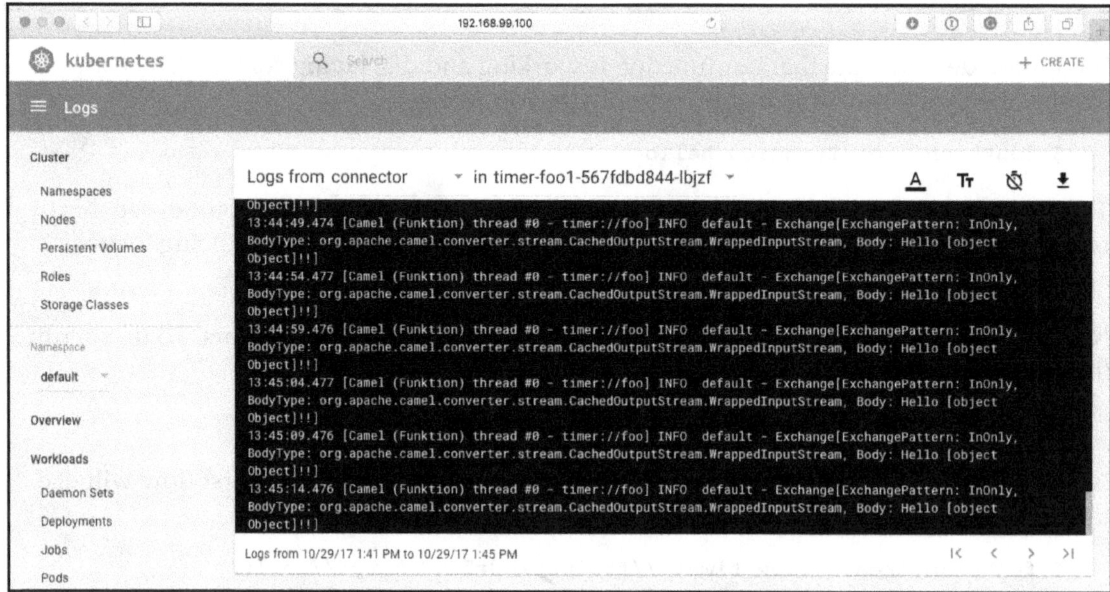

Check the logs for the function by running the following command:

```
$ funktion logs function hello
```

You should see that there is a page request every five seconds from a client with a user agent of `Apache-HttpClient/4.5.2`. This is the timer flow:

```
.8"
::ffff:172.17.0.6 - - [29/Oct/2017:13:54:29 +0000] "GET / HTTP/1.1" 200 23 "-" "Apache-HttpClient/4.
5.2 (Java/1.8.0_111)"
::ffff:172.17.0.1 - - [29/Oct/2017:13:54:31 +0000] "GET /healthz HTTP/1.1" 200 8 "-" "kube-probe/1.8
"
::ffff:172.17.0.6 - - [29/Oct/2017:13:54:34 +0000] "GET / HTTP/1.1" 200 23 "-" "Apache-HttpClient/4.
5.2 (Java/1.8.0_111)"
::ffff:172.17.0.1 - - [29/Oct/2017:13:54:38 +0000] "GET /healthz HTTP/1.1" 200 8 "-" "kube-probe/1.8
"
::ffff:172.17.0.6 - - [29/Oct/2017:13:54:39 +0000] "GET / HTTP/1.1" 200 23 "-" "Apache-HttpClient/4.
5.2 (Java/1.8.0_111)"
::ffff:172.17.0.1 - - [29/Oct/2017:13:54:41 +0000] "GET /healthz HTTP/1.1" 200 8 "-" "kube-probe/1.8
"
```

To remove the flow simply run:

```
$ funktion delete flow timer-foo1
```

This will remove the pod running the connector and your function will stop receiving automated requests.

Going back to the Kubernetes dashboard and clicking on **Config Maps** should display a list of everything that Funktion has created. As you can see, most parts of Funktion have a ConfigMap:

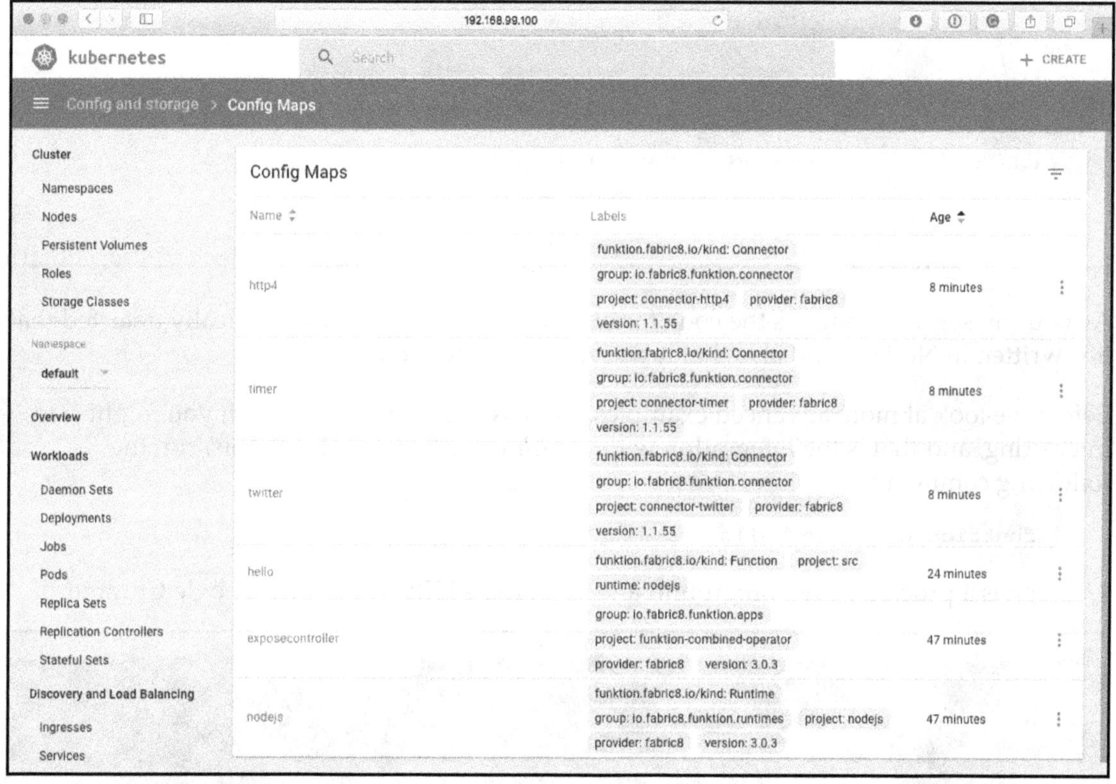

Clicking on the **Config Maps** for `hello` will show you something that looks like the following page:

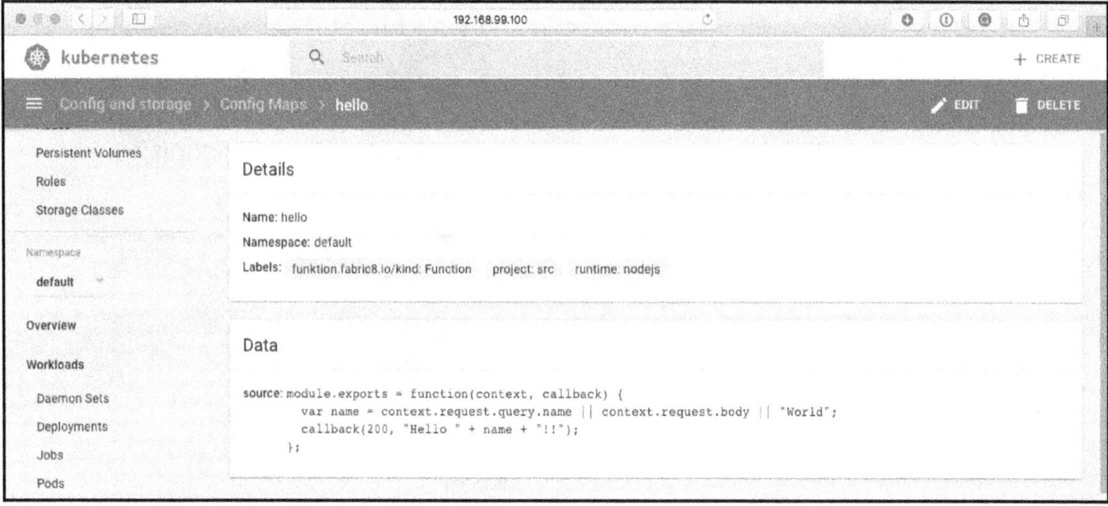

As you can see, this contains the code for our function and it has automatically detected that it is written in Node.js, and also that it was deployed from the `src` folder.

Before we look at more advanced examples, there is one more thing which you might find interesting, and that is the integration with the *Chrome Dev* tools. To do this, run the following command:

```
$ funktion debug fn hello
```

This opens a process in the foreground and give you a URL to put into Google Chrome:

```
2. russ (kubectl)
⚡ funktion debug fn hello

kubectl port-forward hello-84c7bdb4d6-4p89n 5858:5858

To Debug open: chrome-devtools://devtools/bundled/inspector.html?experiments=true&v8only=true&ws=127
.0.0.1:5858/67ad3cd0-0fd6-4e50-a1a4-d468e2071b0c

Forwarding from 127.0.0.1:5858 -> 5858
```

Once you have Google Chrome open and pointed at your function you can perform tasks such as editing the code directly within the browser:

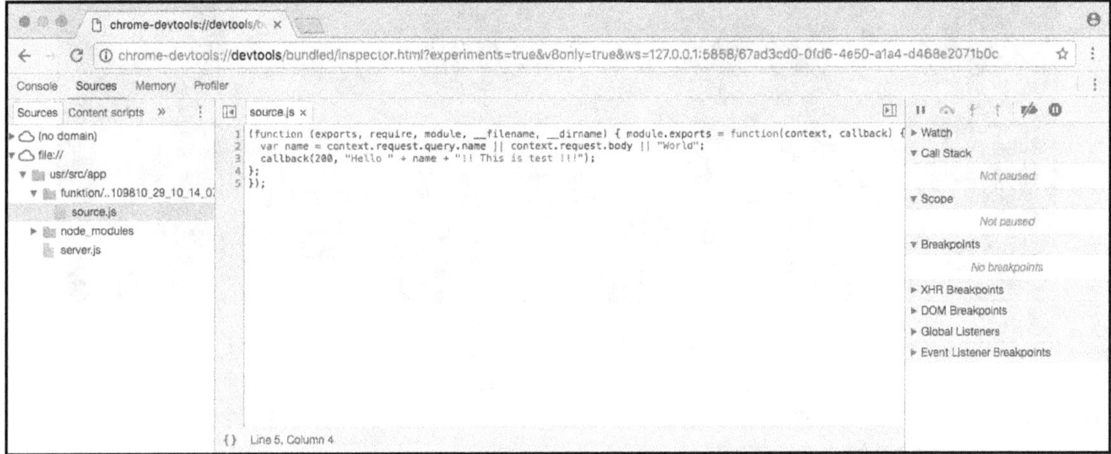

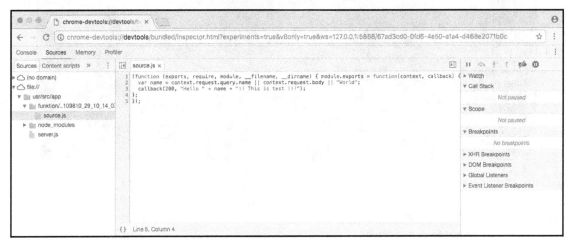

Any changes made using the Chrome Dev tools are made directly within the pod and they will not persist if you relaunch the pod; this should be used purely for testing.

To remove our `hello` function we just need to run:

```
$ funktion delete function hello
```

This should leave us with a clean installation ready for a more advanced example.

Twitter streams

As we installed the Twitter connector in the previous section, let's take a look at configuring it to pull in some data. To start with, you can view all of the configurable options for the connector by running the following command:

```
$ funktion edit connector twitter -l
```

You should see something like the following Terminal output:

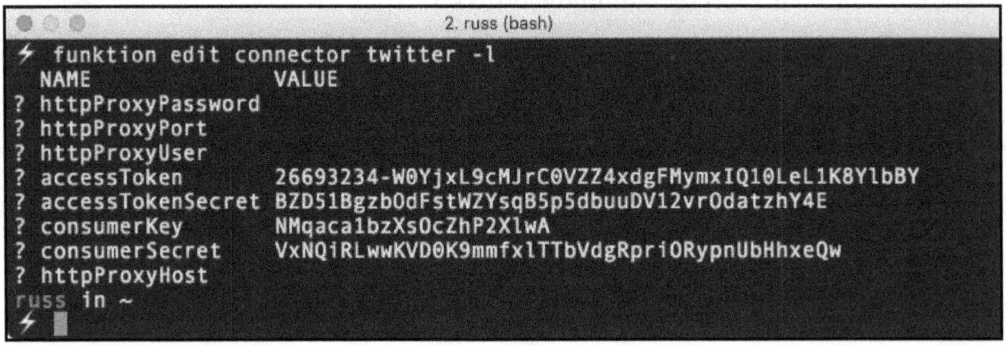

```
2. russ (bash)
⚡ funktion edit connector twitter -l
  NAME                VALUE
? httpProxyPassword
? httpProxyPort
? httpProxyUser
? accessToken         26693234-W0YjxL9cMJrC0VZZ4xdgFMymxIQ10LeL1K8YlbBY
? accessTokenSecret BZD51BgzbOdFstWZYsqB5p5dbuuDV12vrOdatzhY4E
? consumerKey         NMqaca1bzXsOcZhP2XlwA
? consumerSecret      VxNQiRLwwKVD0K9mmfxlTTbVdgRpriORypnUbHhxeQw
? httpProxyHost
russ in ~
⚡
```

As you can see, you can configure a proxy as well as providing an `accessToken`, `accessTokenSecret`, `consumerKey`, and `consumerSecret`. You should have these from the previous chapter. If not then regenerate them using the instructions in `Chapter 4`, *Introducing Kubeless Functioning*.

Like the tokens and secrets I will be using to demonstrate the commands you need to run, the details listed in the preceding screenshot are the default dummy placeholder details and are not valid.

To update the connector with your own details, run the following command, ensuring that you replace the details with your own:

```
$ funktion edit connector twitter \
    accessToken=1213091858-REJvMEEUeSoGA0WPKp7cv8BBTyTcDeRkHBr6Wpj \
    accessTokenSecret=WopER9tbSJtUtASEz62lI8HTCvhlYBvDHcuCIof5YzyGg \
    consumerKey=aKiWFB6Q7Ck5byHTWu3zHktDF \
    consumerSecret=uFPEszch9UuIlHt6nCxar8x1DSYqhWw8VELqp3pMPB571DwnDg
```

You should receive confirmation that the connector has been updated. Now, we are able to launch a flow that uses the Twitter adapter. To do this we should run the following command:

```
$ funktion create flow --name twitsearch
"twitter://search?type=polling&keywords=kubernetes&delay=120s"
$ funktion get flows
```

We will see the following:

```
1. russ (bash)
⚡ funktion edit connector twitter \
→     accessToken=1213091858-REJvMEEUeSoGA0WPKp7cv8BBTyTcDeRkHBr6Wpj \
→     accessTokenSecret=WopER9tbSJtUtASEz62lI8HTCvhlYBvDHcuCIof5YzyGg \
→     consumerKey=aKiWFB6Q7Ck5byHTWu3zHktDF \
→     consumerSecret=uFPEszch9UuIlHt6nCxar8x1DSYqhWw8VELqp3pMPB571DwnDg
Connector twitter updated
russ in ~
⚡ funktion create flow --name twitsearch "twitter://search?type=polling&keywords=kubernetes&delay=1
20s"
2017/11/04 17:23:50 Flow twitsearch created twitter://search?type=polling&keywords=kubernetes&delay=
120s
russ in ~
⚡ funktion get flows
NAME                              PODS      STEPS
twitsearch                        1/1       twitter://search?type=polling&keywords=kubernetes&delay=1
20s
russ in ~
⚡
```

Once you have started the pod, you can check the logs by running the following:

```
$ funktion logs flow twitsearch
```

Or by viewing the logs for the `twitsearch` pod in the dashboard:

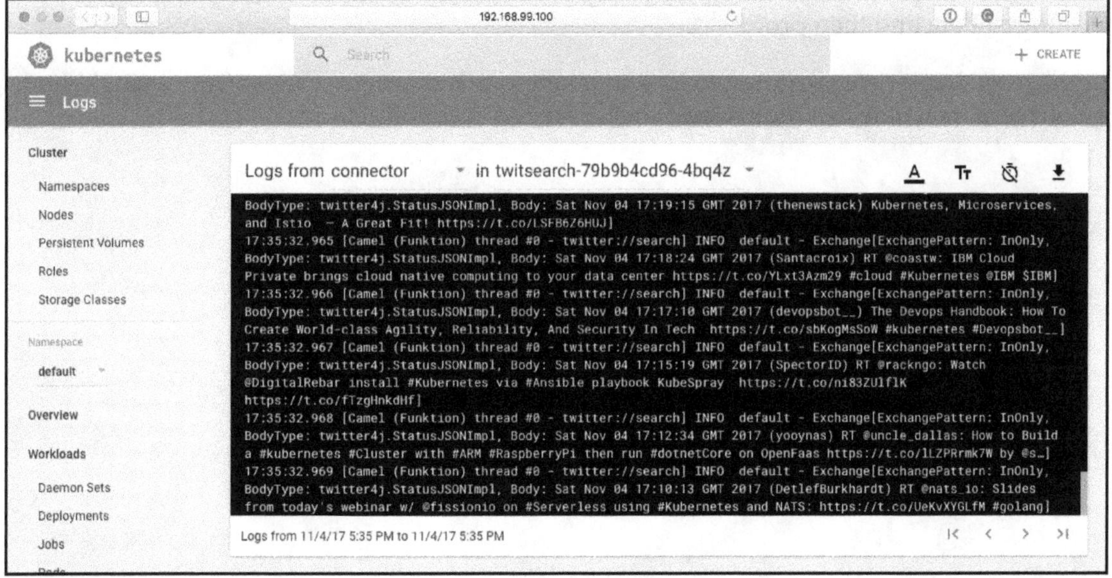

As you can see, Camel is printing a stream of tweets that contain the work Kubernetes. Your application can subscribe to this stream and you can then process the tweets. Finally, running the following command will delete the flow:

```
$ funktion delete flow twitsearch
```

You can then remove your Minikube machine using the `minikube delete` command.

Summary

In this chapter, we have taken a brief look at Funktion. We installed the command-line client and then installed it on our single-node Kubernetes cluster. Once deployed we launched a test function and interacted with it before using one of the many event streams to search for tweets containing Kubernetes.

Funktion is still in its early stages of development and it currently has a small, but active, community making contributions on the project's GitHub pages. Because of this, at the time of writing there are not too many practical examples of full-blown applications that take advantage of the many flows that Funktion supports via Apache Camel. I would recommend keeping an eye on Funktion if you are planning on writing any applications that ingest data and then process it.

In the next chapter we are going to look at taking our Kubernetes cluster from a single-node on our local machine to a multi-node cluster hosted on public clouds.

6
Installing Kubernetes in the Cloud

So far, we have been running Kubernetes on our local machines. This does have some drawbacks, one of which is processing power. We are going to start looking at some more complex and powerful frameworks, so we need some additional power. Because of this, we are going to look at installing Kubernetes on a few different public clouds, each time using a different tool:

- Launching Kubernetes in DigitalOcean
- Launching Kubernetes in AWS
- Launching Kubernetes in Microsoft Azure
- Launching Kubernetes on the Google Cloud Platform

We will then take a look at the differences between public cloud providers and look at installing Kubeless on one of the platforms.

Launching Kubernetes in DigitalOcean

The first public cloud platform we are going to look at is DigitalOcean. DigitalOcean is a little different from the big three we are going to be looking at in the following sections as it has fewer features. For example, on the product page DigitalOcean has eight features listed, whereas the AWS product page has eighteen main areas listed and each of these areas is split into six or more features and services.

Don't let this fool you into thinking that DigitalOcean is any less of a service than the other public cloud providers we are going to be looking at this in this chapter.

DigitalOcean's strong point is that it is an extremely simple-to-use hosting platform. With its straightforward API and command-line tools, its supporting services, and excellent management interface it is easy to bring up powerful yet very competitively priced virtual machines in less than a minute.

Creating Droplets

Droplets are DigitalOcean's term for its compute resource. For our Kubernetes, we are going to be launching three Ubuntu 17.04 Droplets, each with 1 GB of RAM, 1 CPU, and 30 GB of SSD storage.

This three Droplet cluster, at the time of writing, will cost approximately $30 per month to keep online. If you are planning on keeping it online while you need it then it will cost $0.045 per hour for the three Droplets.

Before you can create any Droplets you will need an account; you can sign up for DigitalOcean at `https://cloud.digitalocean.com/registrations/new`. Once you have signed up, and before you do anything else, I recommend that you immediately enable two-factor authentication on your account. You can enable this on the account security page at `https://cloud.digitalocean.com/settings/security/`.

Enabling two-factor authentication will give you an additional level of security and help protect your account from any unauthorized access and also unexpected cost. After all, you don't want someone logging in and using your account to create 25 of the most expensive Droplets available for them to use as they please with you footing the bill.

Two-factor authentication works by introducing a second level of authentication to your account; typically this is a four- or six-digit code which is either generated by an application, such as Google Authenticator, on your mobile device or a text message sent by the service you are attempting to log in to. This means that even if your password is compromised an attacker still needs access to your mobile device or number.

Next up, we need to generate an SSH key and upload it to DigitalOcean. If you already have an account with an SSH key uploaded, you can skip this task. If you don't have a key, then follow the given instructions.

If you are using macOS High Sierra or Ubuntu 17.04 then you can run the following command:

```
$ ssh-keygen -t rsa
```

This will ask you for a location to store your newly generated private and public key, and also a passphrase. The passphrase is optional, but it does add another layer of security should the private portion of your SSH key fall into the wrong hands:

```
1. russ (bash)
⚡ ssh-keygen -t rsa
Generating public/private rsa key pair.
Enter file in which to save the key (/Users/russ/.ssh/id_rsa):
Enter passphrase (empty for no passphrase):
Enter same passphrase again:
Your identification has been saved in /Users/russ/.ssh/id_rsa.
Your public key has been saved in /Users/russ/.ssh/id_rsa.pub.
The key fingerprint is:
SHA256:X6jXVMUbLTXhysDb0sgaSzQvbPBSKyQ4LK2wLmVTLdA russ@Russs-iMac.local
The key's randomart image is:
+---[RSA 2048]----+
|  ..          ==|
|  o.E.    .   oo+|
|.. =o..o + o  .oo|
|..o...o * =.B... |
|..+     oSO.*o=  |
|.o .     =o=+.   |
|..       .oo .   |
|.         .      |
|                 |
+----[SHA256]-----+
russ in ~
⚡
```

Once you have generated your key, you will need to make a note of the public portion of your key. To do this, run the following command, making sure to update the path of the key to match your own:

```
$ cat /Users/russ/.ssh/id_rsa.pub
```

You should see something like the following:

```
1. russ (bash)
⚡ cat /Users/russ/.ssh/id_rsa.pub
ssh-rsa AAAAB3NzaC1yc2EAAAADAQABAAABAQCuq8wpzZD3a+oo+PcRL0zJ0FsUe7Q+fJ28yzCrJIorZi3u4eRTMhg9gWeMx25e
5hmJ+VKusfP0VAYzL/NU5Bo1JEHjp3KWQLpvTgskOr16QS31gW2NpjPvtET8loUzDvwMLzlf79hX2VTcMsqbLfed+S8rFkChgSCM
rkbNJxB2DHt0EnNrzosI2nilSP0na6J/3S28irf6K1uJme2g8u/noZD3yBADQ66yATvDTwxub8jy9yzOOPaD63kHOSGirXGUfxWS
jJTOtLJd+vZSHZ/IF5cifyXb2FoSMTcgBVLY1XttXnnFfn9WxxZpZ/2+6Nemuw1XS1JCLi90/o8oSyDp russ@Russs-iMac.loc
al
russ in ~
⚡
```

Please make sure you do not share or publish the private portion of your SSH key (the file that does not contain `.pub` in the filename). This is used to authenticate you against the public portion of the key. If this falls into the wrong hands they will be able to access your server/services.

For Windows 10 Professional users' odds are that you are using PuTTY as your SSH client. If you don't have PuTTY you can install it using Chocolatey by running the following:

```
$ choco install putty
```

Once PuTTY is installed you can open the PuTTYgen program by running the following command:

```
$ PUTTYGEN.exe
```

Once open, click on **Generate** and follow the prompt to move your cursor around the blank area. After a second you should have a key generated:

As you can see from the preceding screenshot, you have the option of adding a passphrase, which will be used to unlock the private portion of your key; again, this is optional.

Click on **Save public key** and also **Save private key**, and make a note of the contents of the public key.

Now that you have your public key we need to let DigitalOcean have a copy. To do this, go to the security page, which you can find at `https://cloud.digitalocean.com/settings/security/` and click on **Add SSH Key**. This will pop up a dialog box where you are asked to provide the content of your public key and name it. Fill in the two form fields and then click on the **Add SSH Key** button.

Now that you have an SSH key assigned to your account you can use it to create your Droplets and have passwordless access to them. To create your Droplets, click on the **Create** button in the top right-hand corner of the screen and select **Droplets** from the drop-down menu.

There are several options on the Droplet creation page:

- **Choose an image**: Select the Ubuntu 16.04 image
- **Choose a size**: Select the **$10/mo** option, which has 1 GB, 1 CPU, and 30 GB SSD
- **Add block storage**: Leave as-is
- **Choose a datacenter region**: Select the region closest to you; I selected **London** as I am based in the UK
- **Select additional options**: Select **Private networking**
- **Add your SSH keys**: Choose your SSH key
- **Finalize and create**: Increase the number of Droplets to `3` and for now leave the hostname as-is

Once you have filled out the preceding sections, click on the **Create** button at the bottom of the page. This will launch your three Droplets and give you feedback on how far through the creation process they are. Once they have launched, you should see something similar to the following page:

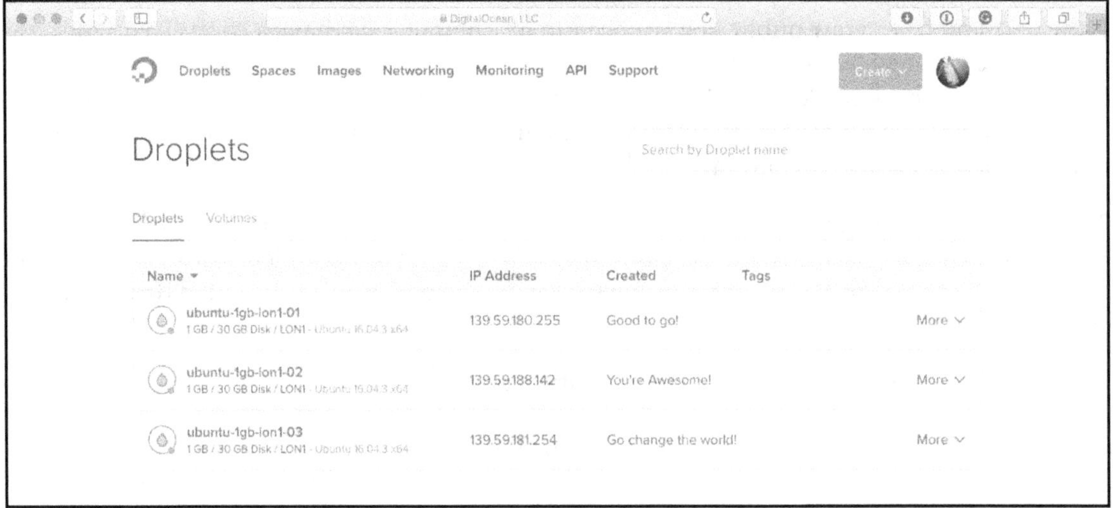

As you can see, I have three Droplets, their IP addresses, and a nice little motivational message. Now we can start deploying our Kubernetes cluster using `kubeadm`.

Deploying Kubernetes using kubeadm

First of all, we need to log in to one of our three Droplets; the first machine we log into will be our Kubernetes master:

```
$ ssh root@139.59.180.255
```

Once logged in, the following two commands check for any updates to the packages and apply them:

```
$ apt-get update
$ apt-get upgrade
```

Now that we are up-to-date we can install the prerequisite packages. To do this run the following:

```
$ apt-get install docker.io curl apt-transport-https
```

You may notice that we are using the version of Docker that is distributed as part of the core Ubuntu 16.04 package repositories rather than the official Docker release. This is because `kubeadm` doesn't have official support for newer versions of Docker and the recommended version is 1.12. At present, the version of Docker supported by Ubuntu 16.04 is 1.12.6.

Now that we have the prerequisites installed we can add the Kubernetes repository by running the following commands:

```
$ curl -s https://packages.cloud.google.com/apt/doc/apt-key.gpg | apt-key
add -
$ cat <<EOF >/etc/apt/sources.list.d/kubernetes.list
deb http://apt.kubernetes.io/ kubernetes-xenial main
EOF
```

The `curl` command adds the GPG key for the repository and the `cat` command creates the repository file. Now that the repository is in place we need to update our package list and install `kubeadm`, `kubelet`, and `kubectl` by running the following:

```
$ apt-get update
$ apt-get install kubelet kubeadm kubectl
```

Once installed, you can check the version of `kubeadm` that was installed by running the following:

```
$ kubeadm version
```

Now that we have everything we need installed we can bootstrap our Kubernetes master node by running the following:

```
$ kubeadm init
```

This will take a few minutes to run and you will get some quite verbose output letting you know what tasks `kubeadm` has completed:

```
1. root@ubuntu-1gb-lon1-01: ~ (ssh)
root@ubuntu-1gb-lon1-01:~# kubeadm init
[kubeadm] WARNING: kubeadm is in beta, please do not use it for production clusters.
[init] Using Kubernetes version: v1.8.3
[init] Using Authorization modes: [Node RBAC]
[preflight] Running pre-flight checks
[kubeadm] WARNING: starting in 1.8, tokens expire after 24 hours by default (if you require a non-ex
piring token use --token-ttl 0)
[certificates] Generated ca certificate and key.
[certificates] Generated apiserver certificate and key.
[certificates] apiserver serving cert is signed for DNS names [ubuntu-1gb-lon1-01 kubernetes kuberne
tes.default kubernetes.default.svc kubernetes.default.svc.cluster.local] and IPs [10.96.0.1 139.59.1
80.255]
[certificates] Generated apiserver-kubelet-client certificate and key.
[certificates] Generated sa key and public key.
[certificates] Generated front-proxy-ca certificate and key.
[certificates] Generated front-proxy-client certificate and key.
[certificates] Valid certificates and keys now exist in "/etc/kubernetes/pki"
```

Once complete you should see the following message, but with your tokens and so on:

```
1. root@ubuntu-1gb-lon1-01: ~ (ssh)
Your Kubernetes master has initialized successfully!

To start using your cluster, you need to run (as a regular user):

  mkdir -p $HOME/.kube
  sudo cp -i /etc/kubernetes/admin.conf $HOME/.kube/config
  sudo chown $(id -u):$(id -g) $HOME/.kube/config

You should now deploy a pod network to the cluster.
Run "kubectl apply -f [podnetwork].yaml" with one of the options listed at:
  http://kubernetes.io/docs/admin/addons/

You can now join any number of machines by running the following on each node
as root:

  kubeadm join --token 0c74f5.4d5492bafe1e0bb9 139.59.180.255:6443 --discovery-token-ca-cert-hash sh
a256:3331ba91e4a3a887c99e59d792b9f031575619b4646f23d8fe2938dc50f89491
```

Make a note of the `kubeadm join` command at the bottom, we will look at that shortly. We should run the commands mentioned in the message:

```
$ mkdir -p $HOME/.kube
$ sudo cp -i /etc/kubernetes/admin.conf $HOME/.kube/config
$ sudo chown $(id -u):$(id -g) $HOME/.kube/config
```

Next, we need to enable pod networking. There are several options you can choose from, all of which provide multihost container networking for your Kubernetes cluster:

- **Calico**: `https://www.projectcalico.org/`
- **Canal**: `https://github.com/projectcalico/canal`
- **flannel**: `https://coreos.com/flannel/docs/latest/`
- **Kube-router**: `https://github.com/cloudnativelabs/kube-router/`
- **Romana**: `https://github.com/romana/romana/`
- **Weave Net**: `https://www.weave.works/oss/net/`

For our installation we are going to be using Weave Net. To install this simply run the following commands:

```
$ export kubever=$(kubectl version | base64 | tr -d '\n')
$ kubectl apply -f "https://cloud.weave.works/k8s/net?k8s-version=$kubever"
```

```
1. root@ubuntu-1gb-lon1-01: ~ (ssh)
root@ubuntu-1gb-lon1-01:~# export kubever=$(kubectl version | base64 | tr -d '\n')
root@ubuntu-1gb-lon1-01:~# kubectl apply -f "https://cloud.weave.works/k8s/net?k8s-version=$kubever"
serviceaccount "weave-net" created
clusterrole "weave-net" created
clusterrolebinding "weave-net" created
daemonset "weave-net" created
root@ubuntu-1gb-lon1-01:~#
```

As you can see, this used the `kubectl` command to deploy the pod networking. This means that we have our basic Kubernetes cluster up-and-running, albeit on a single node.

To prepare the other two cluster nodes, open an SSH session for both and run the following commands on them both:

```
$ apt-get update
$ apt-get upgrade
$ apt-get install docker.io curl apt-transport-https
$ curl -s https://packages.cloud.google.com/apt/doc/apt-key.gpg | apt-key
add -
$ cat <<EOF >/etc/apt/sources.list.d/kubernetes.list
deb http://apt.kubernetes.io/ kubernetes-xenial main
EOF
$ apt-get update
$ apt-get install kubelet kubeadm kubectl
```

As you can see, these are the exact set of commands we executed on the master node to get us to the point where we can execute the `kubeadm` command. As you may have already guessed, rather than running `kubeadm init` we are going to be running the `kubeadm join` command we received when we initialized our master node. For me that command was as follows:

```
$ kubeadm join --token 0c74f5.4d5492bafe1e0bb9 139.59.180.255:6443 --
discovery-token-ca-cert-hash
sha256:3331ba91e4a3a887c99e59d792b9f031575619b4646f23d8fe2938dc50f89491
```

You will need to run the command you received, as the tokens will be tied to your master node. Run the command on both nodes and you should see something like the following Terminal output:

```
2. root@ubuntu-1gb-lon1-02: ~ (ssh)
root@ubuntu-1gb-lon1-02:~# kubeadm join --token 0c74f5.4d5492bafe1e0bb9 139.59.180.255:6443 --discov
ery-token-ca-cert-hash sha256:3331ba91e4a3a887c99e59d792b9f031575619b4646f23d8fe2938dc50f89491
[kubeadm] WARNING: kubeadm is in beta, please do not use it for production clusters.
[preflight] Running pre-flight checks
[discovery] Trying to connect to API Server "139.59.180.255:6443"
[discovery] Created cluster-info discovery client, requesting info from "https://139.59.180.255:6443
"
[discovery] Requesting info from "https://139.59.180.255:6443" again to validate TLS against the pin
ned public key
[discovery] Cluster info signature and contents are valid and TLS certificate validates against pinn
ed roots, will use API Server "139.59.180.255:6443"
[discovery] Successfully established connection with API Server "139.59.180.255:6443"
[bootstrap] Detected server version: v1.8.3
[bootstrap] The server supports the Certificates API (certificates.k8s.io/v1beta1)

Node join complete:
* Certificate signing request sent to master and response
  received.
* Kubelet informed of new secure connection details.

Run 'kubectl get nodes' on the master to see this machine join.
root@ubuntu-1gb-lon1-02:~#
```

Once you have run the command on both of your remaining nodes, return to your master node and run the following command:

```
$ kubectl get nodes
```

This should return a list of the nodes within your Kubernetes cluster:

```
1. root@ubuntu-1gb-lon1-01: ~ (ssh)
root@ubuntu-1gb-lon1-01:~# kubectl get nodes
NAME                 STATUS    ROLES     AGE       VERSION
ubuntu-1gb-lon1-01   Ready     master    34m       v1.8.3
ubuntu-1gb-lon1-02   Ready     <none>    3m        v1.8.3
ubuntu-1gb-lon1-03   Ready     <none>    3m        v1.8.3
root@ubuntu-1gb-lon1-01:~#
```

As you can see, we have a cluster made up of our three Droplets. The only downside is that at present we have to log in to our master node to interact with our cluster. Luckily this is easy to resolve, we just need to download a copy of the cluster `admin.conf` file.

To do this on macOS High Sierra or Ubuntu 17.04 run the following command, making sure to replace the IP address with that of your master node:

```
$ scp root@139.59.180.255:/etc/kubernetes/admin.conf
```

If you are using Windows 10 Professional you will need to use a program such as WinSCP. To install this run the following command:

```
$ choco install winscp
```

Once installed, launch it by typing `WINSCP.exe` and then follow the on-screen prompts to connect to your master node and download the `admin.conf` file, which can be found in `/etc/kubernetes/`.

Once you have a copy of the `admin.conf` file you will be able to run the following command locally to see your three-node Kubernetes cluster:

```
$ kubectl --kubeconfig ./admin.conf get nodes
```

Once we have confirmed that we can connect using our local copy of `kubectl` we should put the configuration file in place, so we don't have to use the `--kubeconfig` flag each time. To do this run the following commands (macOS and Ubuntu only):

```
$ mv ~/.kube/config ~/.kube/config.mini
$mv admin.conf ~/.kube/config
```

Now run the following:

```
$ kubectl get nodes
```

This should show your three Droplets:

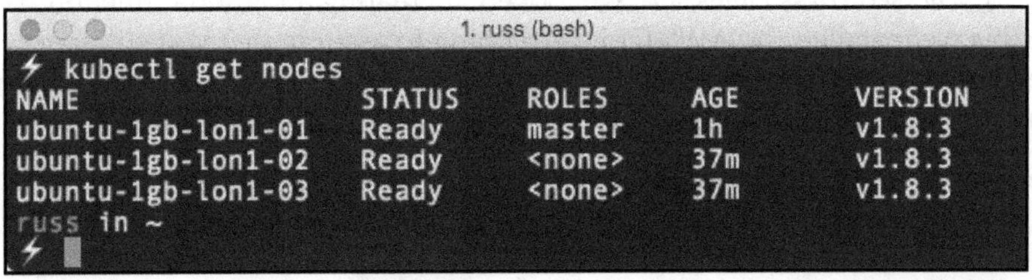

```
1. russ (bash)
⚡ kubectl get nodes
NAME                  STATUS    ROLES     AGE       VERSION
ubuntu-1gb-lon1-01    Ready     master    1h        v1.8.3
ubuntu-1gb-lon1-02    Ready     <none>    37m       v1.8.3
ubuntu-1gb-lon1-03    Ready     <none>    37m       v1.8.3
russ in ~
⚡
```

Removing the cluster

To remove the cluster, simply log in to your DigitalOcean control panel and click on the **Destroy** link, which can be found in the **More** drop-down menu to the right of each Droplet. Follow the on-screen instructions from there. Make sure you destroy all three Droplets as they will be incurring cost while they are online.

This has been a manual deployment of Kubernetes on low-spec servers. In the next few sections, we are going to look at how to deploy Kubernetes in other public clouds, starting with AWS.

Launching Kubernetes in AWS

There are several tools we can use to launch a Kubernetes cluster on AWS; we are going to be covering one called `kube-aws`. Unfortunately, `kube-aws` does not support Windows-based machines so the following instructions will only apply to macOS High Sierra and Ubuntu 17.04.

`kube-aws` is a command-line tool that is used to generate an AWS CloudFormation template, which is then used to launch and manage a CoreOS cluster. Kubernetes is then deployed to the cluster of CoreOS instances.

AWS CloudFormation is Amazon's native scripting tool and allows you to programmatically launch AWS services; it covers pretty much all of the AWS API. CoreOS is an operating system that is focused on one thing, running containers. It has an extremely small footprint and is designed to be clustered and configured on cloud providers out-of-the-box.

Getting set up

In `Chapter 1`, *The Serverless Landscape*, we looked at creating a Lambda function. To configure this we installed the AWS CLI. I am going to assume that you still have this configured and the IAM user you have configured has administrator privileges. You can test this by running the following:

```
$ aws ec2 describe-instances
```

This should return something like the following:

```
1. russ (bash)
⚡ aws ec2 describe-instances
{
    "Reservations": []
}
russ in ~
⚡
```

We need to import our SSH key in to AWS. To do this, open the AWS Console (`https://console.aws.amazon.com/`). Once logged in, select **EC2** from the **Service** menu at the top of the page. Once you are on the **EC2** page, make sure you have the correct region selected by using the region drop-down menu in the top-right corner of the page. I am going to be using **EU (Ireland)**, which is also known as **eu-west-1**.

Now that we are in the correct region click on the **Key Pairs** option, which can be found under the **NETWORK & SECURITY** section in the left-hand menu. Once the page loads, click on the **Import Key Pair** button and then, like DigitalOcean, enter the name of your key pair and enter the contents of your `id_rsa.pub` file in there.

Next up, we need an AWS KMS store. To create this, run the following command, making sure to update your region as required:

```
$ aws kms --region=eu-west-1 create-key --description="kube-aws assets"
```

This will return several pieces of information, including an **Amazon Resource Name** (**ARN**). Make a note of this and also the `KeyId`:

```
1. russ (bash)
russ in ~
⚡ aws kms --region=eu-west-1 create-key --description="kube-aws assets"
{
    "KeyMetadata": {
        "AWSAccountId": "687011238589",
        "KeyId": "2d54175d-41e1-4865-ac57-b3c40d0c4c3f",
        "Arn": "arn:aws:kms:eu-west-1:687011238589:key/2d54175d-41e1-4865-ac57-b3c40d0c4c3f",
        "CreationDate": 1510416145.84,
        "Enabled": true,
        "Description": "kube-aws assets",
        "KeyUsage": "ENCRYPT_DECRYPT",
        "KeyState": "Enabled",
        "Origin": "AWS_KMS",
        "KeyManager": "CUSTOMER"
    }
}
russ in ~
⚡
```

Next up, we need an Amazon S3 bucket. To create one using the AWS CLI run the following command, making sure to update the region, and also make the bucket name unique to you:

```
$ aws s3api --region=eu-west-1 create-bucket --bucket kube-aws-russ --
create-bucket-configuration LocationConstraint=eu-west-1
```

```
1. russ (bash)
⚡ aws s3api --region=eu-west-1 create-bucket --bucket kube-aws-russ --create-bucket-configuration L
ocationConstraint=eu-west-1
{
    "Location": "http://kube-aws-russ.s3.amazonaws.com/"
}
russ in ~
⚡
```

Now that we have our public SSH key imported, a KMS ARN, and an S3 bucket, we just need to decide on a DNS name for our cluster.

I am going to be using `kube.mckendrick.io` for mine as I have `mckendrick.io` already hosted on the Amazon Route 53 DNS service. You should choose a domain or subdomain you can configure a CNAME on, or one that is hosted on Route 53.

Now that we have the basics covered we need to install the `kube-aws` binary. To do this, if you are running macOS High Sierra you simply need to run the following:

```
$ brew install kube-aws
```

If you are running Ubuntu Linux 17.04 you should run the following:

```
$ cd /tmp
$ wget
https://github.com/kubernetes-incubator/kube-aws/releases/download/v0.9.8/k
ube-aws-linux-amd64.tar.gz
$ tar zxvf kube-aws-linux-amd64.tar.gz
$ sudo mv linux-amd64/kube-aws /usr/local/bin
$ sudo chmod 755 /usr/local/bin/kube-aws
```

Once installed, run the following command to confirm that everything is OK:

```
$ kube-aws version
```

At the time of writing the current version is 0.9.8. You can check for newer versions on the release page at: `https://github.com/kubernetes-incubator/kube-aws/releases/`.

Launching the cluster using kube-aws

Before we start to create the cluster configuration, we need to create a working directory, as there are going to be a few artifacts created. Let's create a folder called `kube-aws-cluster` and change to it:

```
$ mkdir kube-aws-cluster
$ cd kube-aws-cluster
```

Now we are in our working directory we can create our cluster configuration file. To do this run the following command, making sure to replace the values with the information you gathered in the previous section:

If you are not using a Route 53-hosted domain, remove the `--hosted-zone-id` flag.

```
kube-aws init \
  --cluster-name=kube-aws-cluster \
  --external-dns-name=kube.mckendrick.io \
  --hosted-zone-id=Z2WSA56Y5ICKTT \
  --region=eu-west-1 \
  --availability-zone=eu-west-1a \
  --key-name=russ \
  --kms-key-arn="arn:aws:kms:eu-west-1:687011238589:key/2d54175d-41e1-4865-
ac57-b3c40d0c4c3f"
```

This will create a file called `cluster.yaml`, which will be the base of our configuration:

```
1. kube-aws-cluster (bash)
russ in ~/kube-aws-cluster
⚡ kube-aws init \
→ --cluster-name=kube-aws-cluster \
→ --external-dns-name=kube.mckendrick.io \
→ --hosted-zone-id=Z2WSA56Y5ICKTT \
→ --region=eu-west-1 \
→ --availability-zone=eu-west-1a \
→ --key-name=russ \
→ --kms-key-arn="arn:aws:kms:eu-west-1:687011238589:key/2d54175d-41e1-4865-ac57-b3c40d0c4c3f"
Success! Created cluster.yaml

Next steps:
1. (Optional) Edit cluster.yaml to parameterize the cluster.
2. Use the "kube-aws render" command to render the CloudFormation stack template and coreos-cloudini
t userdata.
russ in ~/kube-aws-cluster
⚡
```

Next, we need to create the certificates that will be used by our Kubernetes cluster. To do this run the following command:

```
$ kube-aws render credentials --generate-ca
```

```
1. kube-aws-cluster (bash)
russ in ~/kube-aws-cluster
⚡ kube-aws render credentials --generate-ca
Generating credentials...
-> Generating new TLS CA
-> Generating new assets
russ in ~/kube-aws-cluster
⚡
```

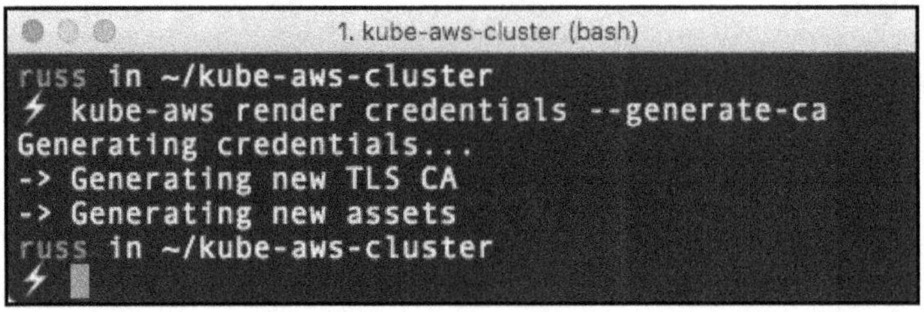

Next up, we need to generate the AWS CloudFormation templates. To do this run the following command:

```
$ kube-aws render stack
```

This will create the templates in a folder called `stack-templates`:

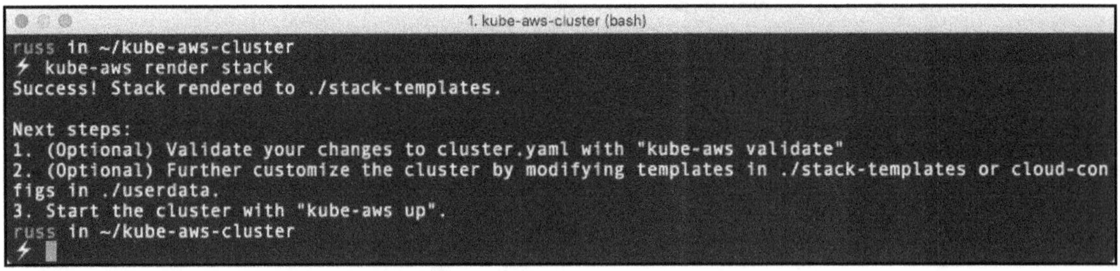

```
1. kube-aws-cluster (bash)
russ in ~/kube-aws-cluster
⚡ kube-aws render stack
Success! Stack rendered to ./stack-templates.

Next steps:
1. (Optional) Validate your changes to cluster.yaml with "kube-aws validate"
2. (Optional) Further customize the cluster by modifying templates in ./stack-templates or cloud-con
figs in ./userdata.
3. Start the cluster with "kube-aws up".
russ in ~/kube-aws-cluster
⚡
```

Running `ls` in your working directory should show you that several files and folders have been created:

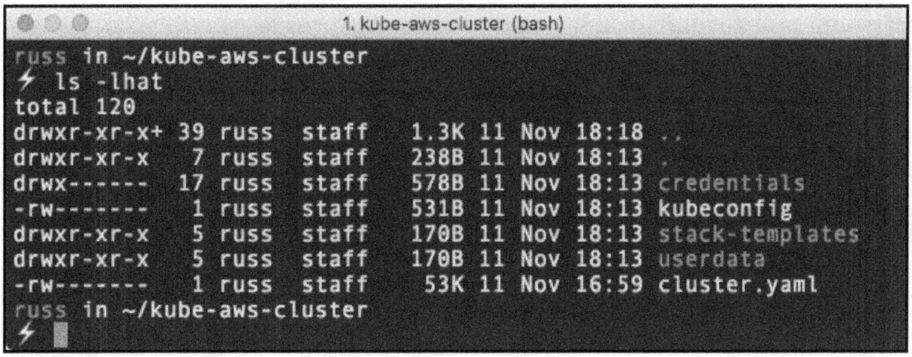

```
1. kube-aws-cluster (bash)
russ in ~/kube-aws-cluster
⚡ ls -lhat
total 120
drwxr-xr-x+ 39 russ  staff   1.3K 11 Nov 18:18 ..
drwxr-xr-x   7 russ  staff   238B 11 Nov 18:13 .
drwx------  17 russ  staff   578B 11 Nov 18:13 credentials
-rw-------   1 russ  staff   531B 11 Nov 18:13 kubeconfig
drwxr-xr-x   5 russ  staff   170B 11 Nov 18:13 stack-templates
drwxr-xr-x   5 russ  staff   170B 11 Nov 18:13 userdata
-rw-------   1 russ  staff    53K 11 Nov 16:59 cluster.yaml
russ in ~/kube-aws-cluster
⚡
```

Finally, we can run the following command to validate and upload the files to our S3 bucket, remembering to update the bucket name with your own:

```
$ kube-aws validate --s3-uri s3://kube-aws-russ/kube-aws-cluster
```

Now we can launch our cluster. To do this simply run the following command, again making sure you update the bucket name:

```
$ kube-aws up --s3-uri s3://kube-aws-russ/kube-aws-cluster
```

This will start to launch our cluster using the AWS CloudFormation tool:

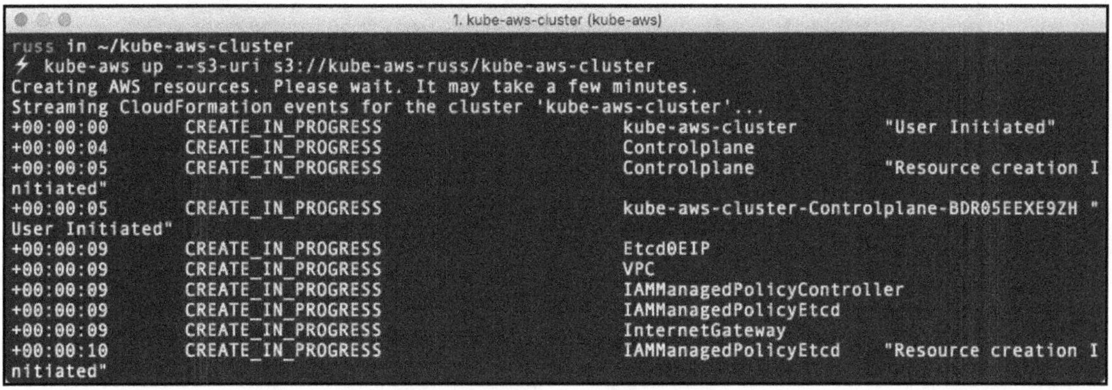

```
1. kube-aws-cluster (kube-aws)
russ in ~/kube-aws-cluster
⚡ kube-aws up --s3-uri s3://kube-aws-russ/kube-aws-cluster
Creating AWS resources. Please wait. It may take a few minutes.
Streaming CloudFormation events for the cluster 'kube-aws-cluster'...
+00:00:00       CREATE_IN_PROGRESS                      kube-aws-cluster        "User Initiated"
+00:00:04       CREATE_IN_PROGRESS                      Controlplane
+00:00:05       CREATE_IN_PROGRESS                      Controlplane            "Resource creation I
nitiated"
+00:00:05       CREATE_IN_PROGRESS                      kube-aws-cluster-Controlplane-BDR05EEXE9ZH "
User Initiated"
+00:00:09       CREATE_IN_PROGRESS                      Etcd0EIP
+00:00:09       CREATE_IN_PROGRESS                      VPC
+00:00:09       CREATE_IN_PROGRESS                      IAMManagedPolicyController
+00:00:09       CREATE_IN_PROGRESS                      IAMManagedPolicyEtcd
+00:00:09       CREATE_IN_PROGRESS                      InternetGateway
+00:00:10       CREATE_IN_PROGRESS                      IAMManagedPolicyEtcd    "Resource creation I
nitiated"
```

This process will take several minutes; you can view its progress on the command line within the AWS Console. To view it in the Console go to the **Services** menu and select **CloudFormation**. Once open, you should see a few stacks listed; select one of them and then click on the **Events** tab:

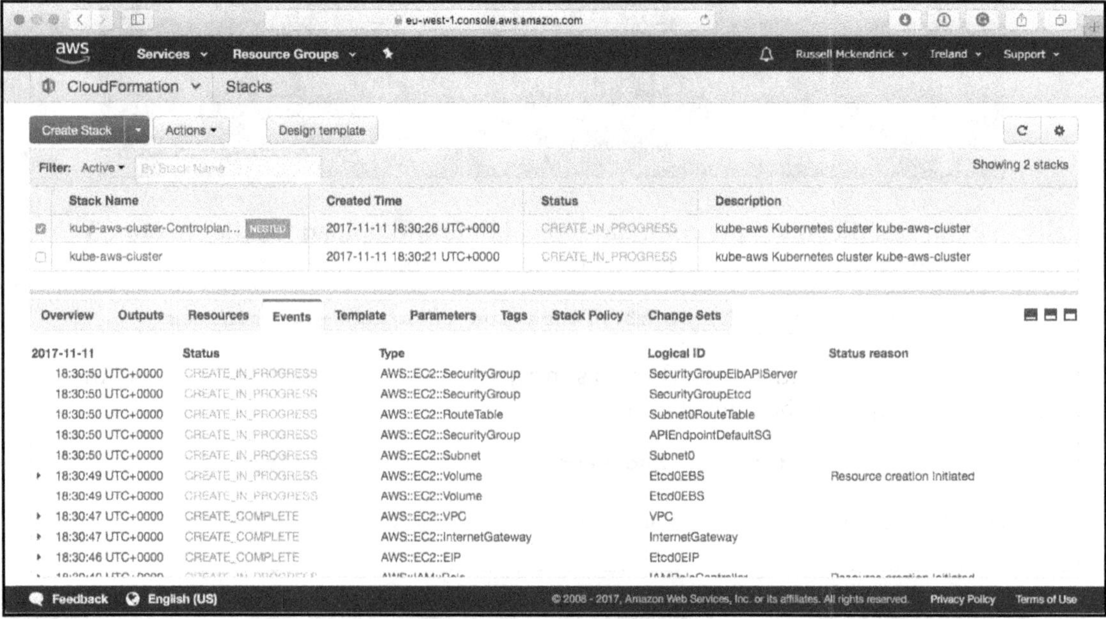

As you can see from the **Events** and also **Resources** tabs, there is a lot going on in the background. There are: IAM roles, VPCs and networking, EC2 instances, Load Balancers, DNS updates, auto scaling groups, and more being created.

Once it has finished, you should see three CloudFormation stacks, one main one called `kube-aws-cluster` and two nested stacks, one called `kube-aws-cluster-Controlplane` and the other `kube-aws-cluster-Nodepool1`. Both of the nested stacks will have a unique ID appended to their name. You will receive confirmation that your cluster has launched on the command line:

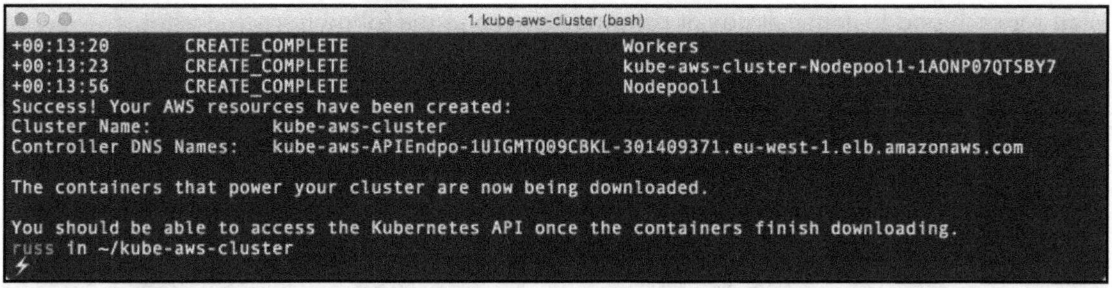

```
1. kube-aws-cluster (bash)
+00:13:20       CREATE_COMPLETE                         Workers
+00:13:23       CREATE_COMPLETE                         kube-aws-cluster-Nodepool1-1AONP07QTSBY7
+00:13:56       CREATE_COMPLETE                         Nodepool1
Success! Your AWS resources have been created:
Cluster Name:           kube-aws-cluster
Controller DNS Names:   kube-aws-APIEndpo-1UIGMTQ09CBKL-301409371.eu-west-1.elb.amazonaws.com

The containers that power your cluster are now being downloaded.

You should be able to access the Kubernetes API once the containers finish downloading.
russ in ~/kube-aws-cluster
⚡
```

Running the following command in our working directory will list the nodes within our AWS Kubernetes cluster:

```
$ kubectl --kubeconfig=kubeconfig get nodes
```

```
1. kube-aws-cluster (bash)
russ in ~/kube-aws-cluster
⚡ kubectl --kubeconfig=kubeconfig get nodes
NAME                                        STATUS    ROLES     AGE       VERSION
ip-10-0-0-69.eu-west-1.compute.internal     Ready     <none>    5m        v1.7.4+coreos.0
ip-10-0-0-75.eu-west-1.compute.internal     Ready     master    10m       v1.7.4+coreos.0
russ in ~/kube-aws-cluster
⚡
```

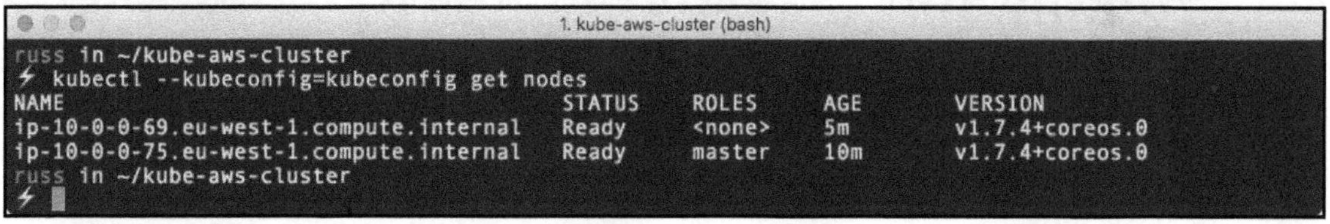

The Sock Shop

To test our deployment we can launch the Sock Shop. This is a demo microservice application written by Weave. You can find its project page at: `https://microservices-demo.github.io/`.

To launch the shop, we need to run the following commands from within our working directory:

```
$ kubectl --kubeconfig=kubeconfig create namespace sock-shop
$ kubectl --kubeconfig=kubeconfig apply -n sock-shop -f
"https://github.com/microservices-demo/microservices-demo/blob/master/deplo
y/kubernetes/complete-demo.yaml?raw=true"
```

It will take a few minutes to launch; you can check the progress by running the following:

```
$ kubectl --kubeconfig=kubeconfig -n sock-shop get pods
```

Wait for each pod to gain a status of running, as seen in the following screenshot:

```
1. kube-aws-cluster (bash)
russ in ~/kube-aws-cluster
⚡ kubectl --kubeconfig=kubeconfig -n sock-shop get pods
NAME                            READY     STATUS    RESTARTS   AGE
carts-2469883122-95vn6          1/1       Running   0          2m
carts-db-1721187500-dndj0       1/1       Running   0          2m
catalogue-4293036822-1bh2v      1/1       Running   0          2m
catalogue-db-1846494424-5lcbl   1/1       Running   0          2m
front-end-2337481689-2pwgf      1/1       Running   0          2m
orders-733484335-49cv9          1/1       Running   0          2m
orders-db-3728196820-wjj50      1/1       Running   0          2m
payment-3050936124-1vphg        1/1       Running   0          2m
queue-master-2067646375-smxjp   1/1       Running   0          2m
rabbitmq-241640118-j178h        1/1       Running   0          2m
shipping-2463450563-mfvjg       1/1       Running   0          2m
user-1574605338-xr65m           1/1       Running   0          2m
user-db-3152184577-h9trv        1/1       Running   0          2m
russ in ~/kube-aws-cluster
⚡
```

Then, we should be able to access our application. To do this we will need to expose it to the internet. As we have our cluster in AWS we can use the following command to launch an Elastic Load Balancer and have it point to our application:

```
$ kubectl --kubeconfig=kubeconfig -n sock-shop expose deployment front-end
--type=LoadBalancer --name=front-end-lb
```

To get information on our Load Balancer we can run the following:

```
$ kubectl --kubeconfig=kubeconfig -n sock-shop get services front-end-lb
```

```
1. kube-aws-cluster (bash)
russ in ~/kube-aws-cluster
⚡ kubectl --kubeconfig=kubeconfig -n sock-shop get services front-end-lb
NAME           TYPE           CLUSTER-IP   EXTERNAL-IP         PORT(S)          AGE
front-end-lb   LoadBalancer   10.3.0.46    a47ecf69fc714...    8079:30086/TCP   8m
russ in ~/kube-aws-cluster
⚡
```

As you can see, the application is being exposed on port `8079`, but we cannot quite see the Elastic Load Balancer URL. To get this we can run the following:

```
$ kubectl --kubeconfig=kubeconfig -n sock-shop describe services front-end-lb
```

```
1. kube-aws-cluster (bash)
russ in ~/kube-aws-cluster
⚡ kubectl --kubeconfig=kubeconfig -n sock-shop describe service front-end-lb
Name:                     front-end-lb
Namespace:                sock-shop
Labels:                   name=front-end
Annotations:              <none>
Selector:                 name=front-end
Type:                     LoadBalancer
IP:                       10.3.0.46
LoadBalancer Ingress:     a47ecf69fc71411e7974802a5d74b8ec-130999546.eu-west-1.elb.amazonaws.com
Port:                     <unset>  8079/TCP
TargetPort:               8079/TCP
NodePort:                 <unset>  30086/TCP
Endpoints:                10.2.8.12:8079
Session Affinity:         None
External Traffic Policy:  Cluster
Events:
  Type    Reason                Age   From                Message
  ----    ------                ----  ----                -------
  Normal  CreatingLoadBalancer  11m   service-controller  Creating load balancer
  Normal  CreatedLoadBalancer   11m   service-controller  Created load balancer
russ in ~/kube-aws-cluster
⚡
```

Now that we know the URL of the Elastic Load Balancer we can enter it, along with the port, into our browser. For me, the full URL was `http://a47ecf69fc71411e7974802a5d74b8ec-130999546.eu-west-1.elb.amazonaws.com:8079/` (this URL is no longer active).

Entering your URL should show you the following page:

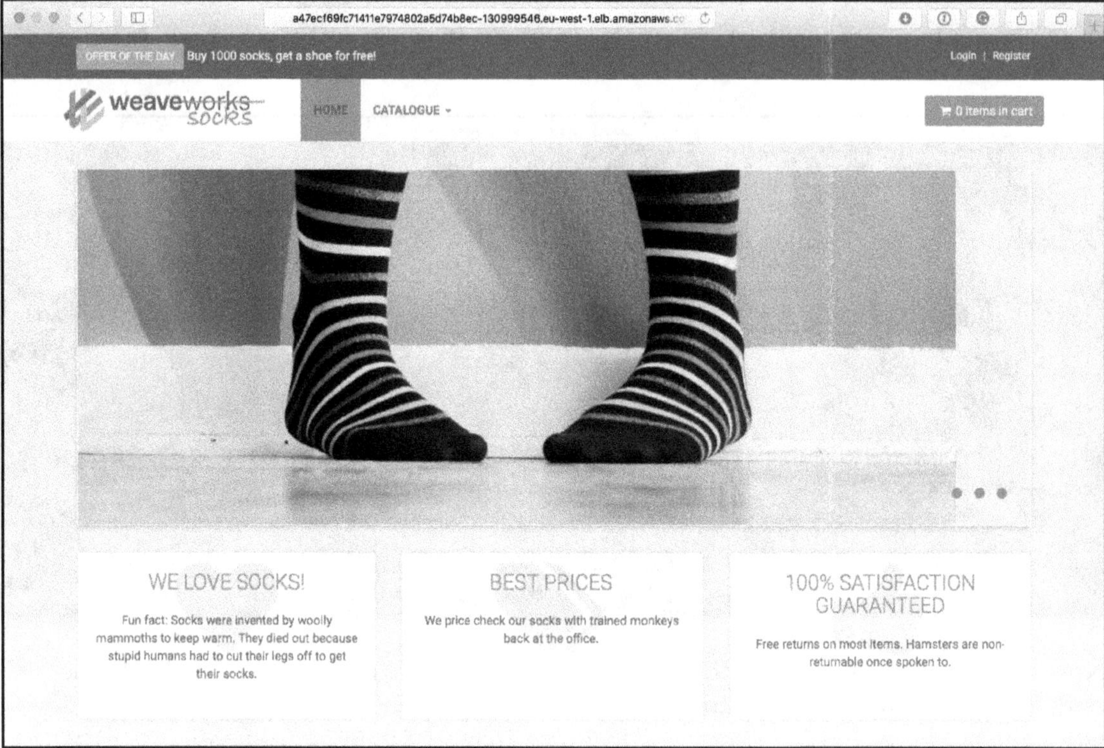

To remove the Sock Shop application simply run:

```
$ kubectl --kubeconfig=kubeconfig delete namespace sock-shop
```

This will remove all of the pods, services, and the Elastic Load Balancer we created.

Removing the cluster

Let's not forget that while the cluster is up-and-running it is costing us money. To remove the cluster and all of the services created by the CloudFormation scripts run the following command:

```
$ kube-aws destroy
```

You will receive confirmation that the CloudFormation stacks are being removed, and that it will take several minutes. I recommend that you double-check in the AWS console on the CloudFormation page to ensure that there have not been any errors during the removal of the stacks, as any resources that are left running may incur costs.

We also need to remove the S3 bucket we created and also the KMS; to do this run the following:

```
$ aws s3 rb s3://kube-aws-russ --force
$ aws kms --region=eu-west-1 disable-key --key-id 2d54175d-41e1-4865-ac57-
b3c40d0c4c3f
```

You can find the `--key-id` from the note you made when we first created the KMS earlier in this section.

While we didn't have to manually configure our cluster, or in fact to log in to any servers this time, the process of launching our cluster was still very manual. For our next public cloud provider, Microsoft Azure, we are going to be looking at a more native deployment.

Launching Kubernetes in Microsoft Azure

In `Chapter 1`, *The Serverless Landscape,* we looked at Microsoft Azure Functions; however, we did not progress much further than the Azure web interface to launch our Function. To use the **Azure Container Service** (**AKS**) we will need to install the Azure command-line client.

It is also worth pointing out at this time that the AKS does not currently support the Windows 10 PowerShell Azure tools. However, if you are using Windows do not worry, as the Linux version of the command-line client is available through the Azure web interface.

Preparing the Azure command-line tools

The Azure command-line tools are available through Homebrew on macOS High Sierra, which makes installing as easy as running the following two commands:

```
$ brew update
$ brew install azure-cli
```

Ubuntu 17.04 users can run the following commands:

```
$ echo "deb [arch=amd64] https://packages.microsoft.com/repos/azure-cli/
wheezy main" | sudo tee /etc/apt/sources.list.d/azure-cli.list
$ sudo apt-key adv --keyserver packages.microsoft.com --recv-keys
52E16F86FEE04B979B07E28DB02C46DF417A0893
$ sudo apt-get install apt-transport-https
$ sudo apt-get update && sudo apt-get install azure-cli
```

Once installed you need to log in to your account. To do this run the following:

```
$ az login
```

When you run the command you will be given a URL, which is `https://aka.ms/devicelogin, and also a code to enter. Open the URL in your browser and enter the code:`

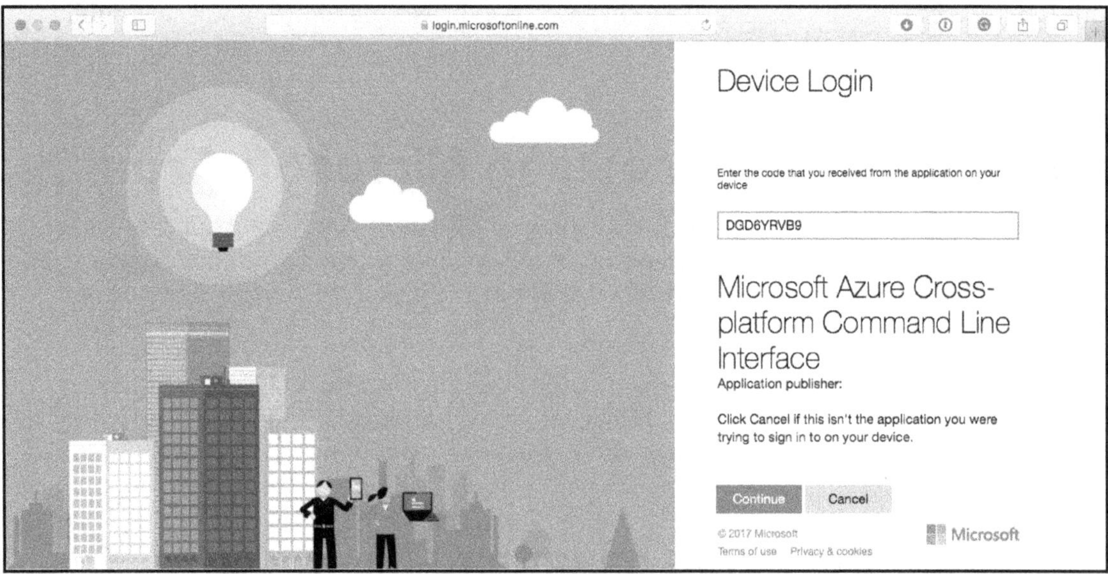

Once logged in, close your browser window and return to the command line, where after a few seconds you will receive confirmation that you are logged in as the user you logged into the browser with. You can double-check this by running the following command:

```
$ az account show
```

As mentioned, Windows users can access their own bash shell using the Azure web interface. To do this, log in and click on the >_ icon in the top menu bar, select bash shell, and then follow the on-screen prompts. At the end of the setup you should see something like the following:

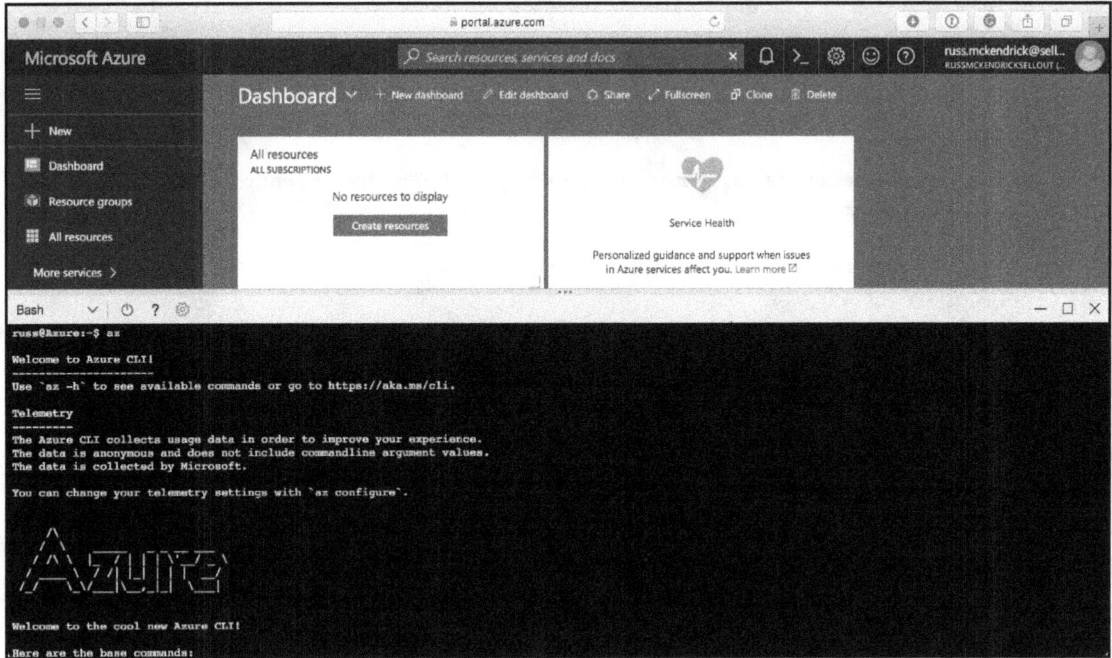

Now we have the command-line tools up, installed, and connected to our account we can launch our Kubernetes cluster.

Launching the AKS cluster

First of all, we need to register for the AKS service. To do this run the following command:

```
$ az provider register -n Microsoft.ContainerService
```

It will take a few minutes for the registration to complete. You can check on the status of the registration by running the following:

```
$ az provider show -n Microsoft.ContainerService
```

Once you see a `registrationState` of `Registered` you are good to go. To launch the cluster, we need to first create a resource group and then create the cluster. At present, AKS is available in either `ukwest` or `westus2`:

```
$ az group create --name KubeResourceGroup --location ukwest
$ az aks create --resource-group KubeResourceGroup --name AzureKubeCluster
--agent-count 1 --generate-ssh-keys
```

Once your cluster has launched you can run the following command to configure your local copy of `kubectl` to authenticate against the cluster:

```
$ az aks get-credentials --resource-group KubeResourceGroup --name
AzureKubeCluster
```

Finally, you can now run the following to start interacting with your cluster as you would any other Kubernetes cluster:

```
$ kubectl get nodes
```

```
1. russ (bash)
⚡ az aks get-credentials --resource-group KubeResourceGroup --name AzureKubeCluster
Merged "AzureKubeCluster" as current context in /Users/russ/.kube/config
russ in ~
⚡ kubectl get nodes
NAME                         STATUS    ROLES     AGE       VERSION
aks-agentpool1-11247062-0    Ready     agent     4m        v1.7.7
russ in ~
⚡
```

You will notice that we only have a single node; we can add two more nodes by running the following:

```
$ az aks scale --resource-group KubeResourceGroup --name AzureKubeCluster -
-agent-count 3
$ kubectl get nodes
```

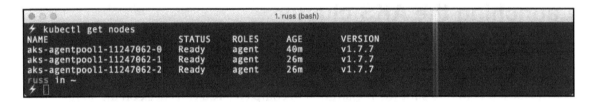

```
1. russ (bash)
⚡ kubectl get nodes
NAME                         STATUS    ROLES     AGE       VERSION
aks-agentpool1-11247062-0    Ready     agent     40m       v1.7.7
aks-agentpool1-11247062-1    Ready     agent     26m       v1.7.7
aks-agentpool1-11247062-2    Ready     agent     26m       v1.7.7
russ in ~
⚡
```

You should be able to see all of the resources that have been launched in the Azure web interface:

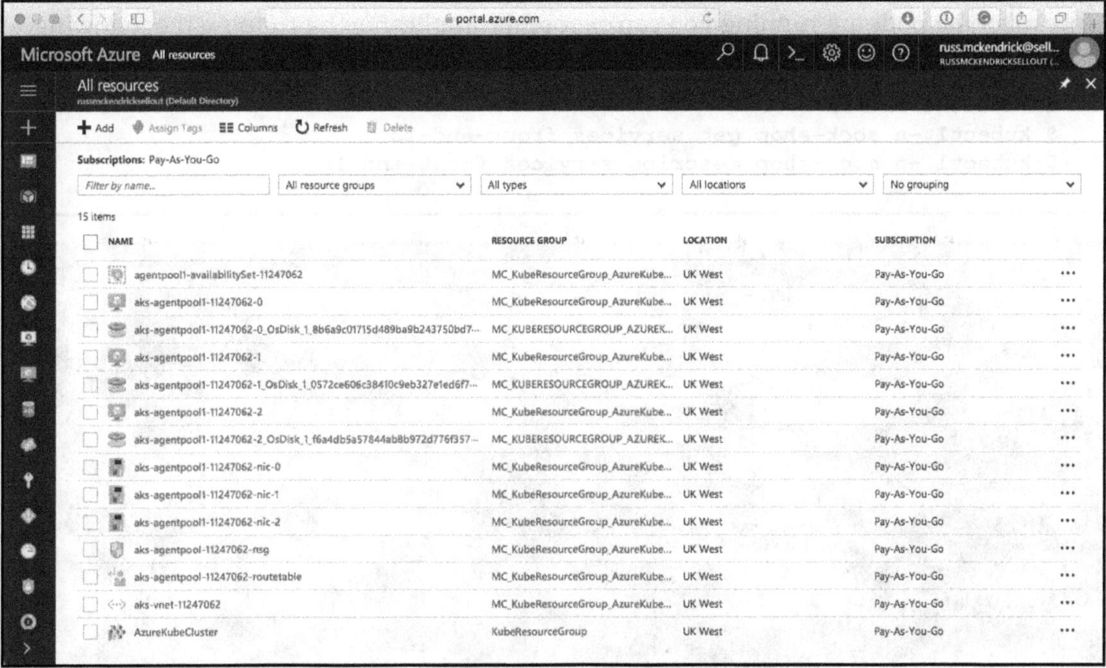

Now that we have three nodes in our cluster, let's launch the *Sock Shop demo* app.

The Sock Shop

The commands are slightly different to the ones we ran before, as we do not have to supply a configuration file for `kubectl`:

```
$ kubectl create namespace sock-shop
$ kubectl apply -n sock-shop -f
"https://github.com/microservices-demo/microservices-demo/blob/master/deplo
y/kubernetes/complete-demo.yaml?raw=true"
```

Again, you can check the status of the pods by running the following:

```
$ kubectl -n sock-shop get pods
```

Once all of the pods are running you can expose the application by running the following:

```
$ kubectl -n sock-shop expose deployment front-end --type=LoadBalancer --
name=front-end-lb
$ kubectl -n sock-shop get services front-end-lb
$ kubectl -n sock-shop describe services front-end-lb
```

```
1. russ (bash)
⚡ kubectl -n sock-shop get services front-end-lb
NAME           TYPE           CLUSTER-IP    EXTERNAL-IP     PORT(S)          AGE
front-end-lb   LoadBalancer   10.0.104.71   51.141.28.140   8079:30286/TCP   4m
russ in ~
⚡ kubectl -n sock-shop describe services front-end-lb
Name:                     front-end-lb
Namespace:                sock-shop
Labels:                   name=front-end
Annotations:              <none>
Selector:                 name=front-end
Type:                     LoadBalancer
IP:                       10.0.104.71
LoadBalancer Ingress:     51.141.28.140
Port:                     <unset>  8079/TCP
TargetPort:               8079/TCP
NodePort:                 <unset>  30286/TCP
Endpoints:                10.244.2.4:8079
Session Affinity:         None
External Traffic Policy:  Cluster
Events:
  Type    Reason                Age   From                Message
  ----    ------                ----  ----                -------
  Normal  CreatingLoadBalancer  4m    service-controller  Creating load balancer
  Normal  CreatedLoadBalancer   1m    service-controller  Created load balancer
russ in ~
⚡
```

This should give you a port and IP address. As you can see from the preceding output, this gave me a URL of `http://51.141.28.140:8079/`, putting this into my browser displayed the Sock Shop application:

To remove the application I just needed to run:

```
$ kubectl delete namespace sock-shop
```

Removing the cluster

As per the other cloud services, while your AKS nodes are online you will be charged by the hour. Once you have finished with the cluster you simply need to remove the resource group; this will delete all of the associated services:

```
$ az aks delete --resource-group KubeResourceGroup --name AzureKubeCluster
$ az group delete --name KubeResourceGroup
```

Once deleted, go to the Azure web interface and manually delete any other remaining resources/services. The next and final public cloud we are going to look at is Google Cloud.

Launching Kubernetes on the Google Cloud Platform

As you would expect, Kubernetes is supported natively on Google Cloud. Before progressing, you will need an account, which you can sign up for at `http://cloud.google.com/`. Once you have your account set up, similar to the other public cloud platforms we have been looking at in this chapter, we need to configure the command-line tools.

Installing the command-line tools

There are installers for all three operating systems. If you are using macOS High Sierra then you can use Homebrew and Cask to install the Google Cloud SDK by running the following:

```
$ brew cask install google-cloud-sdk
```

Windows 10 Professional users can use Chocolatey and run the following:

```
$ choco install gcloudsdk
```

Finally, Ubuntu 17.04 users will need to run the following:

```
$ export CLOUD_SDK_REPO="cloud-sdk-$(lsb_release -c -s)"
$ echo "deb http://packages.cloud.google.com/apt $CLOUD_SDK_REPO main" |
sudo tee -a /etc/apt/sources.list.d/google-cloud-sdk.list
$ curl https://packages.cloud.google.com/apt/doc/apt-key.gpg | sudo apt-key
add -
$ sudo apt-get update && sudo apt-get install google-cloud-sdk
```

Once installed, you need to sign into your account by running the following:

```
$ gcloud init
```

This will open your browser and ask you to sign into your Google Cloud account. Once signed in, you will be asked to grant the Google Cloud SDK permission to access your account. Follow the on-screen prompts to grant permissions and you should receive a message confirming you are authenticated with the Google Cloud SDK.

Going back to your terminal, you should now have a prompt asking you to create a project. For testing purposes answer yes (`y`) to this question and enter a project name. This project name must be unique to you so it may take a few attempts. If you fail at first you can use the following command:

```
$ gcloud projects create russ-kubernetes-cluster
```

As you can see, my project is called `russ-kubernetes-cluster`. You should make references to your own project name in the commands. The final steps are to set our new project as the default as well as the region. I used the following commands:

```
$ gcloud config set project russ-kubernetes-cluster
$ gcloud config set compute/zone us-central1-b
```

Now that we have the command-line tools installed, we can move on to launching our cluster.

Launching the Google container cluster

You can launch the cluster with a single command. The following command will launch a cluster named `kube-cluster`:

```
$ gcloud container clusters create kube-cluster
```

When you first run the command you may run into an error that states that the Google container API is not enabled for your project:

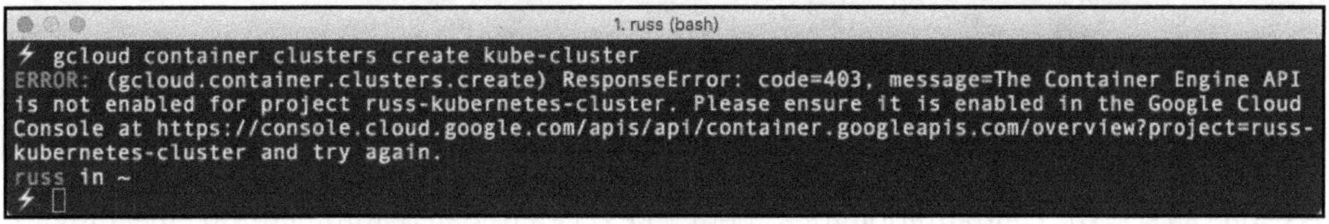

```
1. russ (bash)
⚡ gcloud container clusters create kube-cluster
ERROR: (gcloud.container.clusters.create) ResponseError: code=403, message=The Container Engine API
is not enabled for project russ-kubernetes-cluster. Please ensure it is enabled in the Google Cloud
Console at https://console.cloud.google.com/apis/api/container.googleapis.com/overview?project=russ-
kubernetes-cluster and try again.
russ in ~
⚡ 
```

You can rectify this error by following the link given in the error and following the on-screen instructions to enable the API. You may also find you get an error if your project does not have any billing associated with it:

```
1. russ (bash)
 targetLink: u'https://container.googleapis.com/v1/projects/743337007583/zones/us-central1-b/cluster
s/kube-cluster'
 zone: u'us-central1-b'>] finished with error: Google Compute Engine: Project russ-kubernetes-cluste
r cannot accept requests to setMetadata while in an inactive billing state.  Billing state may take
several minutes to update.
russ in ~
⚡
```

To resolve this, log in to the Google Cloud web interface at `https://console.cloud.google.com/` and select your project from the drop-down list next to where it says **Google Cloud Platform**. Once you have your project selected, click on the **Billing** link in the left-hand side menu and follow the on-screen prompts to link your project to your billing account.

Once you have the API enabled and your project linked to a billing account you should be able to rerun the following:

```
$ gcloud container clusters create kube-cluster
```

It will take several minutes, but once complete you should see something like the following:

```
1. russ (bash)
⚡ gcloud container clusters create kube-cluster
Creating cluster kube-cluster...done.
Created [https://container.googleapis.com/v1/projects/russ-kubernetes-cluster/zones/us-central1-b/cl
usters/kube-cluster].
kubeconfig entry generated for kube-cluster.
NAME          ZONE           MASTER_VERSION  MASTER_IP      MACHINE_TYPE   NODE_VERSION  NUM_NODES
STATUS
kube-cluster  us-central1-b  1.7.8-gke.0     35.192.158.77  n1-standard-1  1.7.8-gke.0   3
RUNNING
russ in ~
```

As you can see, the configuration for `kubectl` has been updated automatically, meaning that we can run the following command to check that we can communicate with our new cluster:

```
1. russ (bash)
⚡ kubectl get nodes
NAME                                         STATUS    ROLES     AGE       VERSION
gke-kube-cluster-default-pool-a23963ed-4wcx  Ready     <none>    2m        v1.7.8-gke.0
gke-kube-cluster-default-pool-a23963ed-7833  Ready     <none>    2m        v1.7.8-gke.0
gke-kube-cluster-default-pool-a23963ed-m6dz  Ready     <none>    2m        v1.7.8-gke.0
russ in ~
⚡
```

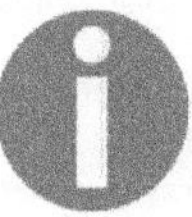

Before running this command please ensure that your local machine has a direct route to the internet and that you are not running through a proxy server or connection which is heavily firewalled, you may not be able to run into difficulties with the `kubectl proxy` command if you are.

You should also be able to see your cluster in the **Container Engine** section of the Google Cloud web interface:

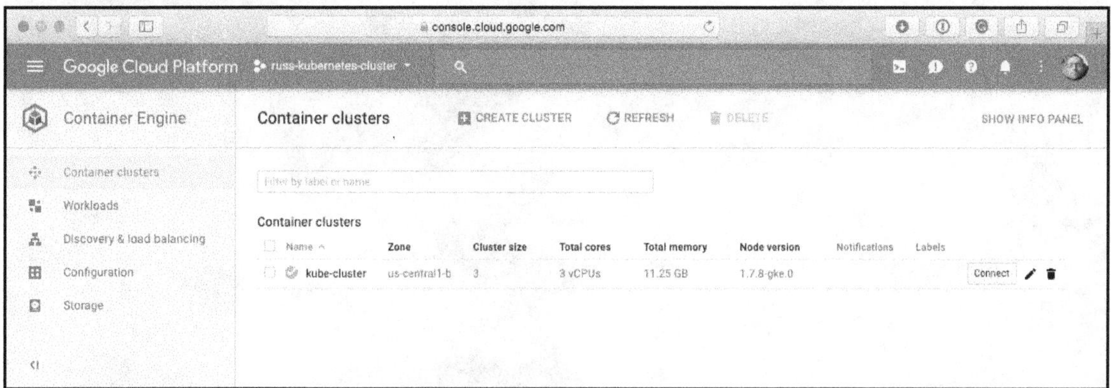

Now that we have our cluster up-and-running, let's launch the Sock Shop application again.

The Sock Shop

As we did with Azure, there is no need to provide a configuration file this time, so we simply need to run the following commands:

```
$ kubectl create namespace sock-shop
$ kubectl apply -n sock-shop -f
"https://github.com/microservices-demo/microservices-demo/blob/master/deplo
y/kubernetes/complete-demo.yaml?raw=true"
$ kubectl -n sock-shop get pods
$ kubectl -n sock-shop expose deployment front-end --type=LoadBalancer --
name=front-end-lb
$ kubectl -n sock-shop get services front-end-lb
$ kubectl -n sock-shop describe services front-end-lb
```

As you can see from the following screenshot, the IP and port give me a URL of `http://104.155.191.39:8079`:

```
1. russ (bash)
⚡ kubectl -n sock-shop get services front-end-lb
NAME           TYPE           CLUSTER-IP    EXTERNAL-IP      PORT(S)          AGE
front-end-lb   LoadBalancer   10.3.255.92   104.155.191.39   8079:32096/TCP   1m
russ in ~
⚡ kubectl -n sock-shop describe services front-end-lb
Name:                     front-end-lb
Namespace:                sock-shop
Labels:                   name=front-end
Annotations:              <none>
Selector:                 name=front-end
Type:                     LoadBalancer
IP:                       10.3.255.92
LoadBalancer Ingress:     104.155.191.39
Port:                     <unset>  8079/TCP
TargetPort:               8079/TCP
NodePort:                 <unset>  32096/TCP
Endpoints:                10.0.1.5:8079
Session Affinity:         None
External Traffic Policy:  Cluster
Events:
  Type    Reason                Age   From                Message
  ----    ------                ----  ----                -------
  Normal  CreatingLoadBalancer  1m    service-controller  Creating load balancer
  Normal  CreatedLoadBalancer   35s   service-controller  Created load balancer
russ in ~
⚡
```

Also, in the Google Cloud web interface, clicking on **Discovery & load balancing** should also show you the Load Balancer we created:

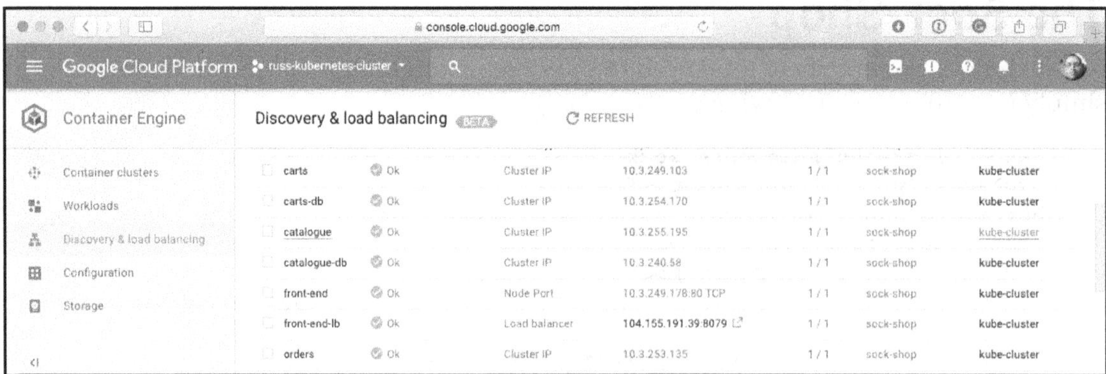

Clicking on the link in the interface, or pasting your URL into a browser should show you the now familiar shop front:

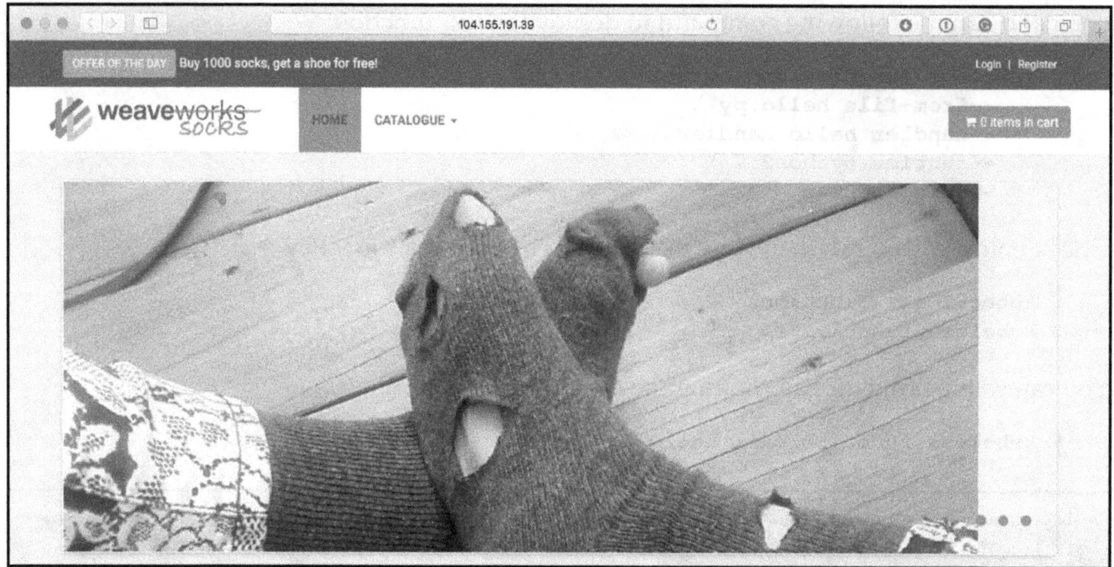

Running the following command should remove the Sock Shop application:

```
$ kubectl delete namespace sock-shop
```

Running Kubeless

Before we remove our Google Cloud, three-node Kubernetes cluster, let's quickly revisit Kubeless. To deploy Kubeless, run the following commands:

```
$ kubectl create ns kubeless
$ kubectl create -f
https://github.com/kubeless/kubeless/releases/download/v0.2.3/kubeless-v0.2
.3.yaml
```

Once deployed, you can check the status by running the following:

```
$ kubectl get pods -n kubeless
$ kubectl get deployment -n kubeless
$ kubectl get statefulset -n kubeless
```

You can also check **Workloads** and **Discovery & load balancing** in the Google **Container Engine** section of the Google Cloud web interface. Once Kubeless has been deployed, return to the `/Chapter04/hello-world` folder in the repository that accompanies this book and run the following command to deploy the test function:

```
$ kubeless function deploy hello \
    --from-file hello.py \
    --handler hello.handler \
    --runtime python2.7 \
    --trigger-http
```

Once deployed, you can then view the function by running the following:

```
$ kubectl get functions
$ kubeless function ls
```

You can call the function by running the following:

```
$ kubeless function call hello
```

```
1. hello-world (bash)
russ in ~/Documents/Code/kubernetes-for-serverless-applications/Chapter04/hello-world on master*
⚡ kubectl get functions
NAME      AGE
hello     2m
russ in ~/Documents/Code/kubernetes-for-serverless-applications/Chapter04/hello-world on master*
⚡ kubeless function ls
NAME    NAMESPACE       HANDLER         RUNTIME         TYPE    TOPIC   DEPENDENCIES
hello   default         hello.handler   python2.7       HTTP
russ in ~/Documents/Code/kubernetes-for-serverless-applications/Chapter04/hello-world on master*
⚡ kubeless function call hello
Forwarding from 127.0.0.1:30000 -> 8080
Forwarding from [::1]:30000 -> 8080
Handling connection for 30000
Hello World!
russ in ~/Documents/Code/kubernetes-for-serverless-applications/Chapter04/hello-world on master*
⚡
```

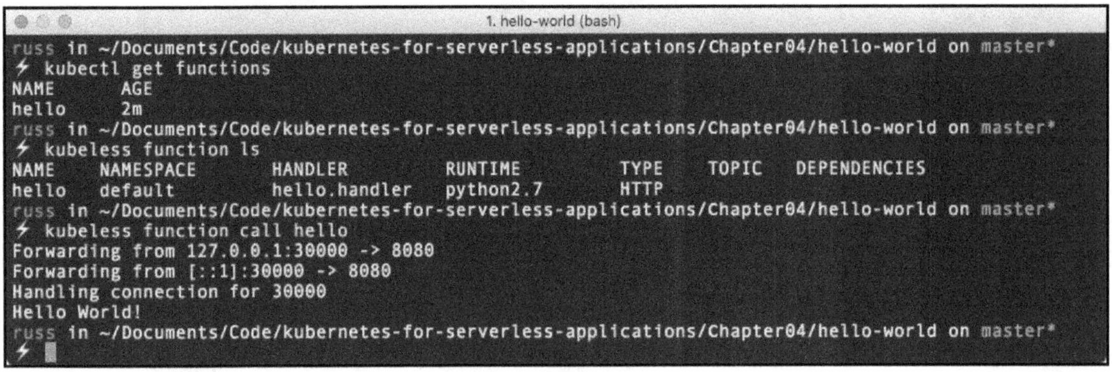

Also, you can expose the function using the following command:

```
$ kubectl expose deployment hello --type=LoadBalancer --name=hello-lb
```

Once the Load Balancer has been created you can run the following to confirm the IP address and port:

```
$ kubectl get services hello-lb
```

Once you know the IP address and port you can open the function in your browser or use curl or HTTPie to view the function:

```
1. hello-world (bash)
russ in ~/Documents/Code/kubernetes-for-serverless-applications/chapter04/hello-world on master*
⚡ kubectl get services hello-lb
NAME       TYPE           CLUSTER-IP     EXTERNAL-IP     PORT(S)          AGE
hello-lb   LoadBalancer   10.3.249.31    35.193.120.24   8080:31799/TCP   1m
russ in ~/Documents/Code/kubernetes-for-serverless-applications/chapter04/hello-world on master*
⚡ http 35.193.120.24:8080
HTTP/1.1 200 OK
Content-Length: 12
Content-Type: text/html; charset=UTF-8
Date: Sun, 12 Nov 2017 13:05:27 GMT
Server: hello-421107193-8w3fj

Hello World!

russ in ~/Documents/Code/kubernetes-for-serverless-applications/chapter04/hello-world on master*
⚡
```

Now that we have tested our cluster with the Sock Shop application and deployed a Kubeless function we should look at terminating our cluster.

Removing the cluster

To remove the cluster just run the following command:

```
$ gcloud container clusters delete kube-cluster
```

It will ask you if you are sure, answer yes and, after a minute or two, your cluster will be deleted. Again, you should double-check in the Google Cloud web interface that your cluster has been correctly deleted so you do not incur any unexpected costs.

Summary

In this chapter, we looked at four cloud providers. The first two, DigitalOcean and AWS, at present do not natively support Kubernetes so we used `kubeadm` and `kube-aws` to launch and configure our clusters. With Microsoft Azure and Google Cloud we used their command-line tools to launch their natively supported Kubernetes services. I am sure you will agree that at the time of writing both of these services are a lot friendlier to use than the first two we looked at.

Once the clusters were up-and-running, interacting with Kubernetes was a pretty consistent experience. We didn't really have to make allowances for where our cluster was running when issuing commands such as `kubectl expose`: Kubernetes was aware of where it was running and used the provider's native services to launch a Load Balancer without us have to intervene with any special settings or considerations.

You may be wondering why we didn't launch the Sock Shop application on DigitalOcean. As the spec of the machines was quite low, the application was really slow to run, and DigitalOcean is the only provider out of the four we looked at where the provider's native Load Balancing service is not currently supported by Kubernetes. I am sure this will be rectified over the coming months.

Also, you might be surprised that there is no native Kubernetes experience on AWS. At the time of writing this is the case; however, there are rumors that since, AWS has joined the Cloud Native Foundation, they are working on developing a native Kubernetes service.

In the next chapter, we are going to take look at Apache OpenWhisk, which is an open source serverless cloud platform originally developed by IBM.

7
Apache OpenWhisk and Kubernetes

In this chapter, we are going to look at Apache OpenWhisk. While not strictly a Kubernetes-only project, like, say, Kubeless and Fission (which are covered in the next chapter), it can be deployed on, and take advantage of, Kubernetes.

We are going to be looking at three main topics:

- An overview of Apache OpenWhisk
- Running Apache OpenWhisk locally using Vagrant
- Running Apache OpenWhisk on Kubernetes

Let's start by finding out more about OpenWhisk.

Apache OpenWhisk overview

Apache OpenWhisk is an open source, serverless cloud computing platform, designed to work in a similar way to all the tools we have been covering in other chapters of this book. Apache OpenWhisk started off life as, and continues to be, Functions as a Service part of IBM's public cloud offering, Bluemix.

It had its general availability release in December 2016. The press release that accompanied the announcement had a quote from Luis Enriquez who is the Head of Platform Engineering and Architecture at Santander Group, one of the customers who had been using IBM Cloud Functions while it was in closed beta, Luis said:

> *"Microservices and containers are changing the way we build apps, but because of serverless, we can take that transformation even further, OpenWhisk provides the instant infrastructure we need for intense tasks and unexpected peaks in workload, and is a key building block as we move to a real-time and event-driven architecture."*

As you may have noticed, this sounds a lot like Lambda from AWS and Microsoft Azure Functions—what sets IBM's service apart from its competitors is that IBM has submitted OpenWhisk to the Apache Incubator, this is the entry point for all externally developed projects to become part of The Apache Software Foundation efforts.

The Apache Software Foundation was founded in 1999 as a charitable organization that oversees the development and management of well over 350 open source software projects, which it does for the public good.

So why would IBM do this? Well, not only is IBM a gold sponsor of The Apache Software Foundation, it makes sense for them to open-source their Functions as a Service offering as it makes it the only public cloud offering where you can avoid vendor lock-in, as you can run Apache OpenWhisk locally or on your own hardware or virtual machines.

This gives you the freedom to run and deploy Apache OpenWhisk anywhere you like. However, if you would like to run it to scale like the Santander Group is, then you have the option of running it on an enterprise-class public cloud supported by IBM.

Running Apache OpenWhisk locally

We are going to be looking at running Apache OpenWhisk locally first. We will do this by using a combination of VirtualBox, which we installed in `Chapter 3`, *Installing Kubernetes Locally*, and Vagrant.

Installing Vagrant

Before we launch our local Apache OpenWhisk server we need to install Vagrant, which is developed by HashiCorp. The best way I can describe Vagrant is as an open source, virtual machine manager, where your machine configuration is written using an easy-to-follow text configuration file.

Installing Vagrant is quite simple. On macOS 10.13 High Sierra we can use Homebrew and Cask:

```
$ brew cask install vagrant
```

If you are running Windows 10 Professional you can use Chocolatey and run the following:

```
$ choco install vagrant
```

Finally, if you are running Ubuntu 17.04 you can install Vagrant directly from the core Ubuntu repositories by running:

```
$ sudo apt-get update
$ sudo apt-get install vagrant
```

Please note, the version supplied by Ubuntu may be a little behind the versions installed using Homebrew and Chocolatey; however for our purposes, this should not present any problems.

You can test your Vagrant installation by running the following commands:

```
$ mkdir vagrant-test
$ cd vagrant-test
$ vagrant init ubuntu/xenial64
$ vagrant up
```

These commands will create a basic Vagrantfile in the `vagrant-test` folder, which uses the official 64-bit Ubuntu 16.04 LTS (Xenial) image from the Vagrant website (`https://app.vagrantup.com/ubuntu/boxes/xenial64/`), downloads the image, launches a virtual machine using VirtualBox, configures networking, and exchanges keys with the server before finally mounting the current folder within the virtual machine at `/vagrant`:

```
1. vagrant-test (bash)
⚡ mkdir vagrant-test
russ in ~
⚡ cd vagrant-test
russ in ~/vagrant-test
⚡ vagrant init ubuntu/xenial64
A `Vagrantfile` has been placed in this directory. You are now
ready to `vagrant up` your first virtual environment! Please read
the comments in the Vagrantfile as well as documentation on
`vagrantup.com` for more information on using Vagrant.
russ in ~/vagrant-test
⚡ vagrant up
Bringing machine 'default' up with 'virtualbox' provider...
==> default: Box 'ubuntu/xenial64' could not be found. Attempting to find and install...
    default: Box Provider: virtualbox
    default: Box Version: >= 0
==> default: Loading metadata for box 'ubuntu/xenial64'
    default: URL: https://vagrantcloud.com/ubuntu/xenial64
==> default: Adding box 'ubuntu/xenial64' (v20171122.0.0) for provider: virtualbox
    default: Downloading: https://vagrantcloud.com/ubuntu/boxes/xenial64/versions/20171122.0.0/provi
ders/virtualbox.box
==> default: Successfully added box 'ubuntu/xenial64' (v20171122.0.0) for 'virtualbox'!
==> default: Importing base box 'ubuntu/xenial64'...
==> default: Matching MAC address for NAT networking...
==> default: Checking if box 'ubuntu/xenial64' is up to date...
==> default: Setting the name of the VM: vagrant-test_default_1511625200087_9940
==> default: Clearing any previously set network interfaces...
==> default: Preparing network interfaces based on configuration...
    default: Adapter 1: nat
==> default: Forwarding ports...
    default: 22 (guest) => 2222 (host) (adapter 1)
```

All of this is defined using the following configuration:

```
Vagrant.configure("2") do |config|
 config.vm.box = "ubuntu/xenial64"
end
```

If you open the Vagrantfile you will notice that there are quite a few configuration options, such as the RAM and CPU allocations, networking, and scripts, which are executed once the virtual machine has successfully launched. You can run the following command to SSH into your Vagrant virtual machine:

```
$ vagrant ssh
```

If you are running Windows 10 Professional you are going to have to install an SSH client. Vagrant will give you some options on how to do this when you execute the preceding command.

Running the following command will power down your virtual machine and remove it:

```
$ vagrant destroy
```

```
1. vagrant-test (bash)
⚡ vagrant ssh
Welcome to Ubuntu 16.04.3 LTS (GNU/Linux 4.4.0-101-generic x86_64)

 * Documentation:  https://help.ubuntu.com
 * Management:     https://landscape.canonical.com
 * Support:        https://ubuntu.com/advantage

  Get cloud support with Ubuntu Advantage Cloud Guest:
    http://www.ubuntu.com/business/services/cloud

0 packages can be updated.
0 updates are security updates.


Last login: Sat Nov 25 16:03:58 2017 from 10.0.2.2
ubuntu@ubuntu-xenial:~$ ls /vagrant/
ubuntu-xenial-16.04-cloudimg-console.log  Vagrantfile
ubuntu@ubuntu-xenial:~$ exit
logout
Connection to 127.0.0.1 closed.
russ in ~/vagrant-test
⚡ vagrant destroy
    default: Are you sure you want to destroy the 'default' VM? [y/N] y

==> default: Forcing shutdown of VM...
==> default: Destroying VM and associated drives...
```

I would also recommend clearing your working folder by running:

```
$ cd ../
$ rm -rf vagrant-test
```

Now that we have Vagrant installed, and have quickly looked at how we can launch and interact with a virtual machine, we can now look at using it to launch our own local installation of Apache OpenWhisk.

Downloading and configuring Apache OpenWhisk

As we have already mentioned, Apache OpenWhisk ships with a Vagrantfile that contains all of the commands to deploy a local Apache OpenWhisk installation from scratch. To download the Apache OpenWhisk repository and deploy the virtual machine, run the following commands:

```
$ git clone --depth=1 https://github.com/apache/incubator-openwhisk.git
openwhisk
$ cd openwhisk/tools/vagrant
$ ./hello
```

This process will take anywhere up to 30 minutes depending on the speed of your internet connectivity; you can find a copy of the Vagrantfile at the following URL: `https://github.com/apache/incubator-openwhisk/blob/master/tools/vagrant/Vagrantfile`.

As you can see, it is just short of 200 lines long, which is a lot different from the three lines in our test Vagrantfile from the last section. The Vagrantfile uses a combination of bash scripts and Ansible to launch, install, and configure our Apache OpenWhisk virtual machine.

Ansible is is an orchestration/configuration tool from Red Hat. It allows you to easily define your deployments in human-readable code, be it interacting with APIs to launch your infrastructure or logging in to servers and executing tasks against them to install and configure your software stack.

At the end of the process, it will execute a basic hello world check as seen in the following console output:

```
1. vagrant (bash)
    default: ++ touch /home/vagrant/.wskprops
    default: ++ chown -R vagrant:vagrant /home/vagrant
    default: +++ cat /home/vagrant/openwhisk/ansible/files/auth.guest
    default: ++ wsk property set --apihost 192.168.33.13 --namespace guest --auth 23bc46b1-71f6-4ed5
-8c54-816aa4f8c502:123zO3xZCLrMN6v2BKK1dXYFpXlPkccOFqm12CdAsMgRU4VrNZ9lyGVCGuMDGIwP
    default: ok: whisk auth set. Run 'wsk property get --auth' to see the new value.
    default: ok: whisk API host set to 192.168.33.13
    default: ok: whisk namespace set to guest
    default: ++ wsk action invoke /whisk.system/utils/echo -p message hello --result
    default: {
    default:     "message": "hello"
    default: }
    default: +++ date
    default: ++ echo 'Sat Nov 25 16:58:19 UTC 2017: build-deploy-end'
```

Before we move on, make a note of the output, which starts with the `wsk property set` command. We will need this to configure the local client, which we are going to look at installing next.

Installing the Apache OpenWhisk client

Each Apache OpenWhisk comes with a download page for the macOS, Windows, and Linux versions of the Apache OpenWhisk client. You can access this from your local installation at the following URL: `https://192.168.33.13/cli/go/download/` or IBM at: `https://openwhisk.ng.bluemix.net/cli/go/download/`.

As your local installation is using a self-signed SSL certificate, you may receive warnings when opening it in your browser. You will need to accept these warnings to proceed to the site. This process varies depending on your browser so you will need to follow the on-screen prompts to progress.

To install the client on macOS 10.13 High Sierra we simply need to run the following commands:

```
$ curl -L --insecure https://192.168.33.13/cli/go/download/mac/amd64/wsk >
/usr/local/bin/wsk
$ chmod +x /usr/local/bin/wsk
$ wsk help
```

This will download the binary using `curl` and ignore the self-signed certificate.

To download on Windows 10 Professional, run the following. I would recommend downloading from IBM to avoid problems with the self-signed SSL certificate and PowerShell. To do this, first of all open a PowerShell window as an admin user. You can do this by selecting **Run as Administrator** from the PowerShell menu in the taskbar. Once open, you should see that you are in the `C:\WINDOWS\system32` folder; if you aren't then run the following:

```
$ cd C:\WINDOWS\system32
$ Invoke-WebRequest -Uri
https://openwhisk.ng.bluemix.net/cli/go/download/windows/amd64/wsk.exe -
UseBasicParsing -OutFile wsk.exe
```

Like the macOS version, you can check that the client is installed by running the following:

```
$ wsk help
```

Finally, on Ubuntu 17.04 you need to run the following commands:

```
$ sudo sh -c "curl -L --insecure
https://192.168.33.13/cli/go/download/linux/amd64/wsk > /usr/local/bin/wsk"
$ sudo chmod +x /usr/local/bin/wsk
```

Once downloaded and made executable you should be able to run:

```
$ wsk help
```

Now that we have the client installed we need to authenticate against our installation. To do this, run the command you made a note of at the end of the last section, minus the `--namespace guest` part. For me, this command was as follows:

```
$ wsk property set --apihost 192.168.33.13 --auth
23bc46b1-71f6-4ed5-8c54-816aa4f8c502:123zO3xZCLrMN6v2BKK1dXYFpXlPkccOFqm12C
dAsMgRU4VrNZ9lyGVCGuMDGIwP
```

If you didn't make a note, then you can dynamically pass the authorization token by running the following command from the folder you launch the Vagrant virtual machine from, as follows:

```
$ wsk property set --apihost 192.168.33.13 --auth `vagrant ssh -- cat
openwhisk/ansible/files/auth.guest`
```

If you don't run it from the folder you launched the machine from, the `vagrant ssh` command will fail, as it will not be able to find your machine configuration. Now that your local client is authenticated against your local installation of Apache OpenWhisk, we can execute the same hello world command that was run by the automation installation by running the following:

```
$ wsk -i action invoke /whisk.system/utils/echo -p message hello --result
```

This should return the message `hello` as per the following Terminal output:

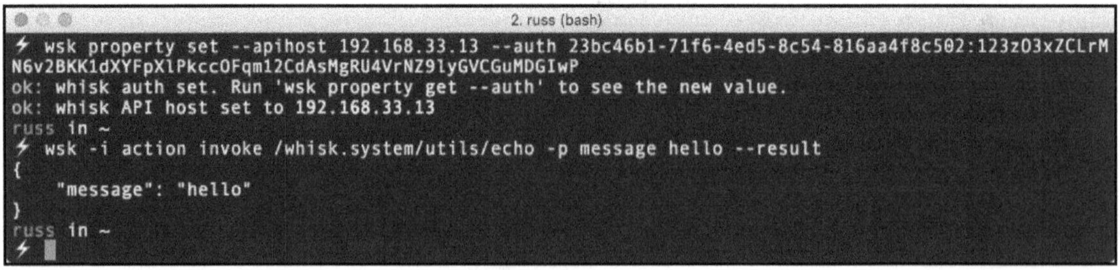

```
2. russ (bash)
⚡ wsk property set --apihost 192.168.33.13 --auth 23bc46b1-71f6-4ed5-8c54-816aa4f8c502:123zO3xZCLrM
N6v2BKK1dXYFpXlPkccOFqm12CdAsMgRU4VrNZ9lyGVCGuMDGIwP
ok: whisk auth set. Run 'wsk property get --auth' to see the new value.
ok: whisk API host set to 192.168.33.13
russ in ~
⚡ wsk -i action invoke /whisk.system/utils/echo -p message hello --result
{
    "message": "hello"
}
russ in ~
⚡
```

Now that we have our local client, we can look at downloading and executing another example.

Hello world

We can now deploy a more complex solution rather than just using the inbuilt `echo` utility to return a message. In a similar way to the previous hello world scripts we used, we are going to deploy a function, written in Node.js, that takes an input and displays it back to us.

First of all, let's create a working directory:

```
$ mkdir openwhisk-http
$ cd openwhisk-http
```

Now we have a working directory, create a file that contains the following code and call it `hello.js`:

```
function main(args) {
    var msg = "you didn't tell me who you are."
    if (args.name) {
        msg = `hello ${args.name}!`
    }
    return {body:
       `<html><body><h3><center>${msg}</center></h3></body></html>`}
}
```

Now that we have the function that we are going to deploy, we first of all need to create a package, and then create the action that is exposed to the web:

```
$ wsk -i package create /guest/demo
$ wsk -i action create /guest/demo/hello hello.js --web true
```

Now that we have created the package and action, your Terminal should look something like the following:

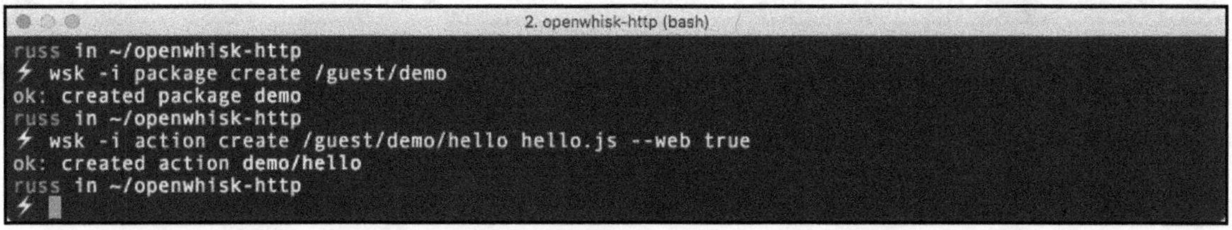

```
2. openwhisk-http (bash)
russ in ~/openwhisk-http
⚡ wsk -i package create /guest/demo
ok: created package demo
russ in ~/openwhisk-http
⚡ wsk -i action create /guest/demo/hello hello.js --web true
ok: created action demo/hello
russ in ~/openwhisk-http
⚡
```

This means that your function can be called using your browser at the following URL:

```
https://192.168.33.13/api/v1/web/guest/demo/hello.http?name=
Kubernetes%20for%20Serverless%20Applications
```

You should see the following page:

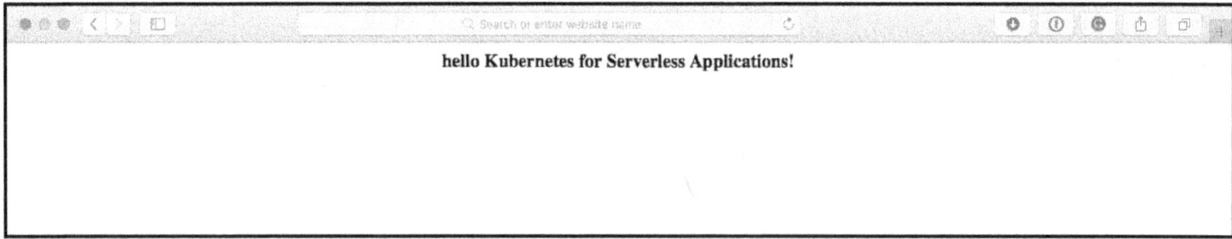

You can see more information using HTTPie on macOS or Ubuntu by running the following:

```
$ http --verify=no
https://192.168.33.13/api/v1/web/guest/demo/hello.http?name=Kubernetes%20fo
r%20Serverless%20Applications
```

This will return the headers and also the output:

```
2. openwhisk-http (bash)
russ in ~/openwhisk-http
⚡ http --verify=no https://192.168.33.13/api/v1/web/guest/demo/hello.http?name=Kubernetes%20for%20S
erverless%20Applications
HTTP/1.1 200 OK
Access-Control-Allow-Headers: Authorization, Content-Type
Access-Control-Allow-Methods: OPTIONS, GET, DELETE, POST, PUT, HEAD, PATCH
Access-Control-Allow-Origin: *
Connection: keep-alive
Content-Length: 97
Content-Type: text/html; charset=UTF-8
Date: Sun, 26 Nov 2017 12:36:41 GMT
Server: nginx/1.11.13

<html><body><h3><center>hello Kubernetes for Serverless Applications!</center></h3></body></html>

russ in ~/openwhisk-http
⚡
```

You can list packages and actions, and remove them by running the following:

```
$ wsk -i list
$ wsk -i action delete /guest/demo/hello
$ wsk -i package delete /guest/demo
```

```
2. openwhisk-http (bash)
russ in ~/openwhisk-http
⚡ wsk -i list
Entities in namespace: default
packages
/guest/demo                                                  private
actions
/guest/demo/hello                                            private nodejs:6
triggers
rules
russ in ~/openwhisk-http
⚡ wsk -i action delete /guest/demo/hello
ok: deleted action demo/hello
russ in ~/openwhisk-http
⚡ wsk -i package delete /guest/demo
ok: deleted package demo
russ in ~/openwhisk-http
⚡
```

Feel free to have a play with your local installation of Apache OpenWhisk; there are more examples at the Awesome OpenWhisk page, which you can find at: `https://github.com/apache/incubator-openwhisk-external-resources/`.

Once you have finished with your local installation, you can run the following command to stop and destroy the virtual machine:

```
$ vagrant destroy
```

Remember, you must be in the `openwhisk/tools/vagrant/` folder to run this command otherwise Vagrant will not be able to find your virtual machine configuration.

Now that we have installed and interacted with Apache OpenWhisk locally, let's look at deploying it on Kubernetes in a public cloud.

Running Apache OpenWhisk on Kubernetes

Now that we have an idea of how to interact with Apache OpenWhisk and the basic concepts behind it, we can look at deploying a copy on top of a Kubernetes cluster. To do this, I am going to launch a three-node cluster in Google Cloud by running the following:

```
$ gcloud container clusters create kube-cluster
```

Once the cluster is up-and-running, you can check that you can see three nodes by running the following:

```
$ kubectl get nodes
```

```
2. russ (bash)
⚡ kubectl get nodes
NAME                                          STATUS    ROLES     AGE       VERSION
gke-kube-cluster-default-pool-e96fe452-8gsg   Ready     <none>    2m        v1.7.8-gke.0
gke-kube-cluster-default-pool-e96fe452-9q7j   Ready     <none>    1m        v1.7.8-gke.0
gke-kube-cluster-default-pool-e96fe452-pzm6   Ready     <none>    2m        v1.7.8-gke.0
russ in ~
⚡
```

Now we have our Kubernetes, we can progress with the Apache OpenWhisk deployment.

Deploying OpenWhisk

All of the configuration needed to deploy Apache OpenWhisk on Kubernetes is available on GitHub, so before we start our deployment we should clone the repository by running the following:

```
$ git clone --depth=1
https://github.com/apache/incubator-openwhisk-deploy-kube.git openwhisk-
kube
$ cd openwhisk-kube
```

Now that we have a copy of the repository, we can make a start on deploying the individual components needed to run Apache OpenWhisk. To start with, we need to create a namespace called `openwhisk`. To do this, run the following:

```
$ kubectl create namespace openwhisk
```

Now we can start our deployment by launching CouchDB.

CouchDB

To deploy CouchDB, run the following command from within the `openwhisk-kube` folder:

```
$ kubectl apply -f kubernetes/couchdb/couchdb.yml
```

This will launch a pod running CouchDB using the parameters defined in the `couchdb.yml` file. You can check that everything is OK with the deployment by getting the name of the pod. You can do this by running the following:

```
$ kubectl -n openwhisk get pods
```

Once you have the name, which for me was `couchdb-1146267775-v0sdm`, you can then run the following, making sure to update the name of the pod with your own:

```
$ kubectl -n openwhisk logs couchdb-1146267775-v0sdm
```

Towards the end of the log output you should see the following message:

```
2. openwhisk-kube (bash)
check for _design/snapshotFilters document in test_whisks database ------ 0.22s
check for _design/whisks-filters.v2 document in test_activations database --- 0.22s
check for _design/whisks.v2 document in test_activations database ------- 0.22s
check for _design/activations document in test_activations database ----- 0.21s
include ------------------------------------------------------------------ 0.19s
/openwhisk /opt/couchdb
+ popd
+ popd
+ echo 'successfully setup and configured CouchDB v2.0'
+ sleep inf
/opt/couchdb
successfully setup and configured CouchDB v2.0
[notice] 2017-11-26T13:20:09.766078Z couchdb@couchdb0 <0.1908.0> 8bacee041a 10.0.2.3:5984 10.0.2.1 u
ndefined GET /test_activations 200 ok 4
[notice] 2017-11-26T13:20:19.763565Z couchdb@couchdb0 <0.2065.0> e2a57c7cac 10.0.2.3:5984 10.0.2.1 u
ndefined GET /test_activations 200 ok 1
[notice] 2017-11-26T13:20:29.763534Z couchdb@couchdb0 <0.2247.0> f0f01fe709 10.0.2.3:5984 10.0.2.1 u
```

Now that our CouchDB pod is running we can move on to the next one, which is Redis.

Redis

To launch the Redis pod, we just need to run the following command:

```
$ kubectl apply -f kubernetes/redis/redis.yml
```

API Gateway

Next up we have the API Gateway; this is launched by running the following:

```
$ kubectl apply -f kubernetes/apigateway/apigateway.yml
```

ZooKeeper

Now we can launch Apache ZooKeeper using the following:

```
$ kubectl apply -f kubernetes/zookeeper/zookeeper.yml
```

Kafka

Now it is time to launch another Apache project, Kafka:

```
$ kubectl apply -f kubernetes/kafka/kafka.yml
```

At this point we should double-check that all of the pods we have launched are running. To do this, run the following:

```
$ kubectl -n openwhisk get pods
```

You should see pods for `couchdb`, `redis`, `apigateway`, `zookeeper`, and `kafka`, all running with no restarts logged and `1/1` in the `READY` column:

```
2. openwhisk-kube (bash)
russ in ~/openwhisk-kube on master*
⚡ kubectl -n openwhisk get pods
NAME                            READY     STATUS    RESTARTS   AGE
apigateway-2549363043-k8fz8     1/1       Running   0          8m
couchdb-1146267775-v0sdm        1/1       Running   0          17m
kafka-3354284012-kqh8b          1/1       Running   0          1m
redis-3845877026-wp9v7          1/1       Running   0          9m
zookeeper-2112860104-krffz      1/1       Running   0          7m
russ in ~/openwhisk-kube on master*
⚡
```

Controller

Next, we have the controller. This is slightly different from the other pods we have deployed, in that it is being deployed in a stateful state:

```
$ kubectl apply -f kubernetes/controller/controller.yml
```

You should see that a StatefulSet has been created rather than a deployment.

Invoker

Again, the next pod we are deploying is going to be a StatefulSet rather than a deployment. Before we deploy the pod we need to make a slight change to the `kubernetes/invoker/invoker.yml` file. This is because, by default, OpenWhisk assumes you are running Ubuntu as your base operating system, which Google Cloud isn't.

To do this, open `kubernetes/invoker/invoker.yml` in your text editor of choice and remove the following block of code:

```
- name: apparmor
  hostPath:
    path: "/usr/lib/x86_64-linux-gnu/libapparmor.so.1"
```

There is also another reference to `apparmor` we need to remove. This time it is towards the bottom of the file:

```
- name: apparmor
  mountPath: "/usr/lib/x86_64-linux-gnu/libapparmor.so.1"
```

Once the two code blocks that reference `apparmor` have been removed, you can deploy the `invoker` by running the following:

```
$ kubectl apply -f kubernetes/invoker/invoker.yml
```

It may take a few minutes to deploy.

NGINX

The final part of the deployment is the NGINX container. We need to do a little more work on this one as we need to generate certificates for our cluster. To generate the certificates, we will need to use OpenSSL. This is not installed by default on Windows machines so you can use the following command to install OpenSSL using Chocolatey:

```
$ choco install openssl.light
```

Once you have OpenSSL installed, you can generate the certificates by running:

```
$ mkdir -p certs
$ openssl req -x509 -newkey rsa:2048 -keyout certs/key.pem -out
certs/cert.pem -nodes -subj "/CN=localhost" -days 365
```

Once we have the certificates, we need to create a `configmap` using the `nginx.conf` file in `kubernetes/nginx`. To do this, run the following command:

```
$ kubectl -n openwhisk create configmap nginx --from-
file=kubernetes/nginx/nginx.conf
```

Now we need to upload the certificate and key we generated as a `secret`:

```
$ kubectl -n openwhisk create secret tls nginx --cert=certs/cert.pem --
key=certs/key.pem
```

Once they have been uploaded, we can launch the NGINX pod by running the following:

```
$ kubectl apply -f kubernetes/nginx/nginx.yml
```

```
russ in ~/openwhisk-kube on master*
⚡ kubectl -n openwhisk create configmap nginx --from-file=kubernetes/nginx/nginx.conf
configmap "nginx" created
russ in ~/openwhisk-kube on master*
⚡ kubectl -n openwhisk create secret tls nginx --cert=certs/cert.pem --key=certs/key.pem
secret "nginx" created
russ in ~/openwhisk-kube on master*
⚡ kubectl apply -f kubernetes/nginx/nginx.yml
service "nginx" created
deployment "nginx" created
russ in ~/openwhisk-kube on master*
⚡
```

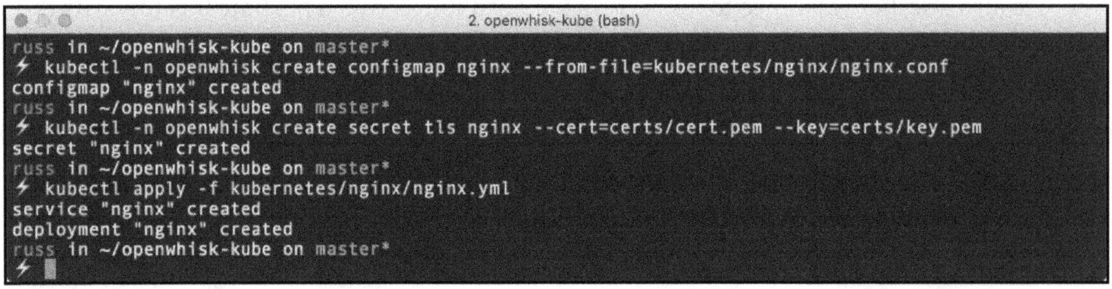

Now that we have all of the pods deployed, you should double-check that they are all running using the following command:

```
$ kubectl -n openwhisk get pods
```

```
⚡ kubectl -n openwhisk get pods
NAME                           READY     STATUS    RESTARTS   AGE
apigateway-2549363043-rc49d    1/1       Running   0          12m
controller-0                   1/1       Running   0          12m
controller-1                   1/1       Running   0          11m
couchdb-1146267775-hwlzs       1/1       Running   0          12m
invoker-0                      1/1       Running   0          12m
kafka-3354284012-26sx2         1/1       Running   1          12m
nginx-2163442153-bnnx1         1/1       Running   0          12m
redis-3845877026-b0mdh         1/1       Running   0          12m
zookeeper-2112860104-9p18b     1/1       Running   0          12m
russ in ~/openwhisk-kube on master*
⚡
```

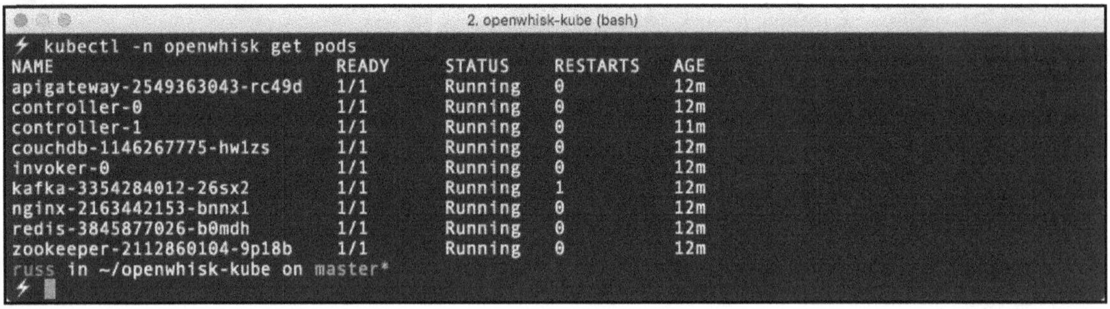

As you can see, everything is running. You can ignore any restarts just so long as the number is not increasing.

Configuring OpenWhisk

Now we have all of the pods deployed, we can start interacting with our deployment. To start with, we need to find out the external IP address of the NGINX pod. You can find information about the pod by running the following:

```
$ kubectl -n openwhisk describe service nginx
```

This is the output:

```
2. openwhisk-kube (bash)
russ in ~/openwhisk-kube on master*
⚡ kubectl -n openwhisk describe service nginx
Name:                     nginx
Namespace:                openwhisk
Labels:                   name=nginx
Annotations:              kubectl.kubernetes.io/last-applied-configuration={"apiVersion":"v1","kind"
:"Service","metadata":{"annotations":{},"labels":{"name":"nginx"},"name":"nginx","namespace":"openwh
isk"},"spec":{"ports":[{"n...
Selector:                 name=nginx
Type:                     NodePort
IP:                       10.3.246.99
Port:                     http  80/TCP
TargetPort:               80/TCP
NodePort:                 http  32643/TCP
Endpoints:                10.0.0.11:80
Port:                     https-api  443/TCP
TargetPort:               443/TCP
NodePort:                 https-api  32427/TCP
Endpoints:                10.0.0.11:443
Port:                     https-admin  8443/TCP
TargetPort:               8443/TCP
NodePort:                 https-admin  30365/TCP
Endpoints:                10.0.0.11:8443
Session Affinity:         None
External Traffic Policy:  Cluster
Events:                   <none>
russ in ~/openwhisk-kube on master*
⚡
```

As you can see, while the ports are exposed they are only exposed on the nodes themselves. As the nodes are on private addresses, we will not be able to access them from our local client. To expose the ports externally we need to create a load-balanced service, to do this run the following command:

```
$ kubectl -n openwhisk expose service nginx --type=LoadBalancer --
name=front-end
```

This will launch a Load Balancer and expose the three ports: `80`, `443`, and `8443`. You can find out the details on the external IP address by running the following:

```
$ kubectl -n openwhisk describe service front-end
```

In the output, you will find a line that says Load Balancer Ingress followed by an IP address:

```
2. openwhisk-kube (bash)
russ in ~/openwhisk-kube on master*
⚡ kubectl -n openwhisk describe service front-end
Name:                     front-end
Namespace:                openwhisk
Labels:                   name=nginx
Annotations:              <none>
Selector:                 name=nginx
Type:                     LoadBalancer
IP:                       10.3.248.65
LoadBalancer Ingress:     35.188.204.73
Port:                     port-1  80/TCP
TargetPort:               80/TCP
NodePort:                 port-1  32767/TCP
Endpoints:                10.0.0.11:80
Port:                     port-2  443/TCP
TargetPort:               443/TCP
NodePort:                 port-2  32169/TCP
Endpoints:                10.0.0.11:443
Port:                     port-3  8443/TCP
TargetPort:               8443/TCP
NodePort:                 port-3  30579/TCP
Endpoints:                10.0.0.11:8443
Session Affinity:         None
External Traffic Policy:  Cluster
Events:
  Type    Reason                Age   From                Message
  ----    ------                ----  ----                -------
  Normal  CreatingLoadBalancer  14m   service-controller  Creating load balancer
  Normal  CreatedLoadBalancer   13m   service-controller  Created load balancer
russ in ~/openwhisk-kube on master*
⚡
```

As you can see from the example output shown previously, I have an IP address of `35.188.204.73`. This will be used as the API endpoint I interact with.

Now that we have the IP address of our installation, we can go ahead and configure the authentication token by running the following command, making sure you update the IP address with that of your own installation:

```
$ wsk -i property set --auth
23bc46b1-71f6-4ed5-8c54-816aa4f8c502:123zO3xZCLrMN6v2BKK1dXYFpXlPkccOFqm12C
dAsMgRU4VrNZ9lyGVCGuMDGIwP --apihost https://35.188.204.73:443
```

Once configured we can then run our hello-world test.

Hello world

This is exactly the same as the hello world in the previous section, so I won't go into too much detail. Simply change to the folder where you have the `hello.js` file and run the following commands:

```
$ wsk -i package create /guest/demo
$ wsk -i action create /guest/demo/hello hello.js --web true
```

Once you have run the commands creating the package and action, you will be able to access the URL. For me, it was the following:

```
https://35.188.204.73/api/v1/web/guest/demo/hello.http?name=Kubernetes%
20for%20Serverless%20Applications
```

This showed the page we expected to see:

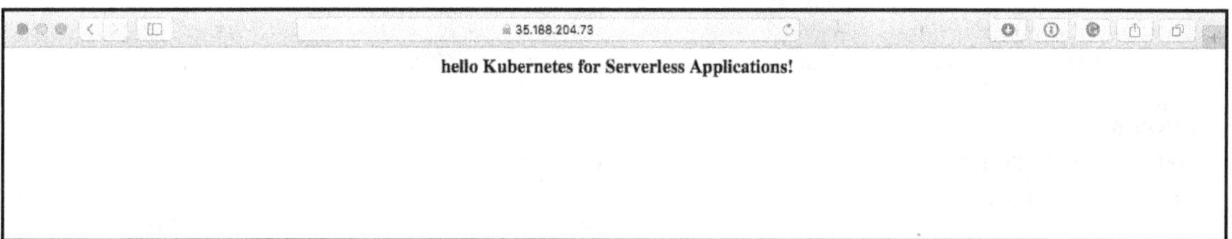

Again, we can see a little more by running HTTPie:

```
$ http --verify=no
https://35.188.204.73/api/v1/web/guest/demo/hello.http?name=Kubernetes%20fo
r%20Serverless%20Applications
```

This shows the following information:

```
2. openwhisk-http (bash)
⚡ http --verify=no https://35.188.204.73/api/v1/web/guest/demo/hello.http?name=Kubernetes%20for%20S
erverless%20Applications
HTTP/1.1 200 OK
Access-Control-Allow-Headers: Authorization, Content-Type
Access-Control-Allow-Methods: OPTIONS, GET, DELETE, POST, PUT, HEAD, PATCH
Access-Control-Allow-Origin: *
Connection: keep-alive
Content-Length: 97
Content-Type: text/html; charset=UTF-8
Date: Sun, 26 Nov 2017 16:07:12 GMT
Server: nginx/1.11.13

<html><body><h3><center>hello Kubernetes for Serverless Applications!</center></h3></body></html>

russ in ~/openwhisk-http
⚡
```

As you can see, once you have deployed Apache OpenWhisk using the provided files, using it is a pretty consistent experience.

Before we finish this chapter we should remove our Kubernetes cluster. To do this run the following command:

```
$ gcloud container clusters delete kube-cluster
```

Once deleted, be sure to check your Google Cloud control panel at `https://console.cloud.google.com/` to make sure there are no leftover resources, which could be incurring unexpected costs.

Summary

In this chapter, we have taken a slight diversion to look at Apache OpenWhisk. We have deployed a copy locally using a standard virtual machine and then we moved onto deploying it to a Kubernetes cluster running on Google Cloud.

As you saw, once the deployment was complete, interacting with Apache OpenWhisk was a consistent experience and we were able to deploy our simple hello-world application with no modifications to both of our installations.

While Kubernetes support for Apache OpenWhisk is still in its infancy, our diversion has shown that it isn't just frameworks that have been designed with Kubernetes in mind, like the tools we have looked at in the previous chapters, which will run on top of a Kubernetes and provide a consistent experience without having to lock you into a single vendor or technology.

In the next chapter, we are going to be looking at probably the most mature Kubernetes Function as a Service offering: Fission.

8
Launching Applications Using Fission

Next up we are going to look at Fission. Fission is a fast-growing, serverless framework for Kubernetes and, of the technologies that we have seen in previous chapters, is probably the most versatile. In this chapter we will cover:

- Who built Fission?
- Installing the prerequisites
- Installing, configuring, and running Fission locally
- Command overview
- Installing, configuring, and running Fission in the cloud
- Deploying a few example Fission applications

By the end of this chapter, we will have worked on installing Fission in two different target environments, and also worked through launching several applications.

Fission overview

Fission is an open source serverless application developed by Platform9. It was designed to run on top of Kubernetes as well as take advantage of some core Kubernetes functionality. Platform9 are a managed service provider whose core business is the deployment, management, and support of open source clouds specializing in OpenStack and Kubernetes.

OpenStack is a collection of open source components that make up a fully functional Infrastructure as a Service offering. It provides compute, networking, block storage, object storage, orchestration, and even container service, to name but a few.

The project's goal is to provide support for a number of different hardware vendors, from vanilla x86 hardware to specialized storage solutions, allowing end users to build out their own AWS and Microsoft Azure style offering.

With services such as AWS Lambda and Azure Functions maturing to the point where they are now commonplace in most enterprises, Platform9 saw an opportunity to provide their own Functions as a Service offering.

Being a company who specialize in complex open source solutions, it made sense for them to contribute their work back to the community, and so they released Fission under the Apache License.

The Apache 2.0 License by The Apache Software Foundation allows developers to release their software for free, giving the end user permission to use that software for any purpose, and modify/redistribute it without the end user having to worry about royalties. To ensure that the License is not breached, the end user must preserve the original copyright notice and disclaimer.

This may seem like a strange decision. However, like OpenWhisk, which we covered in the previous chapter, Platform9 have given their customers, and anyone else who wants to start deploying **Function as a Service** (**FaaS**), a solid foundation to build their applications on top of. Not only are they giving people the freedom to deploy their workloads wherever they want, they are also able to offer support services for installation and the Fission platform.

Installing the prerequisites

Before we install Fission either locally or in a public cloud we need a few supporting tools. The first tool we have already installed and that is the Kubernetes command-line interface, `kubectl`. The second tool needed to run Fission, we have not installed yet: Helm (`http://helm.sh/`).

Installing Helm

Helm is a package manager for Kubernetes and is part of the Cloud Native Computing Foundation, where Bitnami, Google, Microsoft, and the Helm community all contribute to its development.

To install Helm on macOS High Sierra we can use Homebrew; simply run:

```
$ brew install kubernetes-helm
```

If you are running Ubuntu Linux then you can download and install Helm using the installation script:

```
$ curl https://raw.githubusercontent.com/kubernetes/helm/master/scripts/get
| bash
```

Finally, Windows 10 Professional users can download an experimental build of Helm from the canary repository. The direct download link for this build is `https://kubernetes-helm.storage.googleapis.com/helm-canary-windows-amd64.zip`. As this is an experimental build, I recommend running it directly and not putting it in the system folder.

The next step in installing Helm requires you to have a running Kubernetes cluster, as that is where it is launched. I will include the instructions for installing Tiller, the server component of Helm, later in the chapter.

Installing the Fission CLI

The final command-line tool we need to install is the one for Fission itself. You can install this by running the following on macOS High Sierra:

```
$ curl -Lo fission
https://github.com/fission/fission/releases/download/0.3.0/fission-cli-osx
&& chmod +x fission && sudo mv fission /usr/local/bin/
```

For Ubuntu 17.04 you can run:

```
$ curl -Lo fission
https://github.com/fission/fission/releases/download/0.3.0/fission-cli-linu
x && chmod +x fission && sudo mv fission /usr/local/bin/
```

Finally, the Windows executable can be downloaded from `https://github.com/fission/fission/releases/download/0.3.0/fission-cli-windows.exe`. I would recommend using it alongside the executable for Helm rather than installing it in your `System32` folder.

Running the following commands should show you the currently installed versions:

```
$ helm version
$ fission --version
```

```
1. russ (bash)
⚡ helm version
Client: &version.Version{SemVer:"v2.7.2", GitCommit:"8478fb4fc723885b155c924d1c8c410b7a9444e6", GitTreeState:"clean"}
Error: cannot connect to Tiller
russ in ~
⚡ fission --version
fission version 0.3.0
russ in ~
⚡
```

As already mentioned, we have not installed Tiller yet so we can safely ignore the error about not being able to connect to it.

Running Fission locally

Now that we have the prerequisites installed we can look at creating our first function. To do this we are going to use Minikube. To launch the single node cluster we simply need to run the following:

```
$ minikube start
$ kubectl get nodes
```

This should launch your Minikube cluster and also confirm that your local version has been reconfigured to communicate with it:

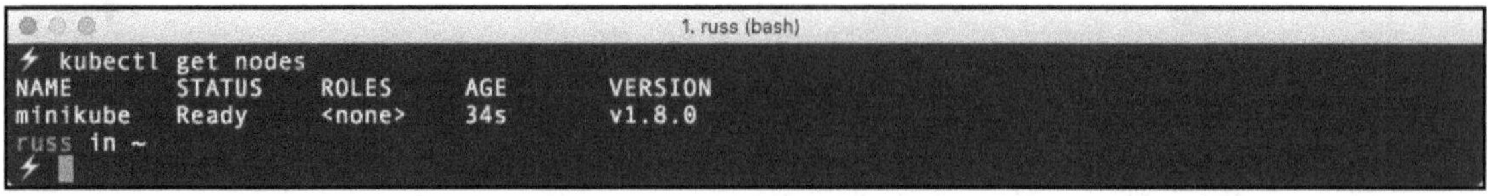

```
1. russ (bash)
⚡ kubectl get nodes
NAME       STATUS    ROLES     AGE       VERSION
minikube   Ready     <none>    34s       v1.8.0
russ in ~
⚡
```

Once we have our cluster running and accessible we need to complete the Helm installation by installing Tiller. To do this we need to run the following:

```
$ helm init
```

You should see something like the following message:

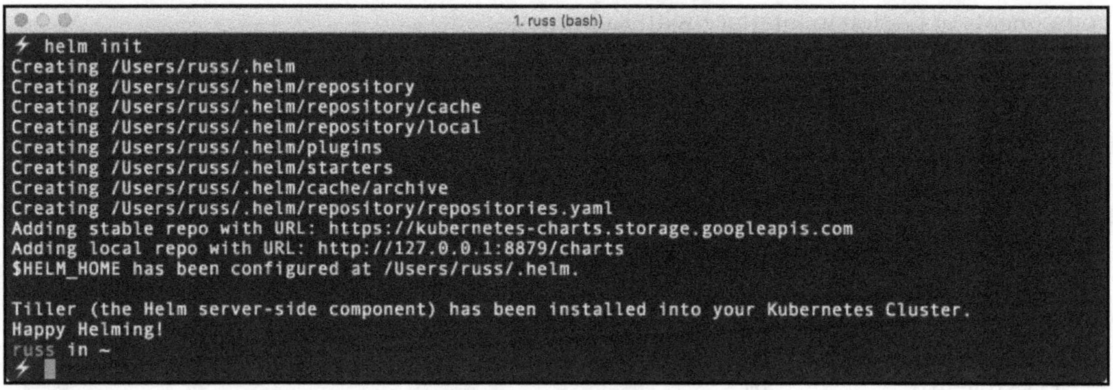

```
1. russ (bash)
⚡ helm init
Creating /Users/russ/.helm
Creating /Users/russ/.helm/repository
Creating /Users/russ/.helm/repository/cache
Creating /Users/russ/.helm/repository/local
Creating /Users/russ/.helm/plugins
Creating /Users/russ/.helm/starters
Creating /Users/russ/.helm/cache/archive
Creating /Users/russ/.helm/repository/repositories.yaml
Adding stable repo with URL: https://kubernetes-charts.storage.googleapis.com
Adding local repo with URL: http://127.0.0.1:8879/charts
$HELM_HOME has been configured at /Users/russ/.helm.

Tiller (the Helm server-side component) has been installed into your Kubernetes Cluster.
Happy Helming!
russ in ~
⚡
```

Launching Fission using Helm

Helm is now configured and we can use it to deploy the remote components of Fission. This can be done by running the following:

```
$ helm install --namespace fission --set serviceType=NodePort
https://github.com/fission/fission/releases/download/0.4.0/fission-all-0.4.
0.tgz
```

After a minute or two, you should receive confirmation that Fission has launched.

Working through the output

Helm is quite verbose with its output. It will give you an overview of everything it has created along with any additional notes the developers have included.

This part of the output contains the basic details of the deployment:

```
NAME: lopsided-fox
LAST DEPLOYED: Sat Dec 9 10:52:19 2017
NAMESPACE: fission
STATUS: DEPLOYED
```

Next up, we get information on what has been deployed within Kubernetes, starting with the service accounts. These provide identity services that run a pod. These allow the various components of Fission to interface with Kubernetes:

```
==> v1/ServiceAccount
NAME            SECRETS AGE
fission-builder 1       1m
fission-fetcher 1       1m
fission-svc     1       1m
```

Then come the bindings. These provide role-based authentication (RBAC) for the cluster:

```
==> v1beta1/ClusterRoleBinding
NAME                 AGE
fission-builder-crd  1m
fission-crd          1m
fission-fetcher-crd  1m
```

Next up are the services themselves:

```
==> v1/Service
NAME           TYPE        CLUSTER-IP   EXTERNAL-IP PORT(S)        AGE
poolmgr        ClusterIP   10.0.0.134   <none>      80/TCP         1m
buildermgr     ClusterIP   10.0.0.212   <none>      80/TCP         1m
influxdb       ClusterIP   10.0.0.24    <none>      8086/TCP       1m
nats-streaming NodePort    10.0.0.161   <none>      4222:31316/TCP 1m
storagesvc     ClusterIP   10.0.0.157   <none>      80/TCP         1m
controller     NodePort    10.0.0.55    <none>      80:31313/TCP   1m
router         NodePort    10.0.0.106   <none>      80:31314/TCP   1m
```

Now we have the deployment details. You will probably notice that, as in the following, some of the pods are still launching, which is why they are showing zero available:

```
==> v1beta1/Deployment
NAME.           DESIRED CURRENT UP-TO-DATE AVAILABLE AGE
timer           1       1       1          1         1m
poolmgr         1       1       1          1         1m
influxdb        1       1       1          1         1m
nats-streaming  1       1       1          1         1m
controller      1       1       1          1         1m
mqtrigger       1       1       1          1         1m
router          1       1       1          0         1m
storagesvc      1       1       1          0         1m
kubewatcher     1       1       1          1         1m
buildermgr      1       1       1          0         1m
```

Next up, we have the pods for the deployments and services:

```
==> v1/Pod(related)
NAME                               READY STATUS            RESTARTS AGE
logger-zp65r                       1/1   Running           0        1m
timer-57f75c486f-9ktbk             1/1   Running           2        1m
poolmgr-69fcff7d7-hbq46            1/1   Running           1        1m
influxdb-c5c6cfd86-wkwrs           1/1   Running           0        1m
nats-streaming-85b9898784-h6j2v    1/1   Running           0        1m
controller-5f964bc987-mmfrx        1/1   Running           0        1m
mqtrigger-c85dd79f7-vj5p7          1/1   Running           0        1m
router-7cfff6794b-gn5pw            0/1   ContainerCreating 0        1m
storagesvc-58d5c8f6-bnqc7          0/1   ContainerCreating 0        1m
kubewatcher-6d784b9987-5wwhv       1/1   Running           0        1m
buildermgr-7ff69c8bb-pvtbx         0/1   ContainerCreating 0        1m
```

Then we have the namespaces:

```
==> v1/Namespace
NAME.            STATUS AGE
fission-builder  Active 1m
fission-function Active 1m
```

Now we have the secrets. These are just for the database being used:

```
==> v1/Secret
NAME     TYPE   DATA AGE
influxdb Opaque 2    1m
```

We are nearing the end: the persistent storage claims. You can see, as we have launched locally, it is just using a folder on the VM rather than creating external storage:

```
==> v1/PersistentVolumeClaim
NAME.                STATUS VOLUME
CAPACITY ACCESS MODES STORAGECLASS AGE
fission-storage-pvc Bound  pvc-082cf8d5-dccf-11e7-bfe6-080027e101f5 8Gi
RWO            standard     1m
```

Now we have the role bindings:

```
==> v1beta1/RoleBinding
NAME                   AGE
fission-function-admin 1m
fission-admin          1m
```

Finally, we have the daemon sets:

```
==> v1beta1/DaemonSet
NAME    DESIRED CURRENT READY UP-TO-DATE AVAILABLE NODE SELECTOR AGE
logger 1        1       1     1          1         <none>        1m
```

Now that we have seen an overview of all the Kubernetes elements of our Fission installation, we get notes on how to interact with the installation.

Launching our first function

The notes are split into three sections; the first section gives instructions on how to install the Fission command-line client. As we have already covered this in the previous section of the chapter we can ignore this step.

Next up, in the second section we are given instructions on environment variables we need to set so that our local Fission client can interact with our Fission installation. To set these variables run the following commands:

```
$ export FISSION_URL=http://$(minikube ip):31313
$ export FISSION_ROUTER=$(minikube ip):31314
```

The `export` command only works with macOS High Sierra and Ubuntu 17.04. Windows 10 Professional users will have to run the following commands:

```
$ for /f "delims=" %%a in ('minikube ip') do @set minikube_ip=%%a
$ set FISSION_URL=http://%minikube_ip%:31313
$ set FISSION_ROUTER=%minikube_ip%:31314
```

As you can see from the commands, our Fission installation is aware that it is running on a Minikube installation and has provided us with commands to dynamically generate the IP address of our Minikube installation.

The third section contains step by step instructions on how to run a hello world function; let's look at running these steps now.

First of all, we need to create an environment. To do this we use the following command:

```
$ fission env create --name nodejs --image fission/node-env
```

This command creates an environment called `nodejs` and then instructs Fission to use the Docker image `fission/node-env` from the Docker Hub—you can find this image at: `https://hub.docker.com/r/fission/node-env/`.

Now that we have the environment created, we need a function to deploy. Run the following command (macOS and Linux only) to download the hello world example:

```
$ curl
https://raw.githubusercontent.com/fission/fission/master/examples/nodejs/he
llo.js > /tmp/hello.js
```

This will download the following code:

```
module.exports = async function(context) {
    return {
        status: 200,
        body: "Hello, world!\n"
    };
}
```

As you can see, it is not dissimilar to the previous examples we have been running in earlier chapters. Now that we have a function downloaded, we can deploy it using the following command:

```
$ fission function create --name hello --env nodejs --code /tmp/hello.js
```

We are almost there; the final step is to create a route to our function. To do this, use the following:

```
$ fission route create --method GET --url /hello --function hello
```

We should now be able to call our function by making an HTTP request. You can use either of the following commands to trigger our function:

```
$ curl http://$FISSION_ROUTER/hello
$ http http://$FISSION_ROUTER/hello
```

For Windows 10 Professional, use the following command to open the example in IE:

```
$ explorer http://%FISSION_ROUTER%/hello
```

HTTPie will give you the headers, as well as the following output:

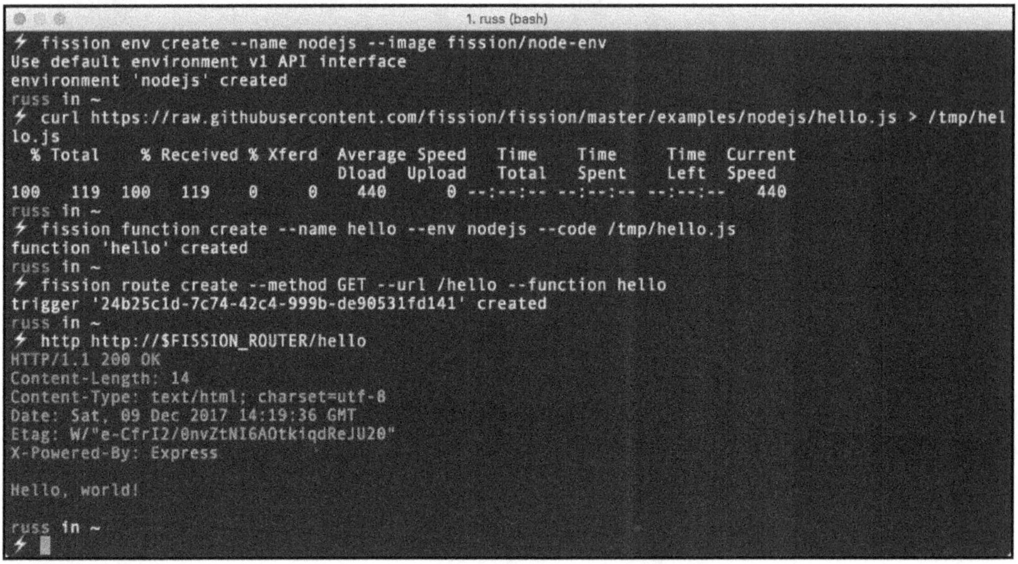

```
1. russ (bash)
⚡ fission env create --name nodejs --image fission/node-env
Use default environment v1 API interface
environment 'nodejs' created
russ in ~
⚡ curl https://raw.githubusercontent.com/fission/fission/master/examples/nodejs/hello.js > /tmp/hel
lo.js
  % Total    % Received % Xferd  Average Speed   Time    Time     Time  Current
                                 Dload  Upload   Total   Spent    Left  Speed
100   119  100   119    0     0    440      0 --:--:-- --:--:-- --:--:--   440
russ in ~
⚡ fission function create --name hello --env nodejs --code /tmp/hello.js
function 'hello' created
russ in ~
⚡ fission route create --method GET --url /hello --function hello
trigger '24b25c1d-7c74-42c4-999b-de90531fd141' created
russ in ~
⚡ http http://$FISSION_ROUTER/hello
HTTP/1.1 200 OK
Content-Length: 14
Content-Type: text/html; charset=utf-8
Date: Sat, 09 Dec 2017 14:19:36 GMT
Etag: W/"e-CfrI2/0nvZtNI6AOtkiqdReJU20"
X-Powered-By: Express

Hello, world!

russ in ~
⚡
```

A guestbook

Now that we have a basic application up and running, let's look at creating something more complex. Fission ships with a demo application that acts as a guestbook. You can find the files we are going to be deploying in the `/Chapter08/guestbook/` folder in the GitHub repository that accompanies this book.

The first step in launching the application is to launch a Redis deployment; this will be used to store the comments being written to the guestbook. To create the deployment, run the following command from within the `/Chapter08/guestbook/` folder:

```
$ kubectl create -f redis.yaml
```

You can see from the following screenshot this has created a `namespace`, `deployment`, and `service`.

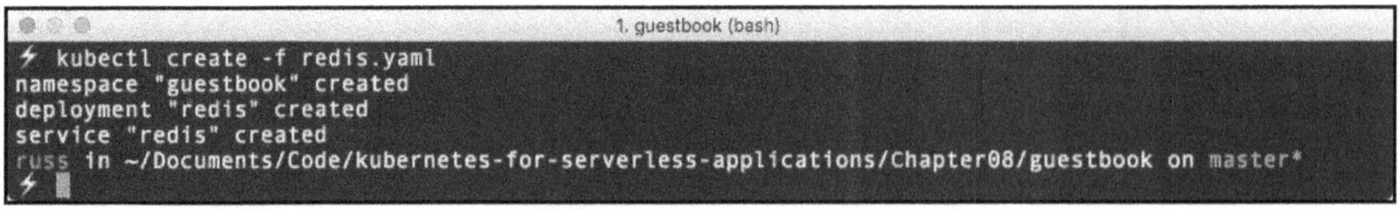

```
1. guestbook (bash)
⚡ kubectl create -f redis.yaml
namespace "guestbook" created
deployment "redis" created
service "redis" created
russ in ~/Documents/Code/kubernetes-for-serverless-applications/Chapter08/guestbook on master*
⚡
```

Now we need to create an environment to launch our functions into. As the application is written in Python, let's run the following:

```
$ fission env create --name python --image fission/python-env
```

The output of the previous command is shown in the following screenshot:

```
1. guestbook (bash)
⚡ fission env create --name python --image fission/python-env
Use default environment v1 API interface
environment 'python' created
russ in ~/Documents/Code/kubernetes-for-serverless-applications/chapter08/guestbook on master*
⚡
```

Now we have created two functions, one for displaying the comments and one for writing the comments. To add these, run the following commands:

```
$ fission function create --name guestbook-get --env python --code get.py -
-url /guestbook --method GET
$ fission function create --name guestbook-add --env python --code add.py -
-url /guestbook --method POST
```

The output of the preceding commands can be seen in the following screenshot:

```
1. guestbook (bash)
russ in ~/Documents/Code/kubernetes-for-serverless-applications/chapter08/guestbook on master*
⚡ fission function create --name guestbook-get --env python --code get.py --url /guestbook --method
 GET
function 'guestbook-get' created
route created: GET /guestbook -> guestbook-get
russ in ~/Documents/Code/kubernetes-for-serverless-applications/chapter08/guestbook on master*
⚡ fission function create --name guestbook-add --env python --code add.py --url /guestbook --method
 POST
function 'guestbook-add' created
route created: POST /guestbook -> guestbook-add
russ in ~/Documents/Code/kubernetes-for-serverless-applications/chapter08/guestbook on master*
⚡
```

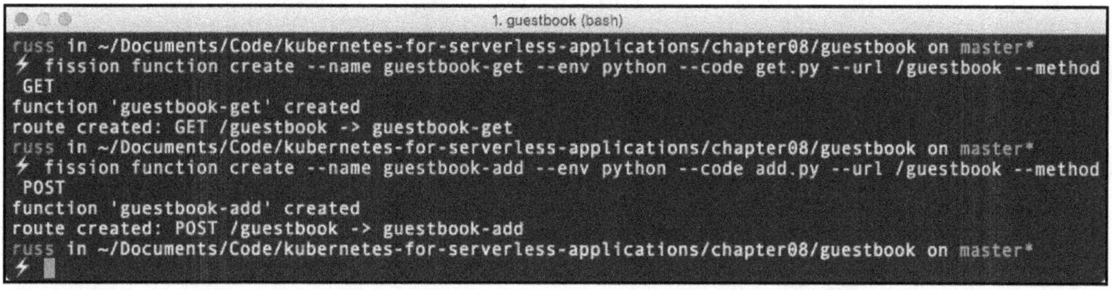

You will notice that the command to add the functions is a little different from the one we used to launch the hello world example in the previous section. In the previous examples, we are both adding the function and creating the route. You might also have noticed that while we have created two functions, they are bound to the same route of `/guestbook`. Rather than discuss this now, let's launch the application and interact with it.

To open the guestbook, run the following command:

```
$ open http://$FISSION_ROUTER/guestbook
```

For Windows 10 Professional, use:

```
$ explorer http://%FISSION_ROUTER%/guestbook
```

This will open your browser at a blank guestbook page, as in the following screenshot:

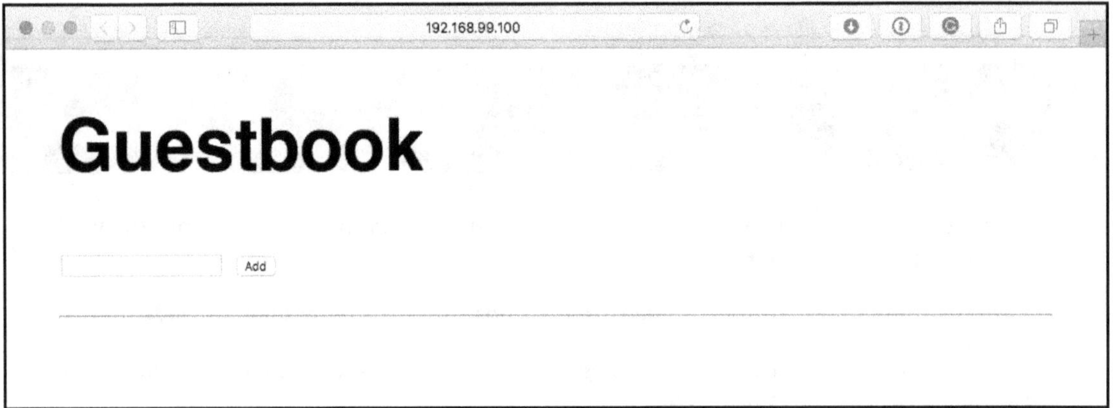

Let's now add a comment by entering some text—say `Testing Fission`—and then click **Add**. Upon refreshing, you should see your comment has been added:

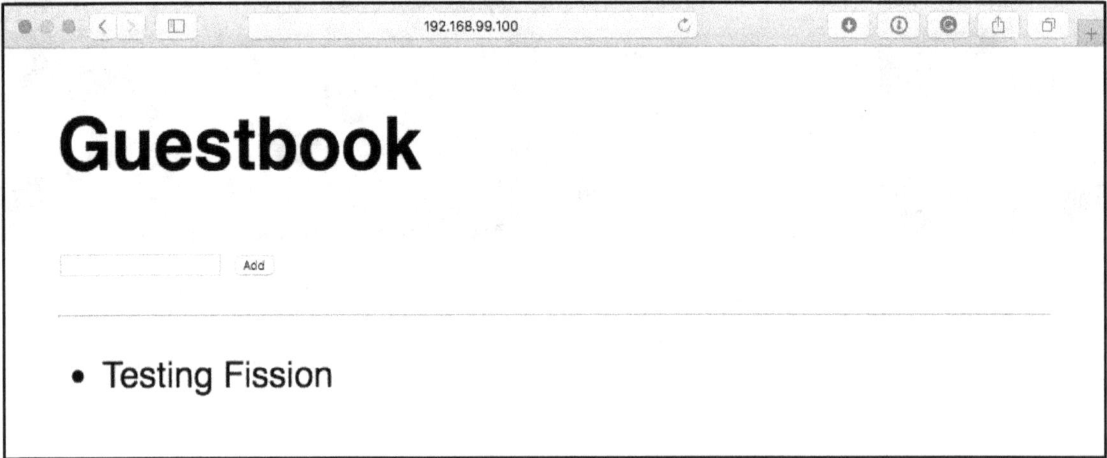

If you receive an internal server error, don't worry—just refresh the page and submit again. Taking a look at the HTML source of the page, you may notice that the form action is configured to `POST` to `/guestbook`:

```
<form action="/guestbook" method="POST">
  <input type="text" name="text">
  <button type="submit">Add</button>
</form>
```

If you look at the command we used to create the two functions, both had a method attached. The `guestbook-add` one, which runs the `add.py`, used the `POST` method, as you can see from the following code:

```
#
# Handles POST /guestbook -- adds item to guestbook
#

from flask import request, redirect
import redis

# Connect to redis.
redisConnection = redis.StrictRedis(host='redis.guestbook', port=6379,
db=0)

def main():
    # Read the item from POST params, add it to redis, and redirect
    # back to the list
    item = request.form['text']
    redisConnection.rpush('guestbook', item)
    return redirect('/guestbook', code=303)
```

The function reads the data posted by the form, pushes the comment to the Redis database, and then takes us back to `/guestbook`. The `303` code is the status code used to redirect after a `POST`.

Whenever your browser requests a page it is sending a `GET` request. In our case, all of the `GET` requests to `/guestbook` are being routed to the `guestbook-get` function, which is the `get.py` code:

```
#
# Handles GET /guestbook -- returns a list of items in the guestbook
# with a form to add more.
#

from flask import current_app, escape
import redis
```

```
# Connect to redis. This is run only when this file is loaded; as
# long as the pod is alive, the connection is reused.
redisConnection = redis.StrictRedis(host='redis.guestbook', port=6379,
db=0)

def main():
    messages = redisConnection.lrange('guestbook', 0, -1)

    items = [("<li>%s</li>" % escape(m.decode('utf-8'))) for m in messages]
    ul = "<ul>%s</ul>" % "\n".join(items)
    return """
      <html><body style="font-family:sans-serif;font-
size:2rem;padding:40px">
          <h1>Guestbook</h1>
          <form action="/guestbook" method="POST">
            <input type="text" name="text">
            <button type="submit">Add</button>
          </form>
          <hr/>
          %s
      </body></html>
      """ % ul
```

As you can see from the preceding code, this connects to the Redis database, reads each entry, formats the results as an unordered HTML list, and then inserts the list below the horizontal rule (`<hr/>`).

Fission commands

Before we look at moving our Fission installation to a public cloud, we should look at the command client a little more. There are several top-level commands available that we can use to manage our functions and routes.

The fission function command

This is pretty much where you will spend most of your time when using Fission. The function command is how you create, manage, and delete your functions. You can use either `fission function <command>` or `fission fn <command>`.

The create command

We have already used this command so we don't need to go into too much detail. The `fission function create` command takes several options; the most common ones are:

- `--name`: This indicates what we want to call our function.
- `--env`: This indicates the environment we want to deploy our function in. More on environments in the next section.
- `--code`: The path or URL to the code we wish to deploy.
- `--url`: The URL we want our function to be available at.
- `--method`: How we access our function on the preceding URL; the options here are `GET`, `POST`, `PUT`, `DELETE`, `HEAD`—if you don't use `--method` but do use `--url` it will always default to `GET`.

As we have already seen in the guestbook example, a `fission function create` command would look something like the following:

```
$ fission function create \
    --name guestbook-get \
    --env python \
    --code get.py \
    --url /guestbook \
    --method GET
```

The get option

This option is a quite a simple one; running `fission function get` will display the source code for your chosen function. It accepts one input: `--name`. This is the name of the function you wish to display the source code for.

Running the following command will display the source code for the hello world function:

```
$ fission function get --name hello
```

```
2. russ (bash)
⚡ fission function get --name hello

module.exports = async function(context) {
    return {
        status: 200,
        body: "Hello, world!\n"
    };
}
russ in ~
⚡
```

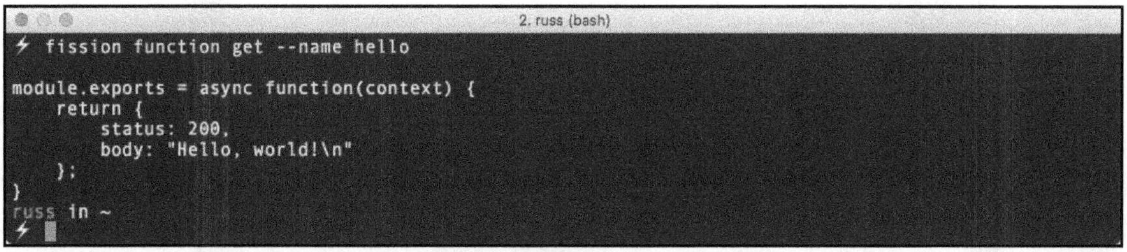

The list and getmeta commands

The following two commands kind of do the same thing:

```
$ fission function list
```

This command will list the functions that are currently installed. In that list is the name of the function, its unique ID, and which environment the function is deployed into:

```
⚡ fission function list
NAME           UID                                  ENV
guestbook-add  c0c9af2f-dcfe-11e7-bfe6-080027e101f5 python
guestbook-get  bbc045f1-dcfe-11e7-bfe6-080027e101f5 python
hello          857368d2-dceb-11e7-bfe6-080027e101f5 nodejs
russ in ~
⚡
```

If we already know the name of the function and we want to remind ourselves of the environment it is running in, or need its UID, then we can use the `fission function getmeta` command and pass it the name of the function:

```
$ fission function getmeta --name hello
```

```
⚡ fission function getmeta --name hello
NAME  UID                                  ENV
hello 857368d2-dceb-11e7-bfe6-080027e101f5 nodejs
russ in ~
⚡
```

The logs command

Although there are not any views at the moment, you can view the logs for your function by using the `fission function logs` command. There are a few different options you can pass:

- `--name`: This is the name of the function you wish to view the logs for, and this is always required
- `--follow`: Keeps the stream open and logs are displayed in real time
- `--detail`: Adds more verbose output

Using the preceding options, the command will look something like the following:

```
$ fission function logs --detail --follow --name hello
```

However, as mentioned, there is not a lot to see at the moment.

The update command

The `fission function update` command deploys an updated version of a function. It uses the same options as the `fission function create` command. For example, if we wanted to update our hello world function to use a different source, we would run the following:

```
$ fission function update \
    --name hello \
    --env nodejs \
    --code hello-update.js \
```

The delete command

The final command we are going to look at is `fission function delete`. This command is pretty self-explanatory. It deletes the function and only accepts a single argument, and that is `--name`.

Please be careful when using `fission function delete`; it does not prompt you in any way, and when you hit *Enter* your function will be deleted.

To delete the hello world function, for example, we should just run the following:

```
$ fission function delete --name hello
```

```
2. russ (bash)
⚡ fission function delete --name hello
function 'hello' deleted
russ in ~
⚡
```

As you can see, and as mentioned, there are no *Are you sure?* prompts so be careful when using the command.

The fission environment command

The next top-level command is environment. As we have already seen, environments are where our functions run and they also define what language our functions are executed in. At the time of writing, Fission supports Node.js, Go, Python, PHP, Ruby, Perl, and .NET C#.

The create command

The `fission environment create` command is one we have already used. For example, when we created the guestbook application we needed a Python environment to run our application on, so we ran the following:

```
$ fission environment create \
    --name python \
    --image fission/python-env
```

A full list of the images, the URLs to use, and the Dockerfiles used to create the images are as follows:

Language	Image name	Source URL
Python 2.7	`fission/python-env`	`https://github.com/fission/fission/tree/master/environments/python`
Python 3.5	`fission/python3-env`	`https://github.com/fission/fission/tree/master/environments/python`
Node.js	`fission/nodejs-env`	`https://github.com/fission/fission/tree/master/environments/nodejs`
.NET C#	`fission/dotnet-env`	`https://github.com/fission/fission/tree/master/environments/dotnet`
.NET 2.0 C#	`fission/dotnet20-env`	`https://github.com/fission/fission/tree/master/environments/dotnet20`
Go	`fission/go-runtime`	`https://github.com/fission/fission/tree/master/environments/go`
PHP	`fission/php7-env`	`https://github.com/fission/fission/tree/master/environments/php7`
Ruby	`fission/ruby-env`	`https://github.com/fission/fission/tree/master/environments/ruby`
Perl	`fission/perl-env`	`https://github.com/fission/fission/tree/master/environments/perl`

The list and get command

Like the function command, environment also has a `list` and `get` command, and they work in the same way.

```
$ fission environment list
```

Running the previous command will list all of the configured environments.

```
$ fission environment get --name nodejs
```

Running the previous command will get the details of the named environment.

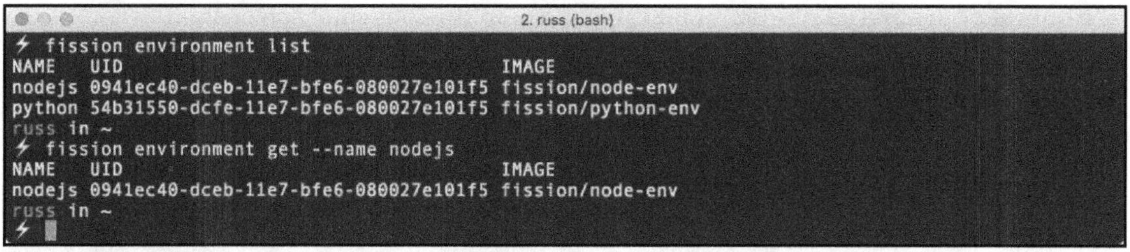

```
2. russ (bash)
⚡ fission environment list
NAME   UID                                  IMAGE
nodejs 0941ec40-dceb-11e7-bfe6-080027e101f5 fission/node-env
python 54b31550-dcfe-11e7-bfe6-080027e101f5 fission/python-env
russ in ~
⚡ fission environment get --name nodejs
NAME   UID                                  IMAGE
nodejs 0941ec40-dceb-11e7-bfe6-080027e101f5 fission/node-env
russ in ~
⚡
```

The delete command

The `delete` command, again, works as you would expect it to (remember it will delete without warning):

```
$ fission environment delete --name nodejs
```

Also, if you have functions within your environment, it will also delete with no warning. However, your functions will remain until you manually delete them. Any attempt to call a function that does not have an environment will result in an internal server error.

Running Fission in the cloud

Now we have an idea of what is involved in launching and interacting with Fission when it is running locally, let's look at launching Kubernetes in the cloud and then configuring Fission to run there.

For the remainder of this section, I will be only providing instructions for macOS High Sierra and Ubuntu 17.04 hosts as this these have a greater level of compatibility with the commands we will be running.

Launching the Kubernetes cluster

I am going to be launching my Kubernetes in Google Cloud using the following command:

```
$ gcloud container clusters create kube-cluster
```

The output of the preceding command can be seen in the following screenshot:

```
1. russ (bash)
russ in ~
⚡ gcloud container clusters create kube-cluster
Creating cluster kube-cluster...done.
Created [https://container.googleapis.com/v1/projects/russ-kubernetes-cluster/zones/us-central1-b/cl
usters/kube-cluster].
kubeconfig entry generated for kube-cluster.
NAME          ZONE           MASTER_VERSION  MASTER_IP       MACHINE_TYPE   NODE_VERSION  NUM_NODES
STATUS
kube-cluster  us-central1-b  1.7.8-gke.0     35.188.126.90   n1-standard-1  1.7.8-gke.0   3
RUNNING
```

Once launched, which should take about 5 minutes at the most, you can check that your cluster is up and running as expected by using the following:

```
$ kubectl get nodes
```

The output of the preceding command can be seen in the following screenshot:

```
1. russ (bash)
⚡ kubectl get nodes
NAME                                          STATUS   ROLES    AGE   VERSION
gke-kube-cluster-default-pool-e1354e15-13xp   Ready    <none>   3m    v1.7.8-gke.0
gke-kube-cluster-default-pool-e1354e15-kksv   Ready    <none>   3m    v1.7.8-gke.0
gke-kube-cluster-default-pool-e1354e15-tv2g   Ready    <none>   3m    v1.7.8-gke.0
russ in ~
⚡
```

Now that we have our three-node cluster up and running, and our local Kubernetes client interacting with it, we can deploy the Kubernetes end of Helm by running the following command again:

```
$ helm init
```

This will return the following message:

```
1. russ (bash)
⚡ helm init
$HELM_HOME has been configured at /Users/russ/.helm.

Tiller (the Helm server-side component) has been installed into your Kubernetes Cluster.
Happy Helming!
russ in ~
⚡
```

Now that we have Helm ready, we can go ahead and launch Fission.

Installing Fission

As before, we will be using Helm to install Fission. The only difference between installing Fission locally and on a public cloud such as Google Cloud, Microsoft Azure, or AWS is that we will not be using the `--set serviceType=NodePort` option and instead just run the following:

```
$ helm install --namespace fission
https://github.com/fission/fission/releases/download/0.4.0/fission-all-0.4.
0.tgz
```

You may notice that it's a lot quicker to run this time, and that the information returned is quite similar to when we launched Fission on our local single node cluster.

You may notice, this time your installation has a different name:

```
NAME: orange-shark
LAST DEPLOYED: Sun Dec 10 13:46:02 2017
NAMESPACE: fission
STATUS: DEPLOYED
```

This name is used to reference the installation throughout, as you can see from the following screen, which is taken from the **Workloads** page of the Google Cloud web console:

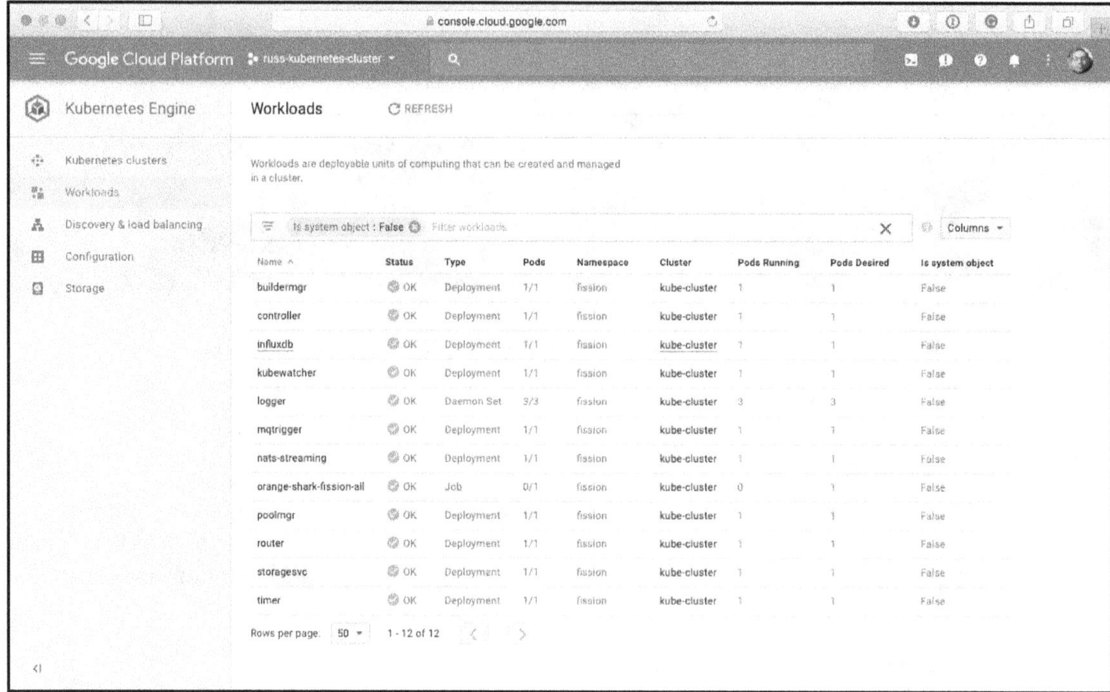

Name	Status	Type	Pods	Namespace	Cluster	Pods Running	Pods Desired	Is system object
buildermgr	OK	Deployment	1/1	fission	kube-cluster	1	1	False
controller	OK	Deployment	1/1	fission	kube-cluster	1	1	False
influxdb	OK	Deployment	1/1	fission	kube-cluster	1	1	False
kubewatcher	OK	Deployment	1/1	fission	kube-cluster	1	1	False
logger	OK	Daemon Set	3/3	fission	kube-cluster	3	3	False
mqtrigger	OK	Deployment	1/1	fission	kube-cluster	1	1	False
nats-streaming	OK	Deployment	1/1	fission	kube-cluster	1	1	False
orange-shark-fission-all	OK	Job	0/1	fission	kube-cluster	0	1	False
poolmgr	OK	Deployment	1/1	fission	kube-cluster	1	1	False
router	OK	Deployment	1/1	fission	kube-cluster	1	1	False
storagesvc	OK	Deployment	1/1	fission	kube-cluster	1	1	False
timer	OK	Deployment	1/1	fission	kube-cluster	1	1	False

While still in the console, clicking on **Discovery & load balancing** will show you all of the external IP addresses that have been assigned to your installation. As we passed the `NodePort` option, external load balancers have been created:

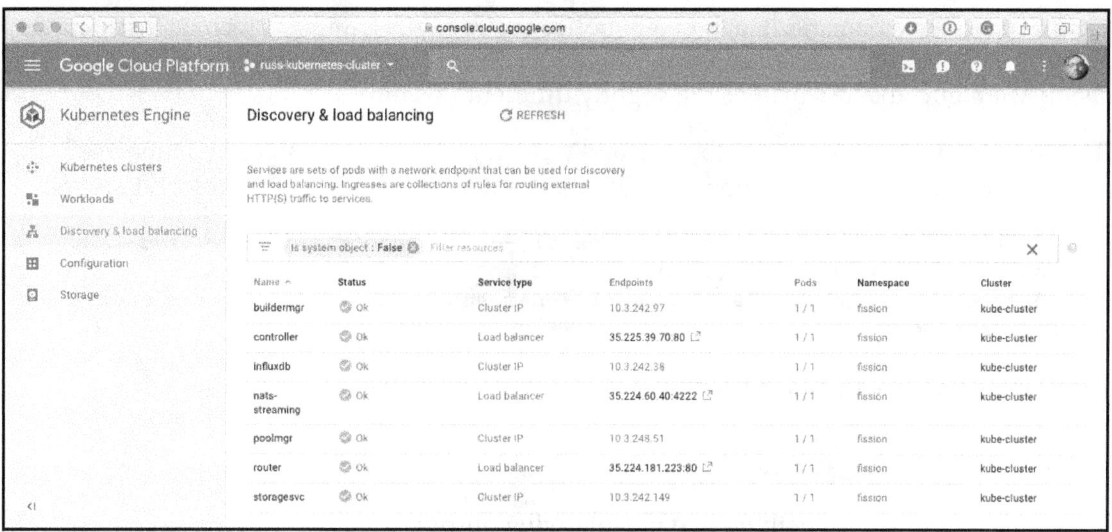

The final thing to look at while in the console is the **Storage** page. As you can see, external block storage has been created and attached to your installation. This is different to when we launched it locally, as the storage was actually that of our single machine:

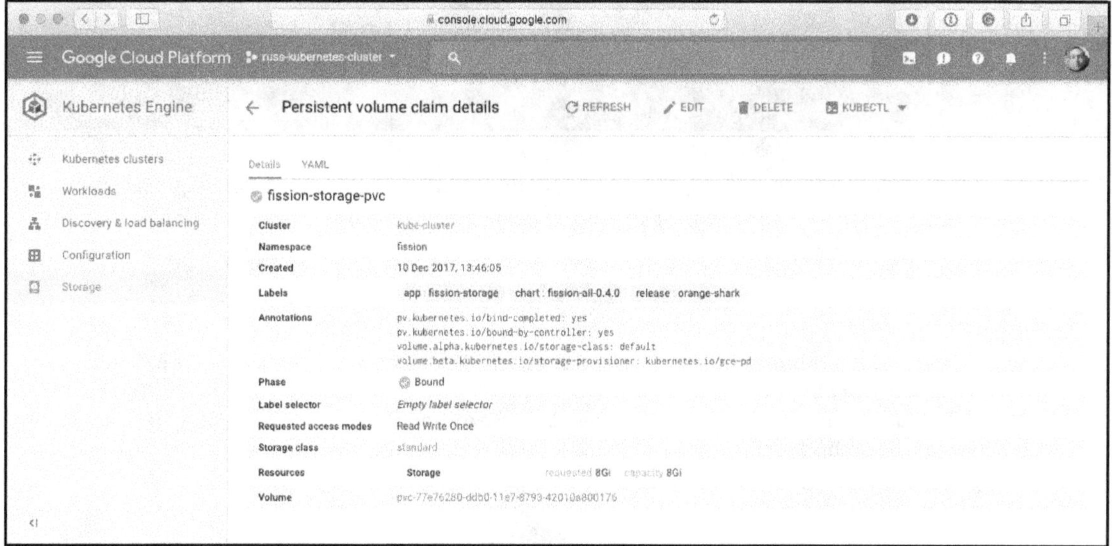

Returning to the command line, you will notice that, again, Helm has given us instructions on how to finish off the configuration of our local Fission client. However, as we were not using Minikube, the instructions are slightly different this time.

The commands to set the `FISSION_URL` and `FISSION_ROUTER` variables this time use `kubectl` to query our installation to find out the external IP address of our load balancers:

```
 $ export FISSION_URL=http://$(kubectl --namespace fission get svc
controller -o=jsonpath='{..ip}')
 $ export FISSION_ROUTER=$(kubectl --namespace fission get svc router -
o=jsonpath='{..ip}')
```

You can check the URLs by running the following commands:

```
$ echo $FISSION_URL
$ echo $FISSION_ROUTER
```

This should give you something like the following output:

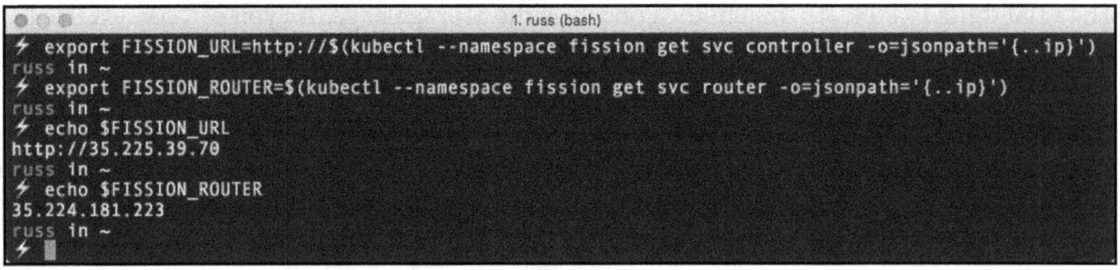

```
1. russ (bash)
⚡ export FISSION_URL=http://$(kubectl --namespace fission get svc controller -o=jsonpath='{..ip}')
russ in ~
⚡ export FISSION_ROUTER=$(kubectl --namespace fission get svc router -o=jsonpath='{..ip}')
russ in ~
⚡ echo $FISSION_URL
http://35.225.39.70
russ in ~
⚡ echo $FISSION_ROUTER
35.224.181.223
russ in ~
⚡
```

Now that we have Fission installed, and our local command-line client configured to interact with our cloud-based installation, we can quickly re-run the hello world example by running the following commands:

```
$ fission env create --name nodejs --image fission/node-env
$ curl
https://raw.githubusercontent.com/fission/fission/master/examples/nodejs/he
llo.js > /tmp/hello.js
$ fission function create --name hello --env nodejs --code /tmp/hello.js --
url /hello --method GET
```

This should give you something like the following output:

```
1. russ (bash)
⚡ fission env create --name nodejs --image fission/node-env
Use default environment v1 API interface
environment 'nodejs' created
russ in ~
⚡ curl https://raw.githubusercontent.com/fission/fission/master/examples/nodejs/hello.js > /tmp/hel
lo.js
  % Total    % Received % Xferd  Average Speed   Time    Time     Time  Current
                                 Dload  Upload   Total   Spent    Left  Speed
100   119  100   119    0     0    484      0 --:--:-- --:--:-- --:--:--   485
russ in ~
⚡ fission function create --name hello --env nodejs --code /tmp/hello.js --url /hello --method GET
function 'hello' created
route created: GET /hello -> hello
russ in ~
⚡
```

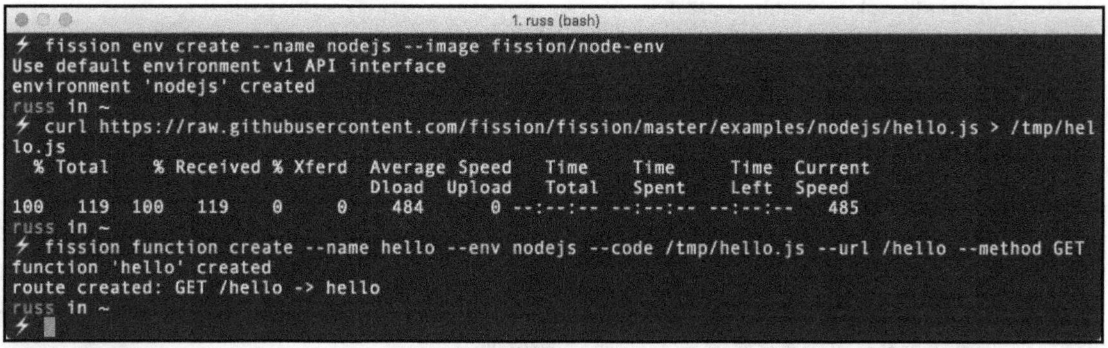

Once launched, you can use either of the following commands to call the function:

```
$ curl http://$FISSION_ROUTER/hello
$ http http://$FISSION_ROUTER/hello
```

This should give you something like the following output:

```
1. russ (bash)
⚡ http http://$FISSION_ROUTER/hello
HTTP/1.1 200 OK
Content-Length: 14
Content-Type: text/html; charset=utf-8
Date: Sun, 10 Dec 2017 14:08:29 GMT
Etag: W/"e-CfrI2/0nvZtNI6A0tkiqdReJU20"
X-Powered-By: Express

Hello, world!

russ in ~
⚡
```

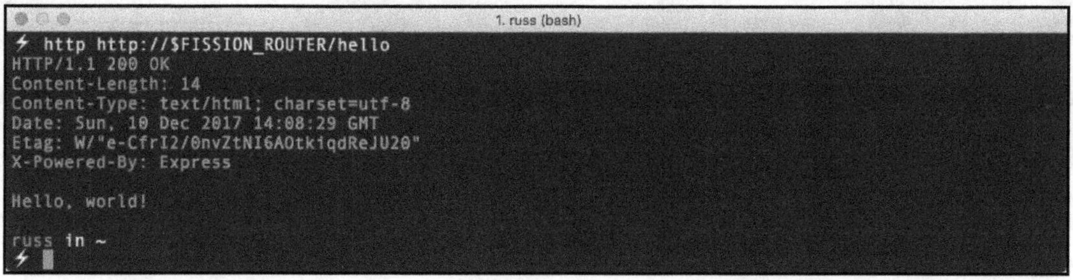

As you can already see, like all of the technologies we have looked at, once installed, interacting and using Fission in a public cloud is no different to how you would interact and use it when running locally. You really don't have to care too much about external access and so on, as Fission and Kubernetes are both sorting this out for you.

The guestbook

Before we move on to a more advanced example, let's quickly launch our guestbook application again. To do this, change to the `/Chapter08/guestbook/` folder in the repository and then run the following commands:

```
$ kubectl create -f redis.yaml
```

```
$ fission env create --name python --image fission/python-env
$ fission function create --name guestbook-get --env python --code get.py -
-url /guestbook --method GET
$ fission function create --name guestbook-add --env python --code add.py -
-url /guestbook --method POST
$ open http://$FISSION_ROUTER/guestbook
```

This should give you something like the following output:

```
1. guestbook (bash)
⚡ kubectl create -f redis.yaml
namespace "guestbook" created
deployment "redis" created
service "redis" created
russ in ~/Documents/Code/kubernetes-for-serverless-applications/Chapter08/guestbook on master*
⚡ fission env create --name python --image fission/python-env
Use default environment v1 API interface
environment 'python' created
russ in ~/Documents/Code/kubernetes-for-serverless-applications/Chapter08/guestbook on master*
⚡ fission function create --name guestbook-get --env python --code get.py --url /guestbook --method
 GET
function 'guestbook-get' created
route created: GET /guestbook -> guestbook-get
russ in ~/Documents/Code/kubernetes-for-serverless-applications/Chapter08/guestbook on master*
⚡ fission function create --name guestbook-add --env python --code add.py --url /guestbook --method
 POST
function 'guestbook-add' created
route created: POST /guestbook -> guestbook-add
russ in ~/Documents/Code/kubernetes-for-serverless-applications/Chapter08/guestbook on master*
⚡ open http://$FISSION_ROUTER/guestbook
russ in ~/Documents/Code/kubernetes-for-serverless-applications/Chapter08/guestbook on master*
⚡
```

This will launch the application and also take you to it in your browser, where you can add a comment:

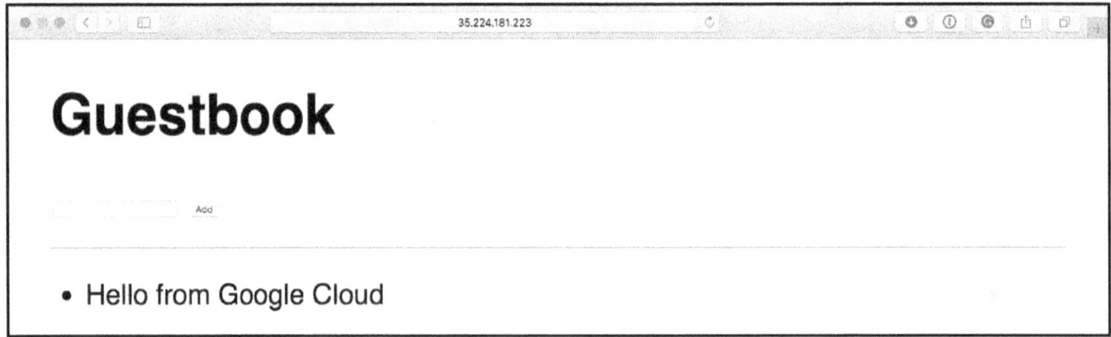

Some more examples

Before we finish off the chapter, let's look at some more example code running in Fission, starting with a weather checker.

Weather

In the `/Chapter08/weather/` folder of the repository, you will find `weather.js`. This is a simple Node.js function that queries the Yahoo weather API to return the current weather for a given location:

```
'use strict';

const rp = require('request-promise-native');

module.exports = async function (context) {
    const stringBody = JSON.stringify(context.request.body);
    const body = JSON.parse(stringBody);
    const location = body.location;

    if (!location) {
        return {
            status: 400,
            body: {
                text: 'You must provide a location.'
            }
        };
    }

    try {
        const response = await
rp(`https://query.yahooapis.com/v1/public/yql?q=select item.condition from
weather.forecast where woeid in (select woeid from geo.places(1) where
text="${location}") and u="c"&format=json`);
        const condition =
JSON.parse(response).query.results.channel.item.condition;
        const text = condition.text;
        const temperature = condition.temp;
        return {
            status: 200,
            body: {
                text: `It is ${temperature} celsius degrees in ${location}
and ${text}`
            },
            headers: {
```

```
                    'Content-Type': 'application/json'
                }
            };
        } catch (e) {
            console.error(e);
            return {
                status: 500,
                body: e
            };
        }
    }
```

As you can see from the preceding code, the function accepts JSON encoded data, which must contain a valid location. Because of this, we will need to deploy the function with a `POST` route, and as it gives an error if no location data is passed, we should also deploy a `GET` route. To do this, simple run the following commands from within the `/Chapter08/weather/` folder:

```
$ fission env create --name nodejs --image fission/node-env
$ fission function create --name weather --env nodejs --code weather.js --
url /weather --method POST
$ fission route create --method GET --url /weather --function weather
```

The first command may result in an error if you already have the environment we originally created for the hello world example up and running, as seen in the following Terminal output:

```
1. weather (bash)
russ in ~/Documents/Code/kubernetes-for-serverless-applications/chapter08/weather on master*
⚡ fission env create --name nodejs --image fission/node-env
Failed to create environment: Resource exists - AlreadyExists
russ in ~/Documents/Code/kubernetes-for-serverless-applications/chapter08/weather on master*
⚡ fission function create --name weather --env nodejs --code weather.js --url /weather --method POS
T
function 'weather' created
route created: POST /weather -> weather
russ in ~/Documents/Code/kubernetes-for-serverless-applications/chapter08/weather on master*
⚡ fission route create --method GET --url /weather --function weather
trigger '199e3e97-6b05-4c6c-a3c8-4c9106809526' created
russ in ~/Documents/Code/kubernetes-for-serverless-applications/chapter08/weather on master*
⚡
```

Now that we have our function deployed we can quickly test it by running one of the following two commands:

```
$ http http://$FISSION_ROUTER/weather
$ curl http://$FISSION_ROUTER/weather
```

Because we haven't supplied the location, you should see the following message:

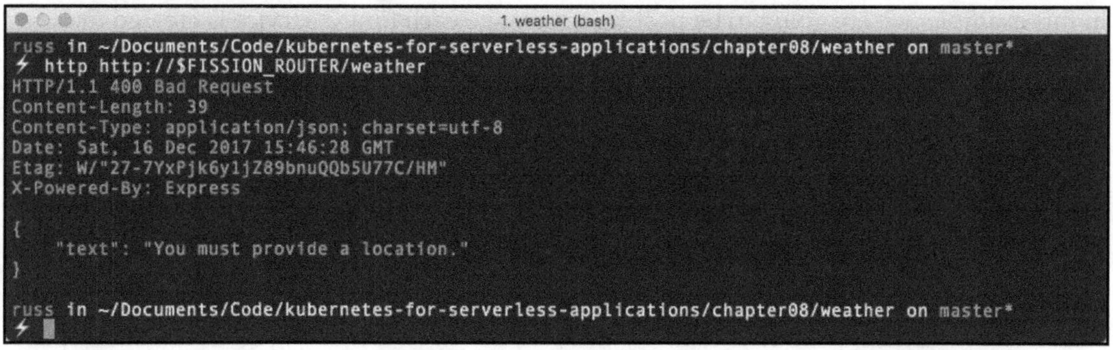

```
1. weather (bash)
russ in ~/Documents/Code/kubernetes-for-serverless-applications/chapter08/weather on master*
⚡ http http://$FISSION_ROUTER/weather
HTTP/1.1 400 Bad Request
Content-Length: 39
Content-Type: application/json; charset=utf-8
Date: Sat, 16 Dec 2017 15:46:28 GMT
Etag: W/"27-7YxPjk6y1jZ89bnuQQb5U77C/HM"
X-Powered-By: Express

{
    "text": "You must provide a location."
}

russ in ~/Documents/Code/kubernetes-for-serverless-applications/chapter08/weather on master*
⚡
```

This is exactly what the code has been programmed to do. As you can see, it has returned a `400` error with the message we expected. Providing a location (I used `Nottingham, England`) by running one of the following commands should tell you what the weather is:

```
$ http POST http://$FISSION_ROUTER/weather location="Nottingham, England"
$ curl -H "Content-Type: application/json" -X POST -d
'{"location":"Nottingham, England"}' http://$FISSION_ROUTER/weather
```

You can see from the following Terminal output, it has confirmed that the weather is currently not that great where I am:

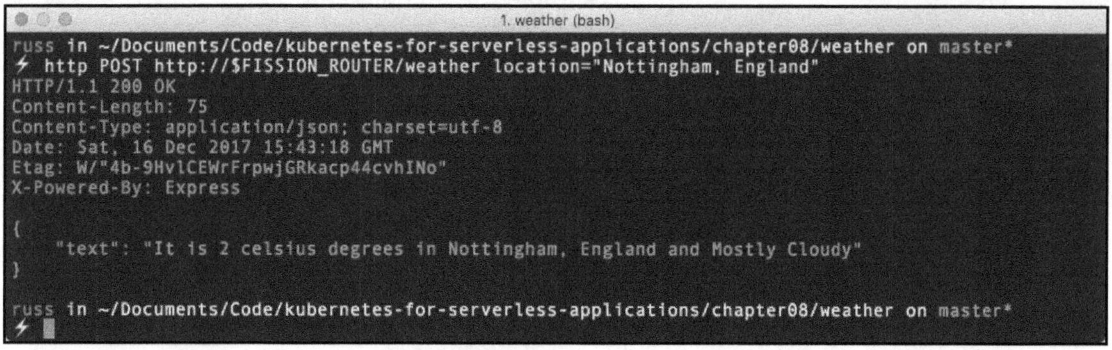

```
1. weather (bash)
russ in ~/Documents/Code/kubernetes-for-serverless-applications/chapter08/weather on master*
⚡ http POST http://$FISSION_ROUTER/weather location="Nottingham, England"
HTTP/1.1 200 OK
Content-Length: 75
Content-Type: application/json; charset=utf-8
Date: Sat, 16 Dec 2017 15:43:18 GMT
Etag: W/"4b-9HvlCEWrFrpwjGRkacp44cvhINo"
X-Powered-By: Express

{
    "text": "It is 2 celsius degrees in Nottingham, England and Mostly Cloudy"
}

russ in ~/Documents/Code/kubernetes-for-serverless-applications/chapter08/weather on master*
⚡
```

Slack

In this example, we are going to be posting a message each time a service is created or deleted in the default namespace of our current Kubernetes installation. The messages will be posted to a group messaging service called Slack using a Webhook.

Slack is an online collaboration tool that allows teams to use an environment to interact with chatbots and each other. It offers free and paid tiers as well as an exhaustive API for your applications to hook into your chat rooms.

I am going to assume that you already have access to a Slack workspace and have permissions to add applications to it. If you don't, then you can configure a new workspace at `https://slack.com/`.

Once you have access to your workspace, click on the name of the workspace in the top-left of the screen and from the drop-down list of options, select **Manage Apps**. This will take you to the Slack **App Directory**. Here, in the search field at the top of the page, enter `Incoming WebHooks`, select the result, and then click on the **Add Configuration** button.

Follow the on-screen instructions to create a Webhook for the channel of your choice. I choose to post my updates in the random channel and I also customized the icon. On this page you will also find a Webhook URL. Mine (which has now been removed) was `https://hooks.slack.com/services/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`.

Make a note of this, as we will need to update the code with it. As you can see in the following code, which you can also find in the repository at `/Chapter08/slack/`, the third line needs to be updated with your Webhook details:

```
'use strict';

let https = require('https');

const slackWebhookPath = "/put/your/url/here"; // Something like
"/services/XXX/YYY/zZz123"

function upcaseFirst(s) {
    return s.charAt(0).toUpperCase() + s.slice(1).toLowerCase();
}

async function sendSlackMessage(msg) {
    let postData = `{"text": "${msg}"}`;
```

```
    let options = {
        hostname: "hooks.slack.com",
        path: slackWebhookPath,
        method: "POST",
        headers: {
            "Content-Type": "application/json"
        }
    };

    return new Promise(function(resolve, reject) {
        let req = https.request(options, function(res) {
            console.log(`slack request status = ${res.statusCode}`);
            return resolve();
        });
        req.write(postData);
        req.end();
    });
}

module.exports = async function(context) {
    console.log(context.request.headers);

    let obj = context.request.body;
    let version = obj.metadata.resourceVersion;
    let eventType = context.request.get('X-Kubernetes-Event-Type');
    let objType = context.request.get('X-Kubernetes-Object-Type');

    let msg = `${upcaseFirst(eventType)} ${objType} ${obj.metadata.name}`;
    console.log(msg, version);

    if (eventType == 'DELETED' || eventType == 'ADDED') {
        console.log("sending event to slack")
        await sendSlackMessage(msg);
    }

    return {
        status: 200,
        body: ""
    }
}
```

To do this, paste everything after `https://hooks.slack.com`, including the slash (/). For me this was `/services/T8F3CR4GG/B8FNRR3PC/wmLSDgS0fl5SGOcAgNjwr6pC`.

The line should read something like the following:

```
const slackWebhookPath =
"/services/T8F3CR4GG/B8FNRR3PC/wmLSDgS0fl5SGOcAgNjwr6pC"; // Something like
"/services/XXX/YYY/zZz123"
```

Make sure the file is called `kubeEventsSlack.js` and once your Webhook details are in the code, we can create and launch the function using the following:

```
$ fission function create --name kubeslack --env nodejs --code
kubeEventsSlack.js
```

Once the function has been created, we need to create something to trigger it. Previously, we have been calling the functions using HTTP calls. This time, though, we want to trigger the function each time something happens within our Kubernetes cluster. To do this, we need to create a watch.

To do this, run the following command:

```
$ fission watch create --function kubeslack --type service --ns default
```

The `fission watch` command is something we have not yet discussed, so let's take a minute to find out a little more about it.

As part of our Fission deployment there is a service called `kubewatcher`. By default, this service is used by Fission to help manage itself by watching the Kubernetes API, but is also exposed to end users. The command used to create the previous watch creates a watcher, which calls our function (`--function kubeslack`) each time changes to a service (`--type service`) are made in the default namespace (`--ns default`). We could also set up a watch that looks for changes to pods, deployments, and so on by changing the type:

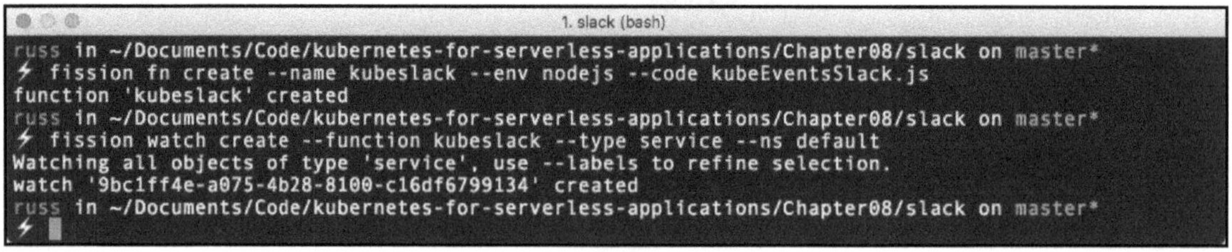

```
1. slack (bash)
russ in ~/Documents/Code/kubernetes-for-serverless-applications/Chapter08/slack on master*
⚡ fission fn create --name kubeslack --env nodejs --code kubeEventsSlack.js
function 'kubeslack' created
russ in ~/Documents/Code/kubernetes-for-serverless-applications/Chapter08/slack on master*
⚡ fission watch create --function kubeslack --type service --ns default
Watching all objects of type 'service', use --labels to refine selection.
watch '9bc1ff4e-a075-4b28-8100-c16df6799134' created
russ in ~/Documents/Code/kubernetes-for-serverless-applications/Chapter08/slack on master*
⚡
```

Now we need to launch a service in the default namespace. To do this, change to the `/Chapter03/` folder and run the following commands:

```
$ kubectl apply -f cli-hello-world.yml
```

Then, delete the service by running the following:

```
$ kubectl delete service cli-hello-world
```

```
1. chapter03 (bash)
russ in ~/Documents/Code/kubernetes-for-serverless-applications/Chapter03 on master*
⚡ kubectl apply -f cli-hello-world.yml
service "cli-hello-world" created
deployment "cli-hello-world" unchanged
russ in ~/Documents/Code/kubernetes-for-serverless-applications/Chapter03 on master*
⚡ kubectl delete service cli-hello-world
service "cli-hello-world" deleted
russ in ~/Documents/Code/kubernetes-for-serverless-applications/Chapter03 on master*
⚡
```

If you check Slack, you should see two messages confirming that a service called `cli-hello-world` has been added and deleted:

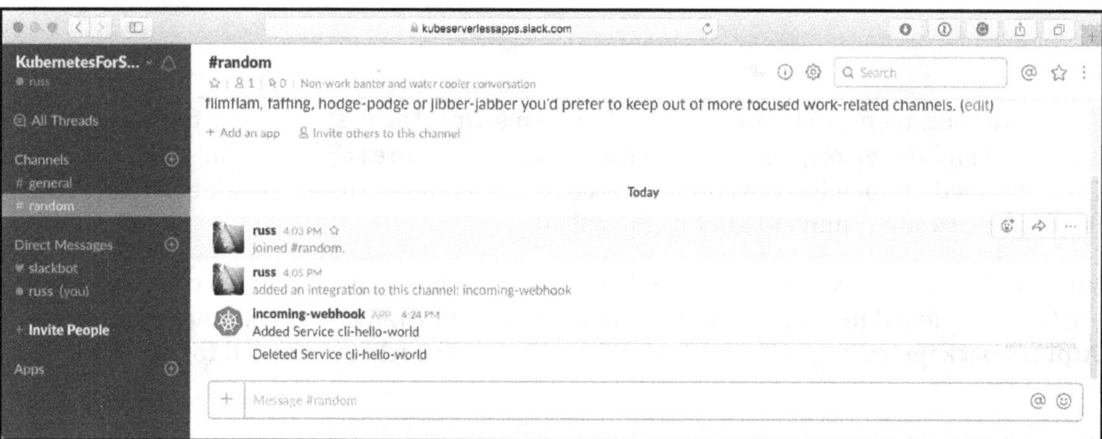

You should see this happen in almost real time, and you might also see messages about other services being started within the default namespace within your cluster.

Whales

The next, and also the last, example we are going to look at is a binary environment. This environment is different to the ones we have been looking at, as it does not contain a programming language as such. Instead, we will be deploying a bash script that installs and configures a Unix tool called `cowsay`. The code for this looks like the following and is available in the `/Chapter08/whale/` folder:

```
#!/bin/sh

if ! hash cowsay 2> /dev/null; then
    apk update > /dev/null
    apk add curl perl > /dev/null
    curl https://raw.githubusercontent.com/docker/whalesay/master/cowsay >
/bin/cowsay 2> /dev/null
    chmod +x /bin/cowsay
    mkdir -p /usr/local/share/cows/
    curl
https://raw.githubusercontent.com/docker/whalesay/master/docker.cow >
/usr/local/share/cows/default.cow 2> /dev/null
fi

cowsay
```

As you can see, there are two sections to the bash script. The first part runs the `cowsay` command and if it errors, which it will do to start with, it uses `apk` to install `curl` and `perl`. Once installed, it downloads a copy of the code, and configures the default behavior. Then it runs the `cowsay` command after it is installed.

You may be thinking to yourself, what is APK and what is `cowsay`? As the containers that are being deployed to run the Fission environments run Alpine Linux, we need to use **Alpines package manager** (**APK**) to install the required packages needed for our code to run.

Alpine Linux is a Linux distribution, which over the last two years has started to gain a lot of traction over the more traditional Ubuntu/CentOS installations—this is because of its size. It is possible to have a base installation of Alpine Linux that uses only 8 MB of space. However, although it is small, it remains just as functional and powerful as other Linux distributions. Its small size coupled with its power makes it the perfect operating system for building containers with.

`cowsay` is a Unix command that repeats whatever input you give it in a speech bubble, coming from a cow, hence the name `cowsay`. We will be installing Docker's own version of `cowsay`, which uses a whale instead of a cow. To deploy the binary function we first need to create the environment:

```
$ fission env create --name binary --image fission/binary-env
```

Now we can deploy the function and create the `POST` and `GET` routes so that we can access it:

```
$ fission function create --name whalesay --env binary --deploy whalesay.sh
--url /whale --method POST
$ fission route create --method GET --url /whale --function whalesay
```

The output of the preceding command can be seen in the following screenshot:

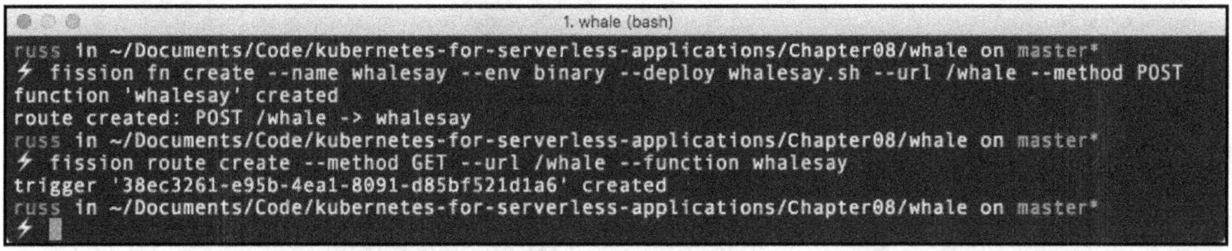

```
1. whale (bash)
russ in ~/Documents/Code/kubernetes-for-serverless-applications/Chapter08/whale on master*
⚡ fission fn create --name whalesay --env binary --deploy whalesay.sh --url /whale --method POST
function 'whalesay' created
route created: POST /whale -> whalesay
russ in ~/Documents/Code/kubernetes-for-serverless-applications/Chapter08/whale on master*
⚡ fission route create --method GET --url /whale --function whalesay
trigger '38ec3261-e95b-4ea1-8091-d85bf521d1a6' created
russ in ~/Documents/Code/kubernetes-for-serverless-applications/Chapter08/whale on master*
⚡
```

Now that we have our function deployed, we can access it using one of the following:

```
$ http http://$FISSION_ROUTER/whale
$ curl http://$FISSION_ROUTER/whale
```

This will return an ASCII whale as seen in the following Terminal output:

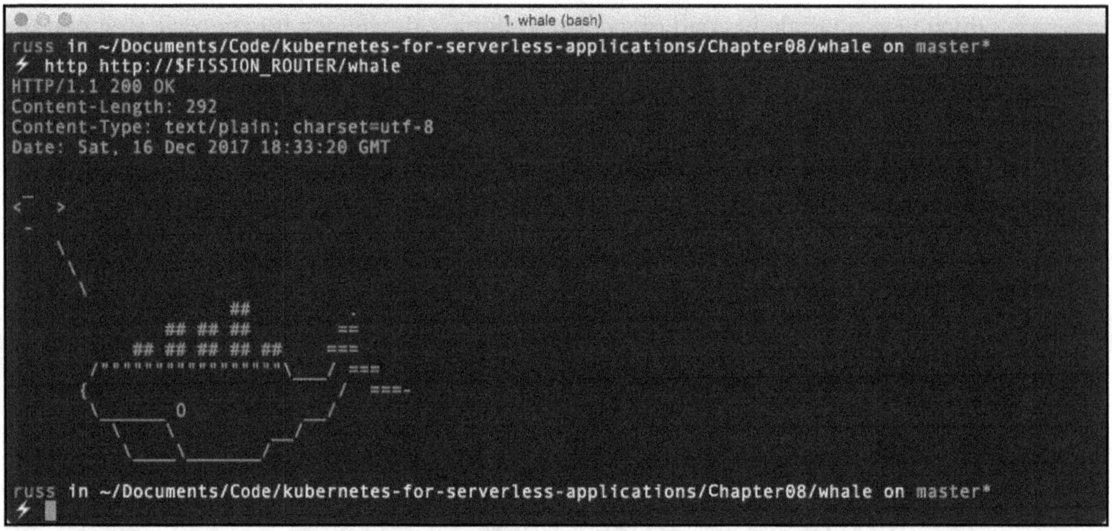

You might notice that there is nothing in the speech bubble; that is because we need to `POST` something. Unlike the previous post examples, the function we have launched will simply repeat whatever we post. So, if we were to `POST` a JSON object, it will return the JSON object. Because of this, we will be posting only plain text:

```
$ echo 'Hello from Whalesay !!!' | http POST http://$FISSION_ROUTER/whale
$ curl -X POST -H "Content-Type: text/plain" --data 'Hello from Whalesay
!!!' http://$FISSION_ROUTER/whale
```

As you can see from the following Terminal output, this returns the message we have posted:

```
russ in ~/Documents/Code/kubernetes-for-serverless-applications/Chapter08/whale on master*
⚡ echo 'Hello from Whalesay !!!' | http POST http://$FISSION_ROUTER/whale
HTTP/1.1 200 OK
Content-Length: 362
Content-Type: text/plain; charset=utf-8
Date: Sat, 16 Dec 2017 18:36:49 GMT

 _________________________
< Hello from Whalesay !!! >
 -------------------------
    \
     \
      \
                    ##        .
              ## ## ##       ==
           ## ## ## ## ##    ===
       /""""""""""""""""\___/ ===
      {                       /  ===-
       \______ O           __/
         \    \         __/
          \____\_______/

russ in ~/Documents/Code/kubernetes-for-serverless-applications/Chapter08/whale on master*
⚡
```

Now, you maybe thinking to yourself that this seems like a pretty silly example. However, what we have done here is taken the content of an HTTP request and posted it to a Linux binary, which was executed with the content we have posted. We then had the output of the command running returned via an HTTP request.

At this point you may want to terminate/power down any Kubernetes clusters you have launched to test Fission with.

Summary

In this chapter, we have looked at Fission. We have installed it using Helm and deployed it both locally and in Google Cloud. We have also launched several test applications, some basic and some that call out to third-party services to both post and return information. During the installation and configuration of the example applications, I hope that you started to see the usefulness of Fission and how it, and other serverless technologies, can be integrated into your own applications.

When I started writing the chapter, I hoped to include some sections on Fission workflows, and also the Fission UI. However, at the time of writing, both those add-ons failed to work. Now, don't get me wrong, Fission is a powerful and simple to use technology; however, it is very new and is still in development, as is Kubernetes—this means that until the code bases get more established, there will be feature breaking updates in new releases.

For example, the version of Fission we installed, version 0.4.0, was released because the latest version of Kubernetes, version 1.8 at the time of writing, removed the `ThirdPartyResources` functionality and replaced it with `CustomResourceDefinitions`, which means that older versions of Fission will not work on current versions of Kubernetes.

We are going to be looking at the Kubernetes release cycle and how this may impact you in the remaining chapters.

9

Looking at OpenFaaS

The final platform we are going to be looking at is called OpenFaaS. This is a relatively new project and has only gained support for Kubernetes, so we will not be going into too much detail. However, the project is gaining a lot of traction and supporters, so I believe it is important we mention it.

In this chapter we will look at:

- What is OpenFaaS and who made it?
- Installing OpenFaaS locally using Minikube

An introduction to OpenFaaS

OpenFaaS was started in December 2016 by Alex Ellis, just over a year to the day before I am writing this. Initially, it was designed to work with Docker swarm.

Docker swarm is Docker's own clustering technology; it allows you to link some hosts running the Docker Engine together. On the face of it, Docker swarm is quite similar to Kubernetes. However, the further you delve into the workings of both technologies, you will find that they not only work differently, but also have been designed to fill different gaps.

Since its first commit in December 2016, OpenFaaS has gotten a lot of attention from the Docker world. Ellis and the other OpenFaaS community members have spoken at DockerCon Europe, Moby Summit, KubeCon, and Gluecon, as well as numerous meetups over the course of the last 12 months. OpenFaaS was also included in the InfoWorld Bossie Awards 2017 as one of the best cloud-computing software projects of 2017.

OpenFaaS is probably the most feature-rich Function as a Service offering, and it supports Docker swarm, so it made sense that a Kubernetes version of the software would eventually be released—this Kubernetes version is called **faas-netes** and it had its first commit in July 2017.

Running OpenFaaS locally

Rather than looking at OpenFaaS on Docker swarm and doing a comparison between running the service on Kubernetes and Docker swarm, we are going to dive straight in and install OpenFaaS on Kubernetes. Like all of the tools we have covered, we are going to need a command-line client, so we are going to start by installing it.

The OpenFaaS command-line client

The OpenFaaS command-line client is available for our three operating systems. Let's work through installing it on each, starting with macOS High Sierra.

As you may have already guessed, we are going to be using Homebrew for this. To install the client, simply run the following command:

```
$ brew install faas-cli
```

For Ubuntu 17.04, the CLI can be installed using the OpenFaaS CLI installation script, which you can run directly from GitHub by running the following command:

```
$ curl -sL cli.openfaas.com | sudo sh
```

This script will also update the installed version of faas-cli if you are running an older version.

To install the CLI on Windows 10 Professional, first of all open a PowerShell window as the admin user; you can do this by selecting **Run as Administrator** from the PowerShell menu in the taskbar. Once open, you should see that you are in the `C:\WINDOWS\system32` folder, if you aren't, then run the following:

```
$ cd C:\WINDOWS\system32
```

Once you are in the `C:\WINDOWS\system32` folder, you can download the OpenFaaS CLI by running the following command:

```
$ Invoke-WebRequest -Uri https://github.com/openfaas/faas-cli/releases/
download/0.5.1/faas-cli.exe -UseBasicParsing -OutFile faas-cli.exe
```

You can find details on the latest release of the OpenFaaS CLI on the project's GitHub release page, which is at `https://github.com/openfaas/faas-cli/releases/`.

Once installed, you should be able to run the following command to confirm the version number of the CLI installed:

```
$ faas-cli version
```

Docker

Next up, we need to locally install Docker. Although I said at the start of this section that we would not be installing on Docker swarm, OpenFaaS still uses the Docker Engine, so we need it installed locally.

If you are running Ubuntu 17.04, you can install Docker using the installation script by Docker, by running the following:

```
$ curl -fsSL get.docker.com -o get-docker.sh
$ sudo sh get-docker.sh
```

To install Docker on macOS High Sierra, we can install it using Homebrew and Cask, by running:

```
$ brew cask install docker
```

For Windows 10 Professional users, you can use Chocolatey and run:

```
$ choco install docker-for-windows
```

Once you have installed Docker for macOS and Docker for Windows, you will need to open the Docker application to complete the installation. If you don't, then Docker will not start and none of the examples we are going to be using Docker for later in the chapter will work. It will take a few minutes to start at first as it needs to download and configure a small virtual machine.

Starting the Minikube cluster

Now that we have the OpenFaaS CLI installed, we can go ahead and launch a single-node Kubernetes cluster using Minikube. To do this, run the following command:

```
$ minikube start
```

This will start the cluster and configure our local Kubernetes CLI to communicate with it, unless you have Windows 10 Professional installed, and then you might see a message like the following:

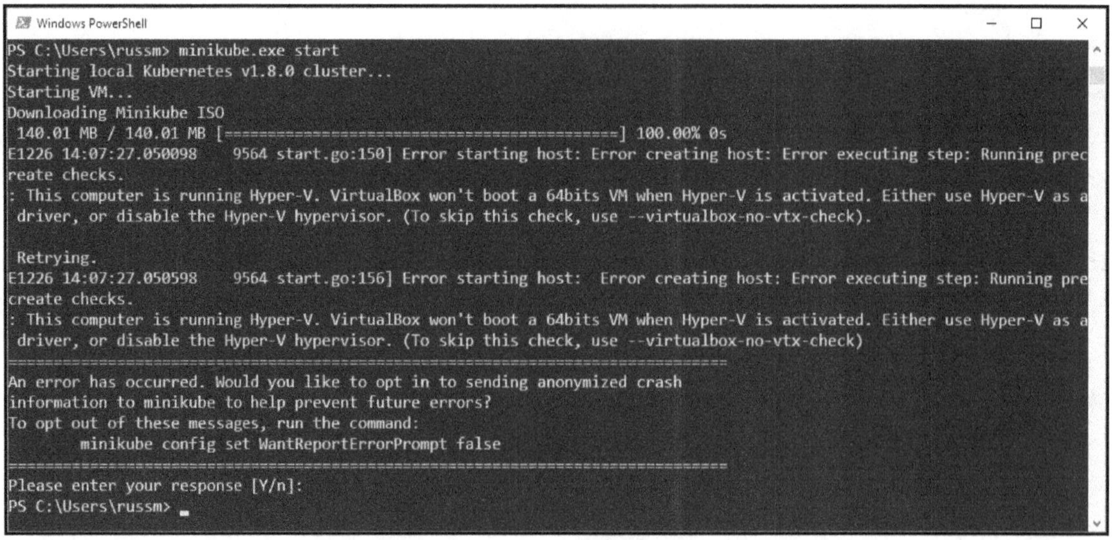

```
Windows PowerShell
PS C:\Users\russm> minikube.exe start
Starting local Kubernetes v1.8.0 cluster...
Starting VM...
Downloading Minikube ISO
 140.01 MB / 140.01 MB [==========================================] 100.00% 0s
E1226 14:07:27.050098    9564 start.go:150] Error starting host: Error creating host: Error executing step: Running prec
reate checks.
: This computer is running Hyper-V. VirtualBox won't boot a 64bits VM when Hyper-V is activated. Either use Hyper-V as a
 driver, or disable the Hyper-V hypervisor. (To skip this check, use --virtualbox-no-vtx-check).

 Retrying.
E1226 14:07:27.050598    9564 start.go:156] Error starting host:  Error creating host: Error executing step: Running pre
create checks.
: This computer is running Hyper-V. VirtualBox won't boot a 64bits VM when Hyper-V is activated. Either use Hyper-V as a
 driver, or disable the Hyper-V hypervisor. (To skip this check, use --virtualbox-no-vtx-check)
================================================================================
An error has occurred. Would you like to opt in to sending anonymized crash
information to minikube to help prevent future errors?
To opt out of these messages, run the command:
        minikube config set WantReportErrorPrompt false
================================================================================
Please enter your response [Y/n]:
PS C:\Users\russm>
```

Part of the Docker for Windows installation enables Hyper-V, and as we found out in `Chapter 3`, *Installing Kubernetes Locally*, when we installed Minikube originally, you cannot run VirtualBox and Hyper-V at the same time. To get around this, we need to configure Minikube to use Hyper-V to power the virtualization rather than VirtualBox.

To do this, open the Hyper-V Manager, select the **Virtual Switch Manager**, and then create a new external virtual switch. Call it `minikube` as in the following screenshot, and make sure that the **Allow management operating system to share this network adapter** checkbox is selected:

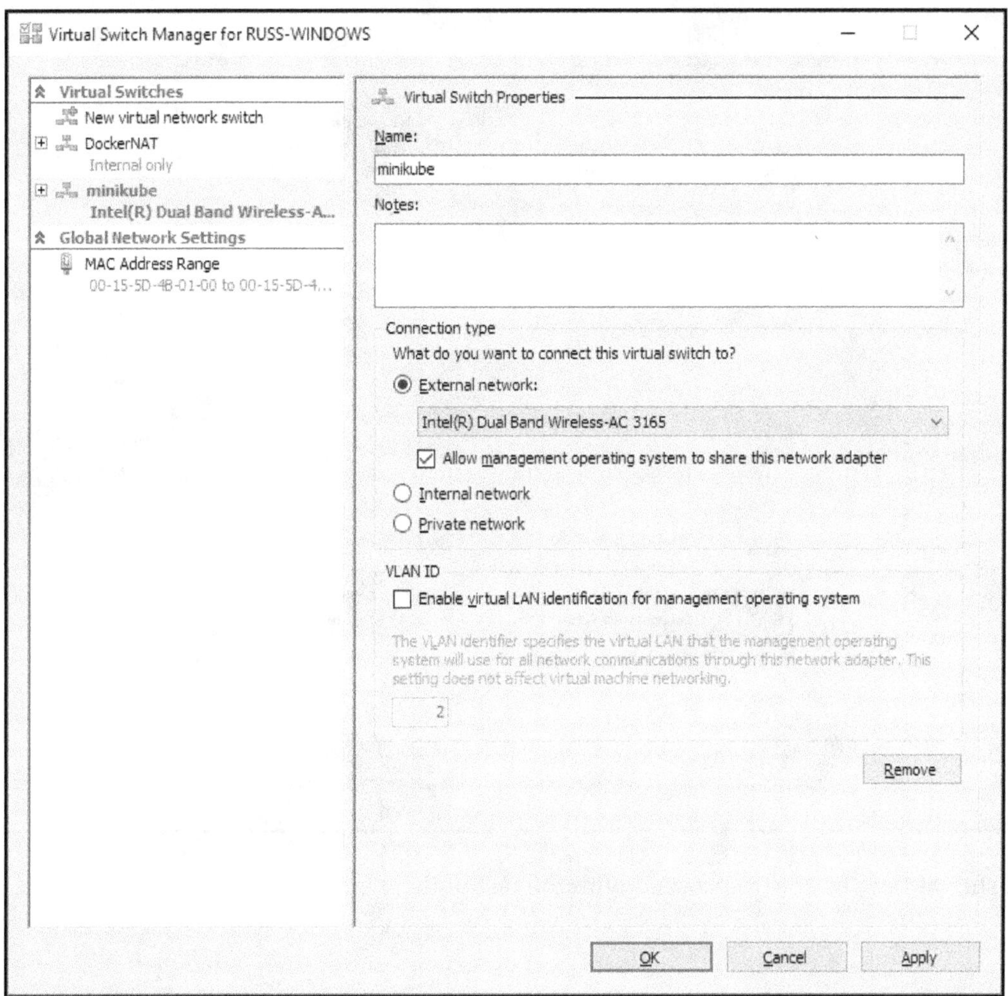

Once you have created the virtual switch, reboot your machine. Once your machine is back online, open a PowerShell window with administrator privileges and run the following command to start the single-node Kubernetes cluster:

```
$ minikube start --vm-driver=hyperv --hyperv-virtual-switch=minikube
```

In the Hyper-V Manager, you should be able to see your `minikube` VM has a status of **Running**, alongside the Docker VM, which is listed as `MobyLinuxVM`:

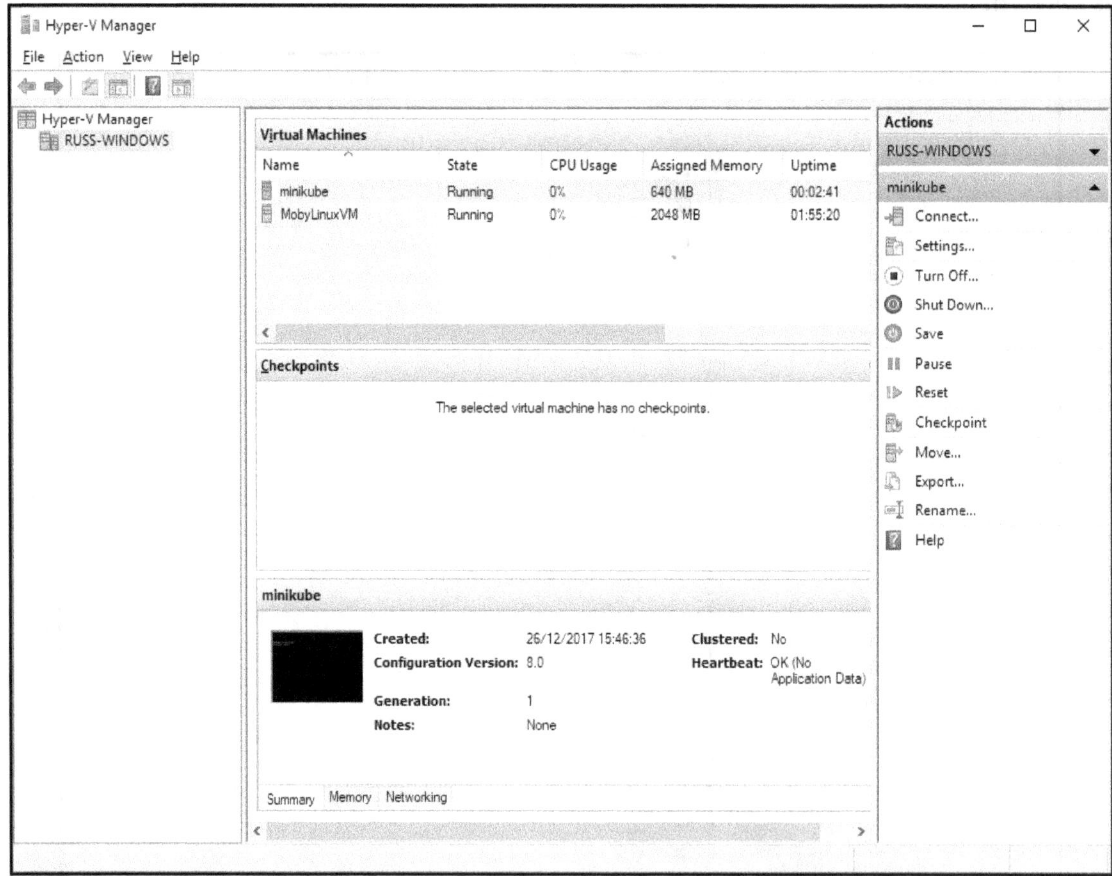

You should now be able to proceed with the rest of the instructions.

Installing OpenFaaS using Helm

Now we have the cluster launched, we need to install the OpenFaaS components. We are going to be using Helm for this. If you didn't install Helm during the previous chapter please refer to the installation instructions there. As with a Helm installation, we need to initialize it, which installs the server-side component Tiller. To do this, run the following command:

```
$ helm init
```

Now that we have Helm configured on our local, single-node Kubernetes cluster, we need to download a copy of the faas-netes code repository from GitHub. To do this, run either of the following commands:

```
$ git clone https://github.com/openfaas/faas-netes
$ cd faas-netes
```

You can also download a copy as a ZIP file from `https://github.com/openfaas/faas-netes`.

Once downloaded, we can install OpenFaaS with Helm using the following command:

```
$ helm upgrade --install --debug --reset-values --set async=false --set
rbac=false openfaas openfaas/
```

This will return quite a bit of output, but the only part that you really to need to pay attention to is the last line, which should contain something similar to the following:

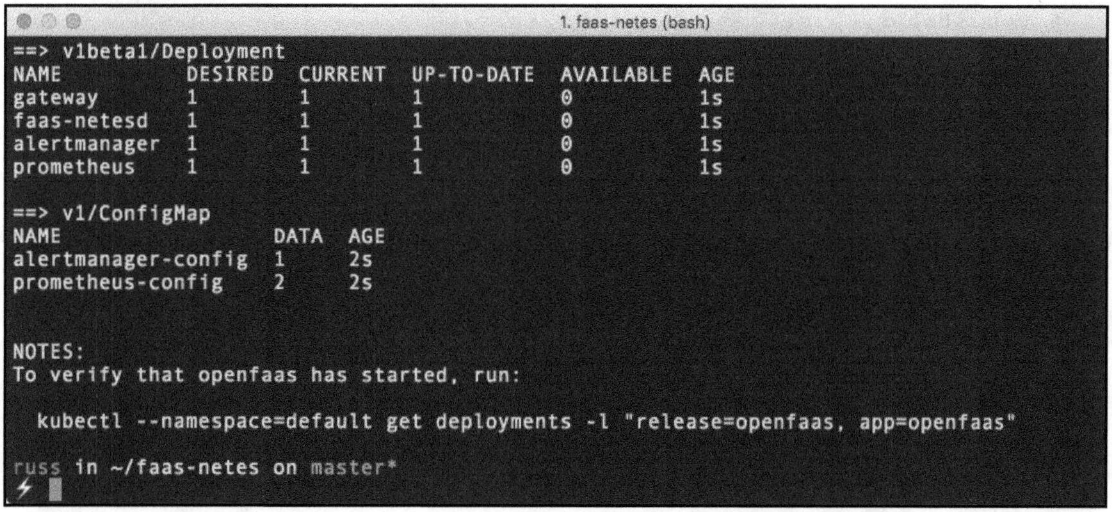

```
1. faas-netes (bash)
==> v1beta1/Deployment
NAME          DESIRED  CURRENT  UP-TO-DATE  AVAILABLE  AGE
gateway       1        1        1           0          1s
faas-netesd   1        1        1           0          1s
alertmanager  1        1        1           0          1s
prometheus    1        1        1           0          1s

==> v1/ConfigMap
NAME                 DATA  AGE
alertmanager-config  1     2s
prometheus-config    2     2s


NOTES:
To verify that openfaas has started, run:

  kubectl --namespace=default get deployments -l "release=openfaas, app=openfaas"

russ in ~/faas-netes on master*
⚡
```

After a minute or two, you can check the status of the installation by running the command at the end of the output:

```
$ kubectl --namespace=default get deployments -l "release=openfaas,
app=openfaas"
```

You should see something like the following Terminal output:

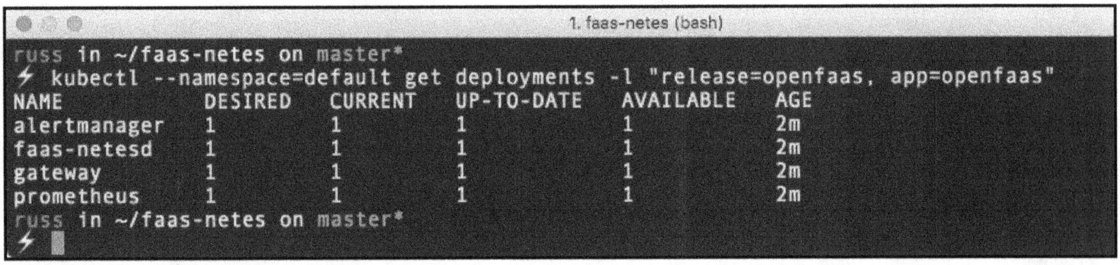

```
1. faas-netes (bash)
russ in ~/faas-netes on master*
⚡ kubectl --namespace=default get deployments -l "release=openfaas, app=openfaas"
NAME           DESIRED   CURRENT   UP-TO-DATE   AVAILABLE   AGE
alertmanager   1         1         1            1           2m
faas-netesd    1         1         1            1           2m
gateway        1         1         1            1           2m
prometheus     1         1         1            1           2m
russ in ~/faas-netes on master*
⚡
```

Now that we have OpenFaaS installed and available, we can look at launching a hello world example.

Hello world!

Like the other services we have covered, we will be running a quick hello world example. This will introduce you to the difference between OpenFaaS and the other tools. We will also find out why we needed to install Docker. To start with, run the following commands:

```
$ mkdir hello
$ cd hello
$ faas-cli new --lang python hello
```

This will create a folder called `hello` and then within it, a file called `hello.yml` and a few folders will be created:

```
russ in ~/hello
⚡ faas-cli new --lang python hello
russ in ~/hello
⚡ faas-cli new --lang python hello
2017/12/26 14:00:49 No templates found in current directory.
2017/12/26 14:00:49 HTTP GET https://github.com/openfaas/faas-cli/archive/master.zip
2017/12/26 14:00:50 Writing 288Kb to master.zip

2017/12/26 14:00:50 Attempting to expand templates from master.zip
2017/12/26 14:00:50 Fetched 10 template(s) : [csharp go-armhf go node-arm64 node-armhf node python-a
rmhf python python3 ruby] from https://github.com/openfaas/faas-cli
2017/12/26 14:00:50 Cleaning up zip file...
Folder: hello created.

Function created in folder: hello
Stack file written: hello.yml
russ in ~/hello
⚡
```

Next, we need to log into a Docker Hub account. To do this, run the following command:

```
$ docker login
```

If you do not have a Docker Hub account, you can sign-up for one at `https://hub.docker.com/` for free:

```
russ in ~/hello
⚡ docker login
Login with your Docker ID to push and pull images from Docker Hub. If you don't have a Docker ID, he
ad over to https://hub.docker.com to create one.
Username: russmckendrick
Password:
Login Succeeded
russ in ~/hello
⚡
```

Opening `hello.yml` in a text editor will show you the following:

```
provider:
  name: faas
  gateway: http://localhost:8080

functions:
  hello:
```

```
    lang: python
    handler: ./hello
    image: hello
```

Edit the file so that the `image` reads `your-dockerhub-username/hello`. In my case, this was `russmckendrick/hello`.

Once edited, run the following command:

```
$ faas-cli build -f hello.yml
```

This will build a container locally, using your local Docker Engine installation containing the code in the `/hello` folder:

```
1. hello (docker)
⚡ faas-cli build -f hello.yml
[0] > Building: hello.
Clearing temporary build folder: ./build/hello/
Preparing ./hello/ ./build/hello/function
Building: russmckendrick/hello with python template. Please wait..
Sending build context to Docker daemon  7.168kB
Step 1/16 : FROM python:2.7-alpine
2.7-alpine: Pulling from library/python
ab7e51e37a18: Pull complete
4a57a4e05b89: Pull complete
765ccb94f933: Pull complete
93cd29df27e5: Pull complete
Digest: sha256:78cee3882c3e4b5e5e98b4cffb558ba0f7f3a68118724d0fb74c99c67321820a
Status: Downloaded newer image for python:2.7-alpine
 ---> 64905abbb69e
Step 2/16 : RUN apk --no-cache add curl     && echo "Pulling watchdog binary from Github."     && cu
rl -sSL https://github.com/openfaas/faas/releases/download/0.6.9/fwatchdog > /usr/bin/fwatchdog
```

Now we have the container image built, which you can see by running the following:

```
$ docker image ls
```

1. hello (bash)
⚡ docker image ls
REPOSITORY TAG IMAGE ID CREATED SIZE
russmckendrick/hello latest 8dd11a2f72ef About a minute ago 84MB
python 2.7-alpine 64905abbb69e 6 days ago 75.3MB
russ in ~/hello
⚡

We can now push the image to our Docker Hub account by running the following:

```
$ faas-cli push -f hello.yml
```

```
1. hello (bash)
⚡ faas-cli push -f hello.yml
[0] > Pushing: hello.
The push refers to a repository [docker.io/russmckendrick/hello]
dfa9e10a5533: Pushed
e9158e6342b8: Pushed
058c7c680ec5: Pushed
be29c652c5c8: Pushed
2ed072e74c54: Pushed
34709e054da1: Pushed
d7943f804991: Pushed
e4cc156c20c5: Pushed
75ff687a2cd0: Pushed
b1dc8ab0e170: Mounted from library/python
c5130c42f015: Mounted from library/python
7c5ea328fb33: Mounted from library/python
52a5560f4ca0: Mounted from library/python
latest: digest: sha256:2d5fae1cdc99461f7d9f2d5776fa6f11c20972a09532feaef73c7af5bdc32f63 size: 3033
[0] < Pushing done.
russ in ~/hello
⚡
```

Now that we have the container image containing our function uploaded to the Docker Hub, you can see this at `https://hub.docker.com/r/russmckendrick/hello/`:

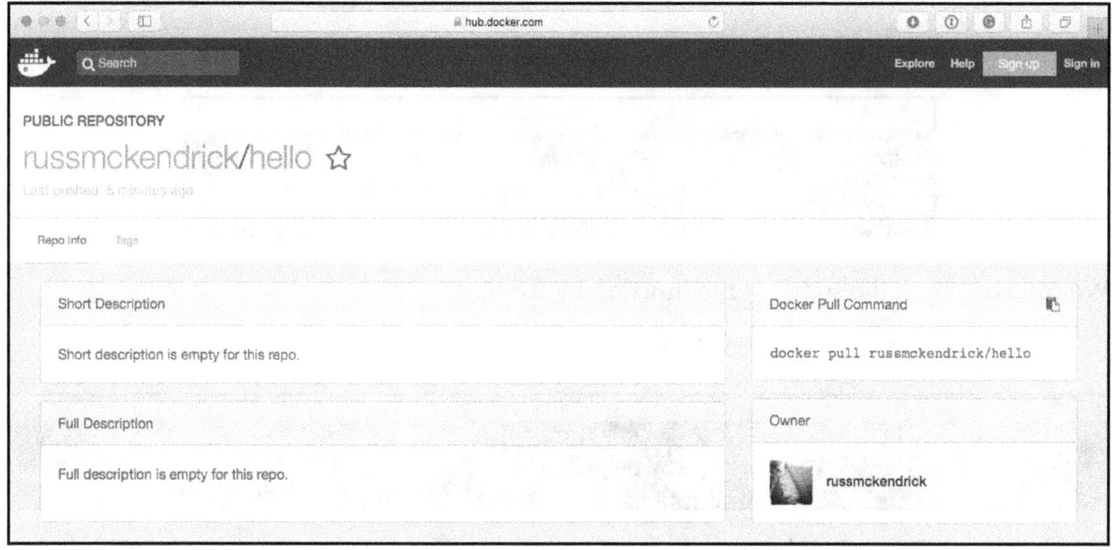

We can launch our function, but to do this, first of all we need to put the IP address of our Minikube VM into a variable so when we run the OpenFaaS CLI, it knows where it is connecting to:

```
$ export gw=http://$(minikube ip):31112
```

Now we can launch our function using the following command:

```
$ faas-cli deploy -f hello.yml --gateway $gw
```

```
1. hello (bash)
⚡ export gw=http://$(minikube ip):31112
russ in ~/hello
⚡ faas-cli deploy -f hello.yml --gateway $gw
Deploying: hello.
No existing function to remove
Deployed.
URL: http://192.168.99.100:31112/function/hello

202 Accepted
russ in ~/hello
```

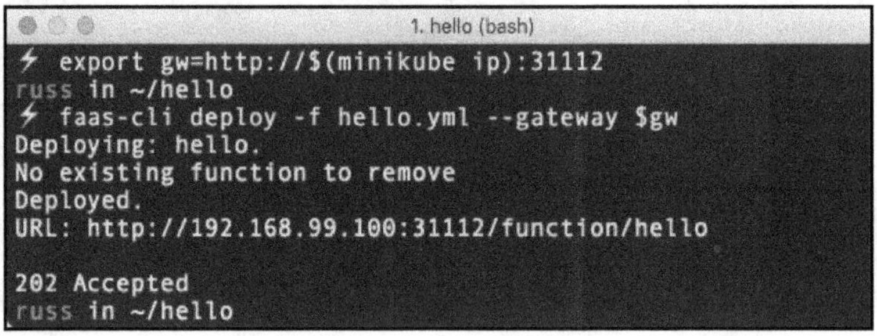

We can invoke the function by running:

```
$ echo test | faas-cli invoke hello --gateway $gw
```

This should return the word `test`:

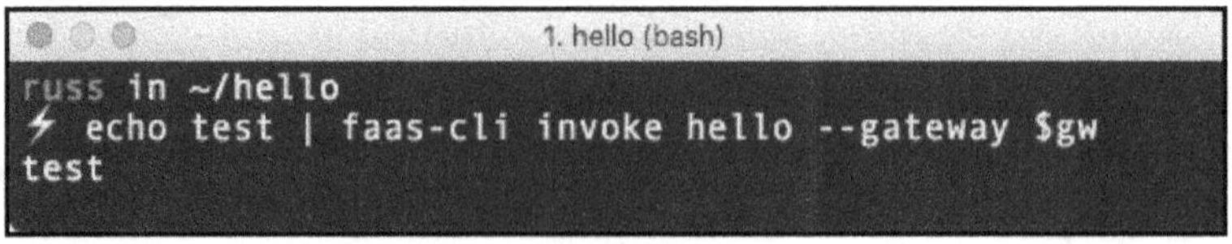

```
1. hello (bash)
russ in ~/hello
⚡ echo test | faas-cli invoke hello --gateway $gw
test
```

We can also check the status of the function by running:

```
$ faas-cli list --gateway $gw
```

```
1. hello (bash)
⚡ faas-cli list --gateway $gw
Function                      Invocations     Replicas
hello                         1               1
russ in ~/hello
```

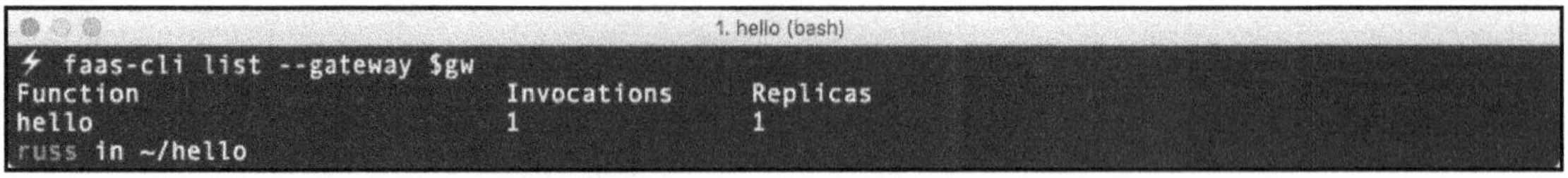

As you can see, we have a single copy of the function running, and it has been called once. Before we move onto the next section, run the function a few more times.

The OpenFaaS UI and store

OpenFaaS comes with a web-based user interface, which can be accessed by running the following command on macOS and Ubuntu:

```
$ open http://$(minikube ip):31112/
```

Windows users can run:

```
$ minikube service gateway-external
```

This will open the OpenFaaS web UI, where you should see the `hello` function we created in the previous section. Selecting the function, entering some text in the **Request Body** form field, and then clicking on **INVOKE** will call the function, as you can see from the following screenshot:

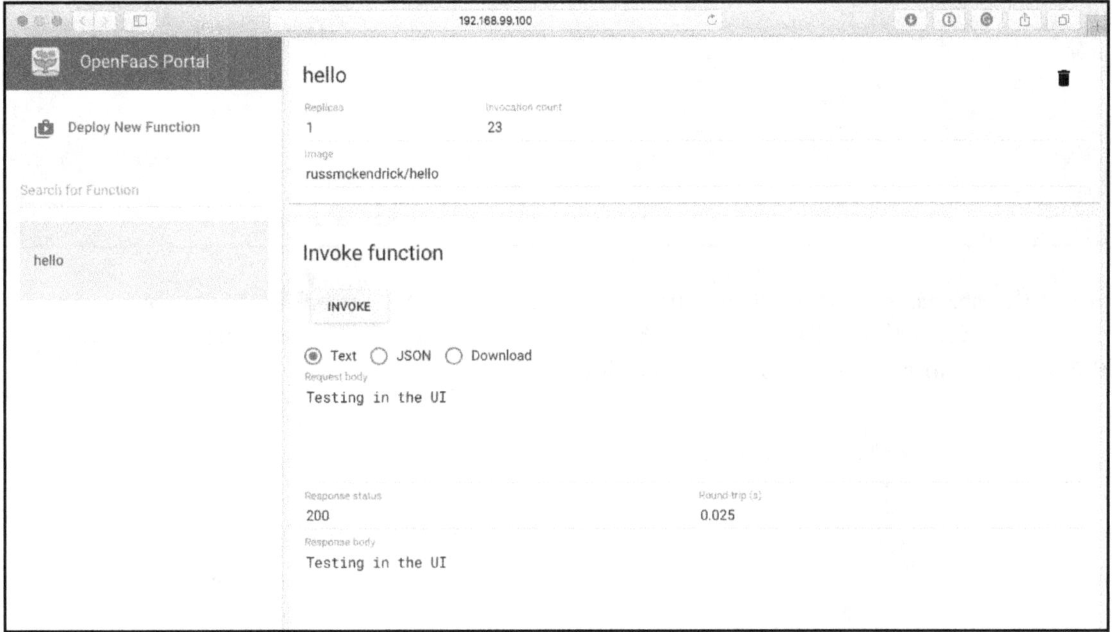

The OpenFaaS UI also includes a store, where you can deploy community-curated functions directly to your OpenFaaS installation. To access the store, click on the **Deploy New Function** button and you will be presented with a list of functions that you can deploy:

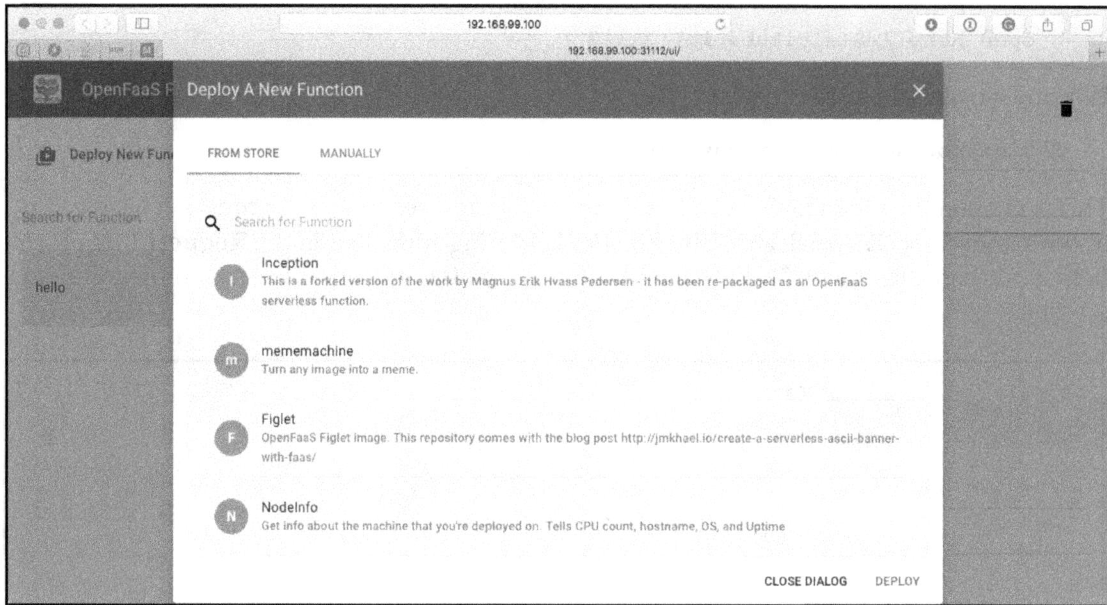

Select the `mememachine` function, and click on the **DEPLOY** button. Once deployed, you should see a function called `mememachine` under your `hello` function, select this and in the **Request Body** form field enter the following:

```
{"image": "http://i.imgflip.com/qiefv.jpg","top": "CREATING A
MEME","bottom": "USING OPENFAAS"}
```

Select **Download** and then click **INVOKE**:

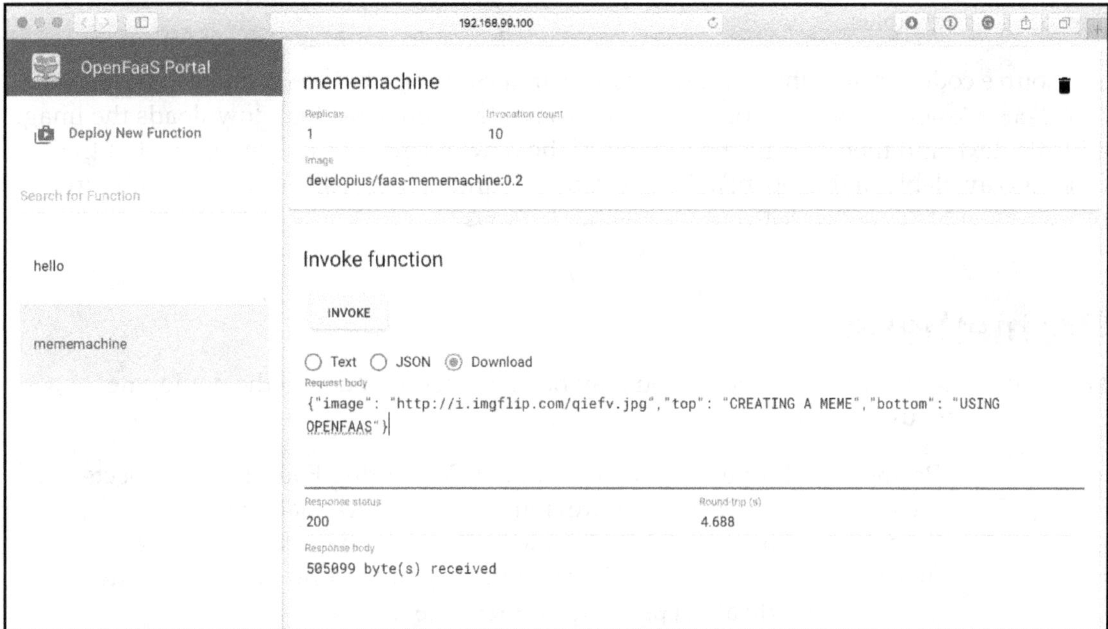

After a second or two, a file will be downloaded and on opening it you should see something like the following screenshot:

As you can see, we have the success baby meme, which is defined in the image field with the URL `http://i.imgflip.com/qiefv.jpg`, and the two lines of text we passed to the `top` and `bottom` variables.

The source code for the function can be found at `https://github.com/faas-and-furious/openfaas-mememachine/`. As you can see, it is a Node.js container that downloads the image, adds the text, and then returns the content of the new image. The source for most of the functions available in the OpenFaaS store can be found on the *FaaS and Furious* GitHub repository at `https://github.com/faas-and-furious/`.

Prometheus

When we first launched OpenFaaS, you may have noticed that one of the deployments was called Prometheus.

Prometheus is one of the Cloud Native Computing Foundation projects we have been discussing in previous chapters. Originally built by SoundCloud, it has quickly become the new standard for collecting metrics on container-based installations—you can find out more at the project's website at `https://prometheus.io/`.

This is logging some basic stats for the OpenFaaS gateway we have been calling throughout the chapter; you can open Prometheus by running one of the two commands (remember, `open` does not work on Windows):

```
$ open http://$(minikube ip):31119/
$ minikube service prometheus-external
```

Once opened, you will be presented with a blank page. Enter the following into the textbox:

```
gateway_function_invocation_total
```

After clicking the **Execute** button, you will see a graph, which breaks down the number of times each function has been called, along with the HTTP status of each function call:

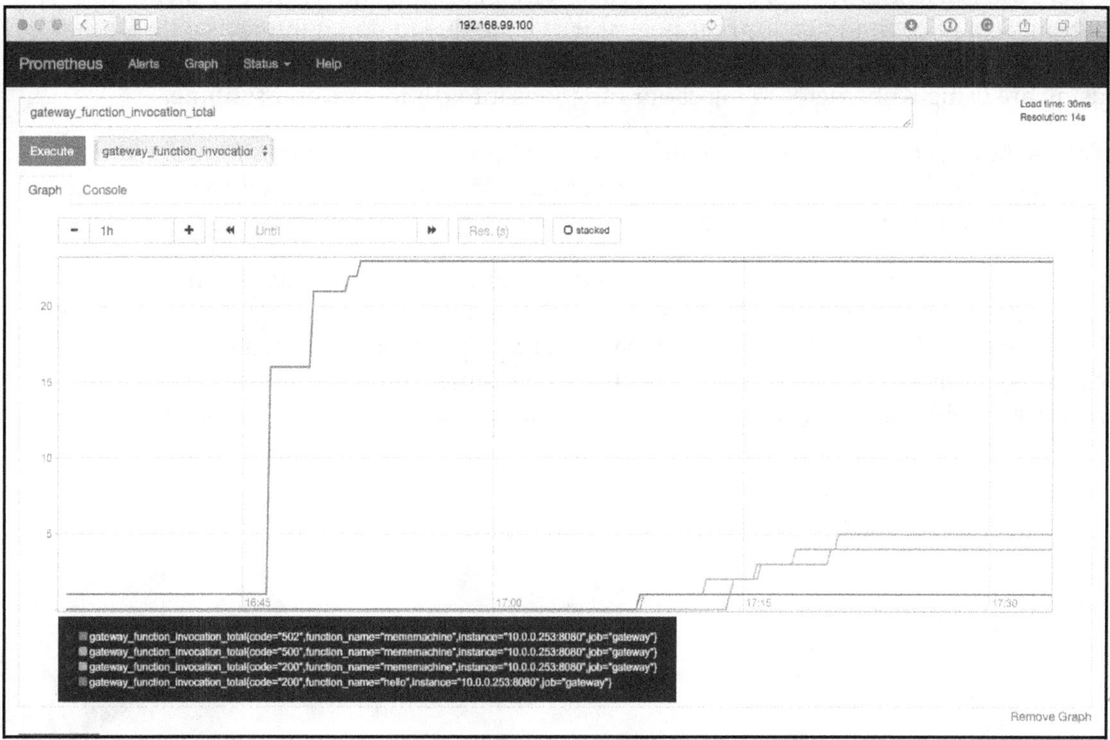

As you can see from the preceding graph, there were a few errors when I ran the `mememachine` function because the image size was too big, causing the function to crash. There are plenty of other metrics being captured. I would recommend having a click around and looking at some of the graphs.

Once you have finished with your OpenFaaS installation, you can remove the installation by running:

```
$ minikube stop
$ minikube delete
```

Summary

OpenFaaS is a fast-growing Functions as a Service platform, and as already mentioned, it is getting a lot of community support behind it. It is unique in that it interacts with Docker locally to build and push images to the Docker Hub, where the other tools we have been using are using Kubernetes to inject our functions into containers and runtime.

This is the advantage of being able to easily distribute container images for use with OpenFaaS, as demonstrated by the `mememachine` example we worked through and the other functions in the OpenFaaS store.

One of the things we didn't do in this chapter is launch Kubernetes cluster in a public cloud and deploy OpenFaaS. One of the reasons for this is, to be able to access it, we would have had to make it available to our host machine via a public IP address, which would have exposed our installation to the world. In the next chapter, we are going to look at the security considerations of running our Kubernetes clusters in public clouds, among other things.

10
Serverless Considerations

At the end of the last chapter, we touched upon securing our serverless installations—and the potential lack of security you get out of the box. In this chapter, we are going to approach that subject head-on and discuss what you should be looking out for when deploying your serverless function services on Kubernetes, as well as how to best monitor your clusters.

We will be looking at:

- Security best practices
- How do you monitor your Kubernetes cluster?

Let's make a start by discussing security.

Security best practices

When talking about security best practices, our ultimate goal should be to ensure that no unauthorized third-party has to access to any part of either our application or infrastructure that we do not want them to have.

For example, I would want an end user to be able to run a script that calls one of my serverless functions via an HTTP request made directly, by a webpage or mobile application. However, I would not want that same user to be able to access my Kubernetes dashboard, for example.

Now, this may seem like a pretty obvious example, but, as we have seen over the past few years, out-of-the-box configurations do not always have this most basic security requirement in mind. A good example of this is MongoDB.

Back in January, June, and September 2017, it was reported by several major news outlets that around 99,000 MongoDB installations were exposed to the internet; these installations were either unpatched or badly configured. This resulted in third parties accessing, copying, and deleting data from them.

In some cases, criminals were copying data, deleting it from the source database, and then sending the database owners a ransom demand for *safe* return of the deleted data—other attackers simply deleted the database and replaced it with an empty database called `PWNED_SECURE_YOUR_STUFF_SILLY` or `DELETED_BECAUSE_YOU_DIDNT_PASSWORD_PROTECT_YOUR_MONGODB`. You can find an example of the ransoms attached to the following tweet: `https://twitter.com/nmerrigan/status/818034565700849664`.

Niall Merrigan, the researcher who posted the previous tweet, pointed out in another tweet that in a single morning the number of compromised MongoDB installations went from 12,000 to around 27,000.

Companies such as Microsoft started to push their own NoSQL database services such as Azure DocumentDB, with blog posts with headings such as *First and foremost, security is our priority*, and images such as the ones in the following link: `https://azure.microsoft.com/en-in/blog/dear-mongodb-users-we-welcome-you-in-azure-documentdb/`, where Microsoft have taken their own DocumentDB logo and the MongoDB logo and put them on rusted locks and modern safe doors.

So what does this have to do with securing our serverless functions? Well, to answer this we must first look at the root cause of the MongoDB problems.

A lot of the versions of MongoDB that were being targeted by the attacks were initially configured out of the box to bind to `0.0.0.0`, which meant that the service attached itself to all IP addresses on a server. Now, this is not a problem if your MongoDB installation was launched on a server that ran only on a private network, but this was not the case for the installations that were being attacked as they were being hosted in public clouds, some of which only provided external IP addresses.

Now, you may be thinking to yourself, surely you would need some sort of authentication to access the database? Well, you would be wrong; authentication, at the time when MongoDB was still being shipped listening on all network interfaces (`0.0.0.0`), was an additional configuration step. This meant that, according to the website Shodan in July 2015, there was a total of 595.2 TB of MongoDB data exposed on the public internet with no authentication.

Also, you read that date right, this was a problem in 2015, and a lot of installations remained unpatched and incorrectly configured.

So how can we avoid these basic configuration issues in our Kubernetes and server function service installations? Let's start by looking at Kubernetes itself.

Securing Kubernetes

Kubernetes is quite secure by default. Both of the cloud providers that provide Kubernetes, Google Cloud and Microsoft Azure, work in a similar way.

A management node is deployed alongside your nodes; this management node controls your entire cluster, and is by default exposed to both the public internet and the cloud provider. We can test what an unauthenticated user sees by launching a cluster with the following command:

```
$ gcloud container clusters create kube
```

Now, by default this command will launch the cluster, including the management node. All of the certificates used to authenticate your local copy of `kubectl` against the cluster are generated on the cloud, and then once the cluster has launched it will configure `kubectl` with all of the information needed to connect. If you have a look in the configuration file, which can be found at `~/.kube/config`, you should see something like the following:

```
apiVersion: v1
clusters:
- cluster:
    certificate-authority-data:
LS0tLS1CRUdJTiBDRVJUSUZJQ0FURS0tLS0tCk1JSURERENDQWZTZ0F3SUJBZ0lSQUpEbDRydFJ
WSENjSlNhL2lxcVN4d0V3RFFZSktvWklodmNOQVFFTEJRQXcKTHpFdE1Dc0dBMVVFQXhNa1pUTm
taRFZtT1dJdE1UVTBPUzAwTlRoa0xXRmxZV010Tnpkak9HTTBOalV5Wm1aaQpNQjRYRFRFM01US
XlOekV4TXpRek0xb1hEVEl5TVRJeU5qRXlNelF6TTFvd0x6RXRNQ3NHQTFVRUF4TWtaVE5rClpE
Vm1PV0l0TVRVME9TMDBOVIhaveEditedThisDoNotW0rryT0dNME5qVXlabVppTUlJQklqQU5CZ
2txaGtpRzl3MEIKQVFFRkFBT0NBUThBTUlJQkNnS0NBUUVBb21pdGF4eE9DMzJwRE5nY3RLQkFK
RXZhVjVBL1ZEMnByU0xYcnpsYwpOL1h1UFI2NWpVR0Z3emVNbkcvMHNrZXZoUklEUncvK3B0elN
DSnR5WFhtNnUysdfsdfsdfsd4LzdHZmxSCmtnRWNPY1pZd2NzS3dIU1lRTXBQVE5Lek51b0JqcD
```

```
lla0ltcnFSNW5qWHRrNU1DS0ROS2lWbVlwTVBBV2dCL1MKakRDYWpNcUxwZU5FdDlRVkluQVI3a
UNTeFRHQkN5cE5ZRHd3R0ZOaFhka3B6b01rcUg2dDhmeXlSTEV1dkZTMgpJVFNOUzJsRVFPc2x4
L1MxaklVVEVlSVlXclFBRlJrRGs2M2VoTnRhVzNubU0rMU9FUCtqT2ZJR3hYWVdtR29FCkgwRER
BRmttRjNrcVEvR3JnbThDb3o0UWdLMlIzMEh0OVlYeUkvckxNSTF5dVFJREFRQUJveU13SVRBT0
JnTsdfsdfsdhxdVCQU1DQWdRd0R3WURWUjBUQVFIL0JBVXdBd0VCL3pBTkJna3Foa2lHOXcwQkF
Rc0ZBQU9DQVFFQQphSnRrdGYyZWFrcVFNQldSV2MrSGJZUzNKYjlzZktTNWFGSW14a2duVkNpMH
BRVXJGWEwzNEt3dk5raG9SQUlkCklBRVpmRTUwT2p3WFdjMnluVW1XL1dMeVU4K0pQZDNWWDBML
0w1SW9oMGdud1c1NU4xK0dQQTZNRWZmSnltenAKVGE3U1NmbUJaTFIyemFaSGNGWDZxeThzMEhV
RHN0L2hTQ0E1WFo5bHp6U1B0WkwxUTVpanhVVUkxbjFsS1p4dwpXTndxaDhtTFBmME1xWE9sejd
MT1g2YmJsQ1B6cUcxRTdRdG5leUpXNk5oL2FmQkY5V2tnT1d3TWlBMlRFMHZ3CmkrMktzdCtWQ1
JkaDlRSVEzUzQvMlRTVHJhMlRCMk9WOWpYY2tYckRaeXJaTThxMzBQQjlnay8zR29pajA4N1EKO
WdleUJUNGRxWXZlT3NyWmNNMWxUT09Ci0tLS0tRU5EIENFUlRJRklDQVRFLS0tLS0K
```


```
    server: https://35.202.202.37
  name: gke_russ-kubernetes-cluster_us-central1-b_kube
contexts:
- context:
    cluster: gke_russ-kubernetes-cluster_us-central1-b_kube
    user: gke_russ-kubernetes-cluster_us-central1-b_kube
  name: gke_russ-kubernetes-cluster_us-central1-b_kube
current-context: gke_russ-kubernetes-cluster_us-central1-b_kube
kind: Config
preferences: {}
users:
- name: gke_russ-kubernetes-cluster_us-central1-b_kube
  user:
    auth-provider:
      config:
        cmd-args: config config-helper --format=json
        cmd-path: /usr/local/Caskroom/google-cloud-sdk/latest/google-cloud-
sdk/bin/gcloud
        expiry-key: '{.credential.token_expiry}'
        token-key: '{.credential.access_token}'
      name: gcp
```

As you can see, there is a certificate store in the `certificate-authority-data` section. This certificate is used to authenticate your cluster, meaning that whenever you run a command such as the following, it will return the list of nodes as expected:

```
$ kubectl get nodes
```

The nodes will appear as follows:

```
1. russ (bash)
russ in ~
⚡ kubectl get nodes
NAME                                     STATUS    ROLES     AGE       VERSION
gke-kube-default-pool-81825d4b-34ml      Ready     <none>    10m       v1.7.8-gke.0
gke-kube-default-pool-81825d4b-bltl      Ready     <none>    10m       v1.7.8-gke.0
gke-kube-default-pool-81825d4b-j66l      Ready     <none>    11m       v1.7.8-gke.0
russ in ~
⚡
```

Now, open your `~/.kube/config` file and remove the certificate from the `certificate-authority-data` section. This will basically create an invalid certificate, meaning that when you run the following command, you will get an error:

```
$ kubectl get nodes
```

The error will appear as follows:

```
1. russ (bash)
russ in ~
⚡ kubectl get nodes
Unable to connect to the server: x509: certificate signed by unknown authority
russ in ~
⚡
```

So, unless you have a copy of the correct certificate, you cannot connect to the cluster. Don't worry, you can still access your certificate by running the following command:

```
$ gcloud container clusters get-credentials kube
```

You will see the following:

```
1. russ (bash)
⚡ gcloud container clusters get-credentials kube
Fetching cluster endpoint and auth data.
kubeconfig entry generated for kube.
russ in ~
⚡
```

This command will connect to your Google Cloud account, download the details, and update your `~/.kube/config` file with the certificate. You can test the freshly downloaded credentials by running:

```
$ kubectl cluster-info
```

This will return details on all of your endpoints:

```
1. russ (bash)
⚡ kubectl cluster-info
Kubernetes master is running at https://35.202.202.37
GLBCDefaultBackend is running at https://35.202.202.37/api/v1/namespaces/kube-system/services/defaul
t-http-backend/proxy
Heapster is running at https://35.202.202.37/api/v1/namespaces/kube-system/services/heapster/proxy
KubeDNS is running at https://35.202.202.37/api/v1/namespaces/kube-system/services/kube-dns/proxy
kubernetes-dashboard is running at https://35.202.202.37/api/v1/namespaces/kube-system/services/kube
rnetes-dashboard/proxy

To further debug and diagnose cluster problems, use 'kubectl cluster-info dump'.
russ in ~
⚡
```

You may notice that the last URL in the list is for the Kubernetes dashboard. How is that secured?

Let's try entering the URL into a browser and see. I entered `https://35.202.202.37/api/v1/namespaces/kube-system/services/kubernetes-dashboard/proxy` (that URL will not be accessible by the time you read this) into my browser, hit return and was instantly greeted by a certificate warning; after accepting the certificates I was shown the following message:

```
User "system:anonymous" cannot get services/proxy in the namespace "kube-
system".: "No policy matched.\nUnknown user \"system:anonymous\""
```

This is great, as it is exactly what we want to see—we do not want unauthenticated users to be able to directly access our dashboard. But, how do we access it? We do not have a username and password, only a certificate—even if we did have a username and password, where would we enter them, given that we were never prompted for any authentication?

Kubernetes has a built-in proxy server. When launched, the proxy server makes a connection to your Kubernetes cluster using the certificate. Once connected, all traffic that is passed through the proxy is authenticated and you will be able to use the services. To start the proxy we simply need to run the following command:

```
$ kubectl proxy
```

You will see the proxy start as follows:

```
1. russ (kubectl)
⚡ kubectl proxy
Starting to serve on 127.0.0.1:8001
```

This will start the proxy process in the foreground. As you can see from the preceding Terminal output, the proxy is listening on your local machine on port `8001`. All we need to do is replace the public part of the URL and put that into our browser. So in my case, I update the following:

```
https://35.202.202.37/api/v1/namespaces/kube-system/services/kubernetes
-dashboard/proxy
```

I change it instead to read as follows:

```
http://127.0.0.1:8001/api/v1/namespaces/kube-system/services/kubernetes
-dashboard/proxy
```

This will take you straight to the dashboard:

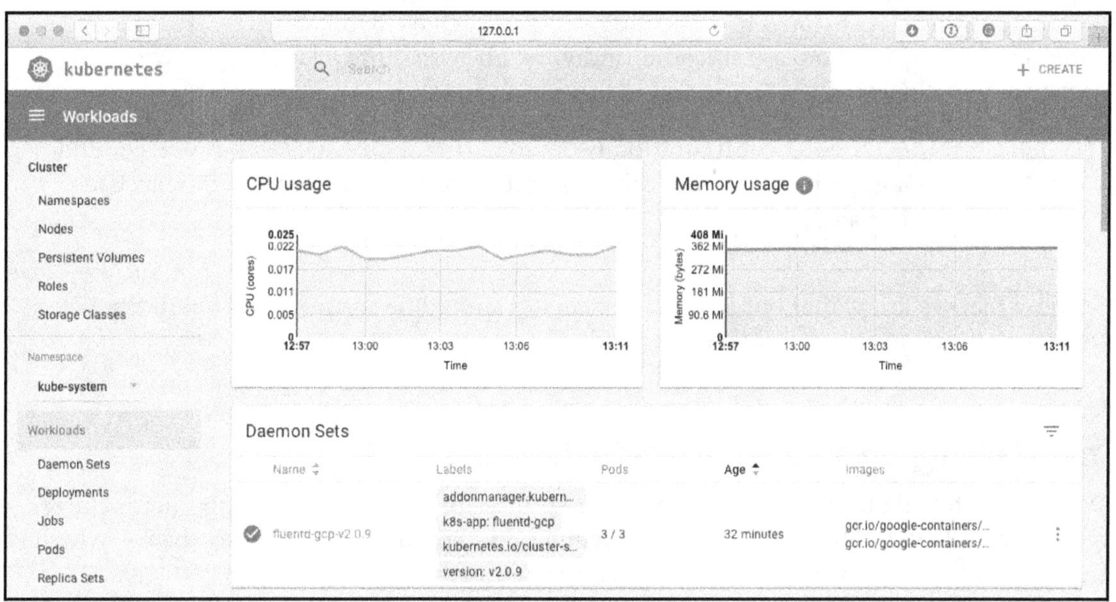

So far, we have demonstrated that Kubernetes on Google Cloud is configured securely. Microsoft Azure clusters work in a similar way—for example, we run the following command to update our local credentials once the cluster had been deployed:

```
$ az aks get-credentials --resource-group KubeResourceGroup --name
AzureKubeCluster
```

When deploying using `kubeadm` and `kube-aws`, certificates are generated and copied to our configuration file.

So, what we have learnt so far is that by default Kubernetes enforces certificate-based authentication to secure your installation, meaning that you would have to go to quite a lot of effort to misconfigure your installation to the point where your installation is exposed to the world. There is, however, one exception to this. It has nothing to do with your installation; it is more about how you manage your `kubectl` configuration file.

Never publish it anywhere (that is, check it into GitHub, for example, or share with colleagues). If it falls into the wrong hands then not only does someone have a copy of your certificate, they also have the rest of your cluster information, meaning that all they have to do is drop it in place on their local machine and they are free to then start launching applications. Additionally, as most cloud-based Kubernetes installations have access to your cloud providers to launch supporting services such as load balancers, storage, and potentially additional nodes, you could find yourself with quite a large bill as well as a compromised cluster.

The `kubectl` configuration I shared earlier in this section has been edited making it invalid—also the cluster it is configured to connect to has been terminated.

So, now that we know that our Kubernetes cluster should be secure, what about the serverless function services we have looked at?

Securing serverless services

We have installed and connected each of our services on both our local Kubernetes cluster and the cloud. So far, though, we haven't really had to think about securing them—which is the question we raised at the end of the last chapter.

The following sections will discuss how secure each tool is in its default configuration and what potential risks this configuration exposes you to. I won't be going into much detail about how to secure each tool, though where appropriate I will provide links to documentation.

OpenFaaS

Let's start by looking at OpenFaaS. I still have my Google Cloud cluster running, so I will deploy OpenFaaS there using the following command from within the `faas-netes` folder I cloned in the previous chapter:

```
$ kubectl apply -f ./faas.yml,monitoring.yml
```

As you can see, this time I have used just `kubectl` rather than `helm`. We can check the services deployed by running:

```
$ kubectl get services
```

This will return the following:

```
1. faas-netes (bash)
russ in ~/faas-netes on master*
⚡ kubectl apply -f ./faas.yml,monitoring.yml
service "faas-netesd" created
serviceaccount "faas-controller" created
deployment "faas-netesd" created
service "gateway" created
deployment "gateway" created
service "prometheus" created
deployment "prometheus" created
service "alertmanager" created
deployment "alertmanager" created
russ in ~/faas-netes on master*
⚡ kubectl get services
NAME           TYPE        CLUSTER-IP      EXTERNAL-IP   PORT(S)          AGE
alertmanager   NodePort    10.63.251.253   <none>        9093:31113/TCP   4s
faas-netesd    NodePort    10.63.253.76    <none>        8080:31111/TCP   6s
gateway        NodePort    10.63.254.103   <none>        8080:31112/TCP   5s
kubernetes     ClusterIP   10.63.240.1     <none>        443/TCP          2h
prometheus     NodePort    10.63.240.11    <none>        9090:31119/TCP   4s
russ in ~/faas-netes on master*
⚡
```

The one thing to notice is that by default OpenFaaS uses the `NodePort` rather than load balancer to expose the gateway service. No problem, you may be thinking to yourself; we can just use the following commands to find out the deployment's name and expose it:

```
$ kubectl get deployments
```

Now we know that the deployment is called gateway, we can run:

```
$ kubectl expose deployment gateway --type=LoadBalancer --name=gateway-lb
```

After a minute or two, running the following command should give us the external IP address and port:

```
$ kubectl get services
```

The results will appear as follows:

```
1. faas-netes (bash)
russ in ~/faas-netes on master*
⚡ kubectl get services
NAME           TYPE          CLUSTER-IP     EXTERNAL-IP    PORT(S)          AGE
alertmanager   NodePort      10.63.251.253  <none>         9093:31113/TCP   7m
faas-netesd    NodePort      10.63.253.76   <none>         8080:31111/TCP   7m
gateway        NodePort      10.63.254.103  <none>         8080:31112/TCP   7m
gateway-lb     LoadBalancer  10.63.254.206  35.224.135.38  8080:30810/TCP   1m
kubernetes     ClusterIP     10.63.240.1    <none>         443/TCP          3h
prometheus     NodePort      10.63.240.11   <none>         9090:31119/TCP   7m
russ in ~/faas-netes on master*
⚡
```

Going to the external IP address and port `8080` in a browser—in my case `http://35.224.135.38:8080/ui/`—unfortunately takes us straight to the OpenFaaS UI, no authentication needed. The same goes for using the command-line interface. So, how can you secure your OpenFaaS installation?

There are instructions on the OpenFaaS GitHub repository for using proxy services such as Traefik and Kong.

Kong is an open source API gateway that adds functionality such as traffic control, logging, the transformation of data, analytics, and most importantly, authentication. For more information on the Kong Community Edition, see `https://konghq.com/kong-community-edition/`.

Traefik (pronounced Traffic) is a reverse HTTP proxy which has been designed to work from the ground up with container orchestration tools like Kubernetes. It not only provides load balancing but also supports basic HTTP authentication and SSL termination. To find out more about Traefik, see its website at `https://traefik.io/`.

Both of these tools can be configured to sit in front of your OpenFaaS installation and intercept requests, and when configured, present the end user with a login prompt. The other way you can secure your OpenFaaS installation is by locking it down to your IP address using the networking tools within your public cloud service. The downside of this is that, depending on how your application calls the functions, you may not be able to lock it down completely.

So OpenFaaS, if just deployed, will expose parts of your Kubernetes cluster, meaning that a third party could potentially gain access to your resources if you do not secure them. For more information on securing your OpenFaaS cluster, see the official documentation at `https://github.com/openfaas/faas/tree/master/guide`. Alternatively, you can use the openfaas-gke installation files by Stefan Prodan, which can be found at `https://github.com/stefanprodan/openfaas-gke/`. It is also possible to access your OpenFaaS installation using the `kubectl proxy` command; however, this may limit its usefulness.

There is one more potential security problem with using OpenFaaS, and if you are already a Docker user it should be one you are familiar with. As OpenFaaS uses Docker images and the Docker Hub as its primary delivery method, you need to be careful whenever you push an image, as the image could potentially contain password details, API credentials, custom code, and other information you may not want to access through a public container image repository—the solution to this would be to use a private repository or a private Docker registry.

Please do not see any of this as a negative; OpenFaaS is an excellent piece of software, and I am sure that over time, changes will be introduced by the community to ensure that the steps detailed previously will not be needed as part of the initial configuration for the Kubernetes-hosted version.

Kubeless

Next up, let's take a look at Kubeless. To deploy the latest version in my Google Cloud Kubernetes cluster, I ran the following commands:

```
$ export RELEASE=v0.3.0
$ kubectl create ns kubeless
$ kubectl create -f
https://github.com/kubeless/kubeless/releases/download/$RELEASE/kubeless-$R
ELEASE.yaml
```

Once deployed, I ran the following command to see what services had been exposed:

```
$ kubectl get services -n kubeless
```

As you can see from the following Terminal output, no services were publicly exposed:

```
1. russ (bash)
russ in ~
⚡ kubectl get services -n kubeless
NAME         TYPE        CLUSTER-IP      EXTERNAL-IP   PORT(S)              AGE
broker       ClusterIP   None            <none>        9092/TCP             3m
kafka        ClusterIP   10.63.240.236   <none>        9092/TCP             3m
zoo          ClusterIP   None            <none>        9092/TCP,3888/TCP    3m
zookeeper    ClusterIP   10.63.254.32    <none>        2181/TCP             3m
russ in ~
⚡
```

So far, so good. Let's quickly launch a test function and expose it. From within the `/Chapter04/hello-world/` folder, I ran the following command:

```
$ kubeless function deploy hello --from-file hello.py --handler
hello.handler --runtime python2.7 --trigger-http
```

This created the function as expected. Running the following commands confirms that the function is available and running:

```
$ kubectl get function
$ kubeless function ls
$ kubeless function call hello
```

Running the following command exposes the function to the world:

```
$ kubectl expose deployment hello --type=LoadBalancer --name=hello-lb
```

After a short time, I can see an IP address for the `hello-lb` service when it is running:

```
$ kubectl get services
```

So far, we haven't had to really do anything to lock our installation down, so how secure is it? The short answer to that question is very, but what makes the default installation of Kubeless more secure than the default installation of OpenFaaS?

On the face of it, both technologies are similar in architecture; their server components are deployed on our Kubernetes cluster and we interact with those components using a command-line interface from our local machine. For example, we used the following command for Kubeless:

```
$ kubeless function deploy hello --from-file hello.py --handler
hello.handler
--runtime python2.7 --trigger-http
```

In the previous chapter, we used the following command to launch our function using OpenFaaS:

```
$ export gw=http://$(minikube ip):31112
$ faas-cli deploy -f hello.yml --gateway $gw
```

As you may have already spotted, at no point during our Kubeless configuration or use did we have to provide it with any of the details of our Kubernetes cluster, unlike OpenFaaS, where we had to explicitly tell the command-line interface the IP address and port of our OpenFaaS installation.

Kubeless knows exactly where our cluster is, and more importantly, it is authenticating whenever it needs to access it. As Kubeless is a native Kubernetes framework, rather than installing itself on top of Kubernetes, it is integrating itself into our cluster and adding additional functionality—in this case, functions—and is using other Kubernetes technologies, such as `kubectl` and custom resource definitions, to inject our function's code into the runtime on-demand, meaning that everything is contained within our Kubernetes cluster and all interaction with it is secure.

This can be demonstrated by removing the certificate from the `~/.kube/config` file and then trying to list the functions. You should see the following error:

```
1. hello-world (bash)
russ in ~/Documents/Code/kubernetes-for-serverless-applications/chapter04/hello-world on master*
⚡ kubeless function ls
FATA[0000] Get https://35.202.202.37/apis/k8s.io/v1/namespaces/default/functions: x509: certificate signed by unknown authority
russ in ~/Documents/Code/kubernetes-for-serverless-applications/chapter04/hello-world on master*
⚡
```

All of this means that your Kubeless installation is secure by default.

Funktion

Funktion, like Kubeless, is secure by default, as it tightly integrates itself with your Kubernetes cluster and adds additional functionality, and its command-line interface piggybacks its calls on top of `kubectl`.

Apache OpenWhisk

Apache OpenWhisk, like OpenFaaS, installs itself on top of your Kubernetes cluster rather than fully integrating itself. However, as we covered in `Chapter 7`, *Apache OpenWhisk and Kubernetes*, the CLI needs to be configured to authenticate itself against the installation once the service is exposed to the public internet. In that chapter, we ran the following commands to expose the service and authenticate the client against the API host:

```
$ kubectl -n openwhisk expose service nginx --type=LoadBalancer --
name=front-end
$ wsk -i property set --auth
23bc46b1-71f6-4ed5-8c54-816aa4f8c502:123zO3xZCLrMN6v2BKK1dXYFpXlPkccOFqm12C
dAsMgRU4VrNZ9lyGVCGuMDGIwP --apihost https://35.188.204.73:443
```

So again, this service is secure by default, assuming that you do not publish or share the authentication key.

Fission

During the Fission installation, we have to set two environment variables:

```
$ helm install --namespace
fissionhttps://github.com/fission/fission/releases/download/0.4.0/fission-a
ll-0.4.0.tgz
$ export FISSION_URL=http://$(kubectl --namespace fission get svc
controller -o=jsonpath='{..ip}')
$ export FISSION_ROUTER=$(kubectl --namespace fission get svc router -
o=jsonpath='{..ip}')
$ fission env create --name nodejs --image fission/node-env
$ curl
https://raw.githubusercontent.com/fission/fission/master/examples/nodejs/he
llo.js > hello.js
$ fission function create --name hello --env nodejs --code hello.js
$ fission route create --method GET --url /hello --function hello
$ curl http://$FISSION_ROUTER/hello
```

There is one variable for the `FISSION_URL` and one for the `FISSION_ROUTER`. This would indicate that potentially not everything is secure. First of all, let's take a look at what we get when we access the `FISSION_URL`:

```
russ in ~
⚡ http $FISSION_URL
HTTP/1.1 200 OK
Content-Length: 47
Content-Type: application/json; charset=utf-8
Date: Thu, 28 Dec 2017 12:23:39 GMT

{
    "message": "Fission API",
    "version": "0.4.0"
}

russ in ~
⚡
```

As you can see, we get a response identifying the Fission API and the version number. Remove the certificates from the `~/.kube/config` file and run the following command:

```
$ fission function list
```

We can still interact with our Fission installation; this means that by default Fission has no authentication, and that when we use the recommended installation procedure, the API is exposed to the internet by default:

```
russ in ~
⚡ fission function list
NAME  UID                                  ENV
hello 324a4411-ebc9-11e7-b33d-42010a800121 nodejs
russ in ~
⚡
```

Work is on-going to ship Fission with a more secure default; you can follow its progress at the following GitHub issue: `https://github.com/fission/fission/issues/22/`.

Until then, it is recommend that you update the Helm chart to set the `serviceType` of `ClusterIP` for the controller service. As you can see from the following output, it is currently set to `LoadBalancer`:

```
russ in ~
⚡ kubectl get services --namespace fission
NAME             TYPE           CLUSTER-IP      EXTERNAL-IP      PORT(S)           AGE
buildermgr       ClusterIP      10.3.240.197    <none>           80/TCP            24m
controller       LoadBalancer   10.3.251.55     35.188.59.62     80:30398/TCP      24m
influxdb         ClusterIP      10.3.241.106    <none>           8086/TCP          24m
nats-streaming   LoadBalancer   10.3.246.176    35.193.6.230     4222:30587/TCP    24m
poolmgr          ClusterIP      10.3.249.68     <none>           80/TCP            24m
router           LoadBalancer   10.3.248.69     35.202.104.113   80:32690/TCP      24m
storagesvc       ClusterIP      10.3.252.62     <none>           80/TCP            24m
russ in ~
⚡
```

Once you have configured the service to use `ClusterIP`, you can configure port forwarding from your localhost to the controller using the `kubectl` inbuilt proxy. The command to do this would look something like the following:

```
$ kubectl -n fission port-forward $(kubectl -n fission get pod -o name|grep
controller|cut -f2 -d'/') 8888
```

This would mean that your `FISSION_URL` would be something like `http://localhost:1234`, as opposed to an externally accessible URL with no authentication. The Fission developers are in the process of building this solution into Fission and it should become the default configuration in one of the early 2018 releases.

Conclusions

As you can see, we have a pretty mixed bag when it comes to securing our serverless installations—some of the solutions we have covered are secure by default, while others, such as the old default MongoDB configuration, need a little more work to secure them and make them production-ready. Before you permanently deploy any of the tools we have covered in this book, please ensure that you have reviewed exactly what each tool is exposing and how you can best lock it down.

Monitoring Kubernetes

Before we start to look at various ways we can monitor our Kubernetes cluster we should quickly talk about what we mean by monitoring when it comes to a tool with potentially a lot of moving parts.

Traditionally, monitoring servers has meant keeping a close eye on the availability of applications running on fixed servers. To do this, our monitoring tool would collate information on the CPU, RAM, and disk utilization, as well as which services were running, the number of processes, and also the availability of the services and the server itself.

We would set triggers at certain thresholds so that, for example, if there was an increase of CPU load, we could log in to the server and do some investigation before said CPU load starts to affect our application's performance.

As you can image, monitoring a Kubernetes cluster is a lot different to this. By design, the applications running with the cluster should be fault tolerant and also highly available—in fact, the functions we have been running in previous chapters sometimes only have a lifespan of the time it takes to execute the function.

This changes the way that we monitor our clusters, as we trust that a lot of the things we would traditionally be monitoring for will be handled by Kubernetes itself, rather than needing us to log in and take preventative actions.

With this in mind, we do not need to go too deep into the ins and outs of monitoring your Kubernetes clusters—that is probably a whole different book. Instead, we are going to take a quick look at some of the options for reviewing service metrics for our Kubernetes clusters using first the dashboard and then Google Cloud and Microsoft Azure, as these both natively support Kubernetes clusters.

The dashboard

The Kubernetes dashboard is not just a great resource for managing your cluster; it also gives you a great visual overview of what you have running and how it is currently performing.

For example, selecting **All namespaces** in the **Namespaces** drop-down menu and then clicking on **Pods** in the **Workloads** section of the left-hand side menu will give you a list of all the running pods, along with a breakdown of what each pod is currently using CPU and RAM-wise:

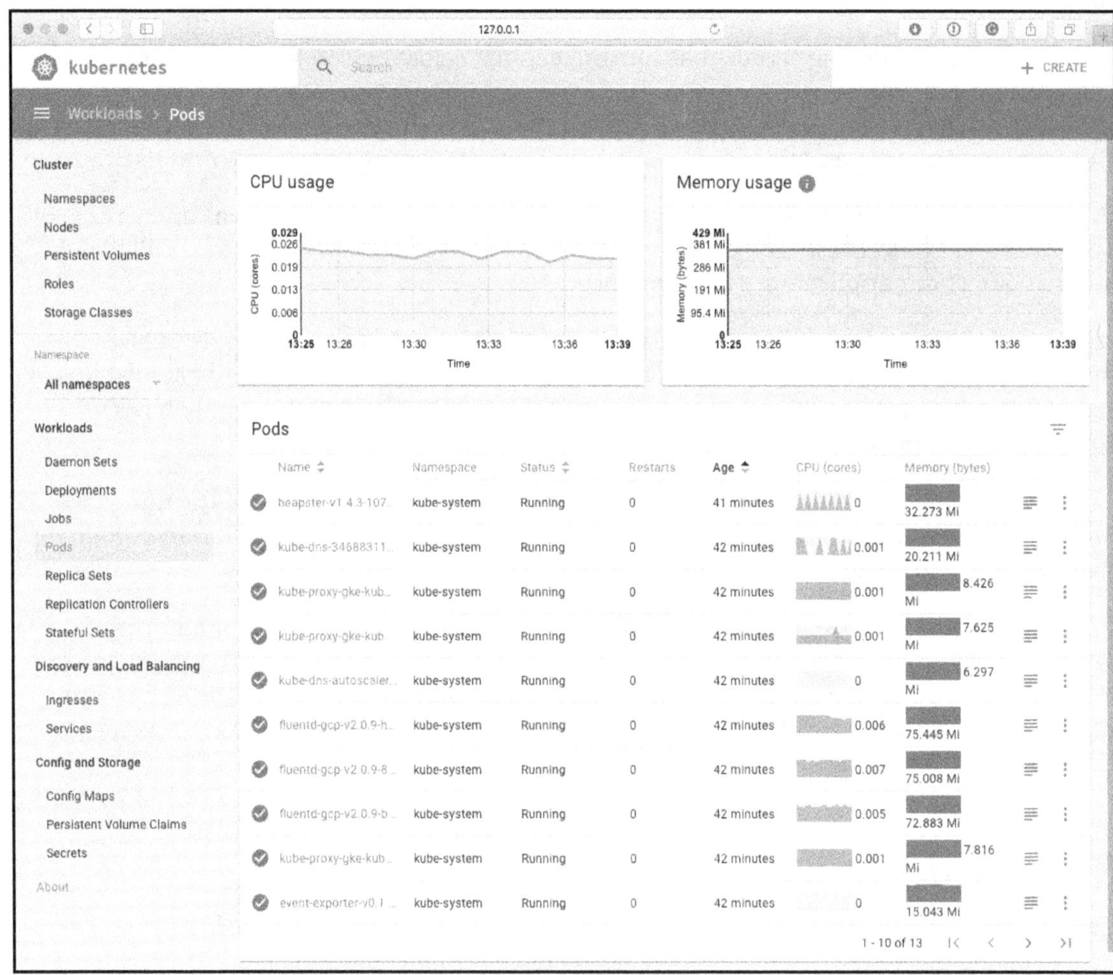

Clicking on a pod—in this case, the heapster one—will give you a more detailed breakdown of the overall resources being used by the containers that make up that pod:

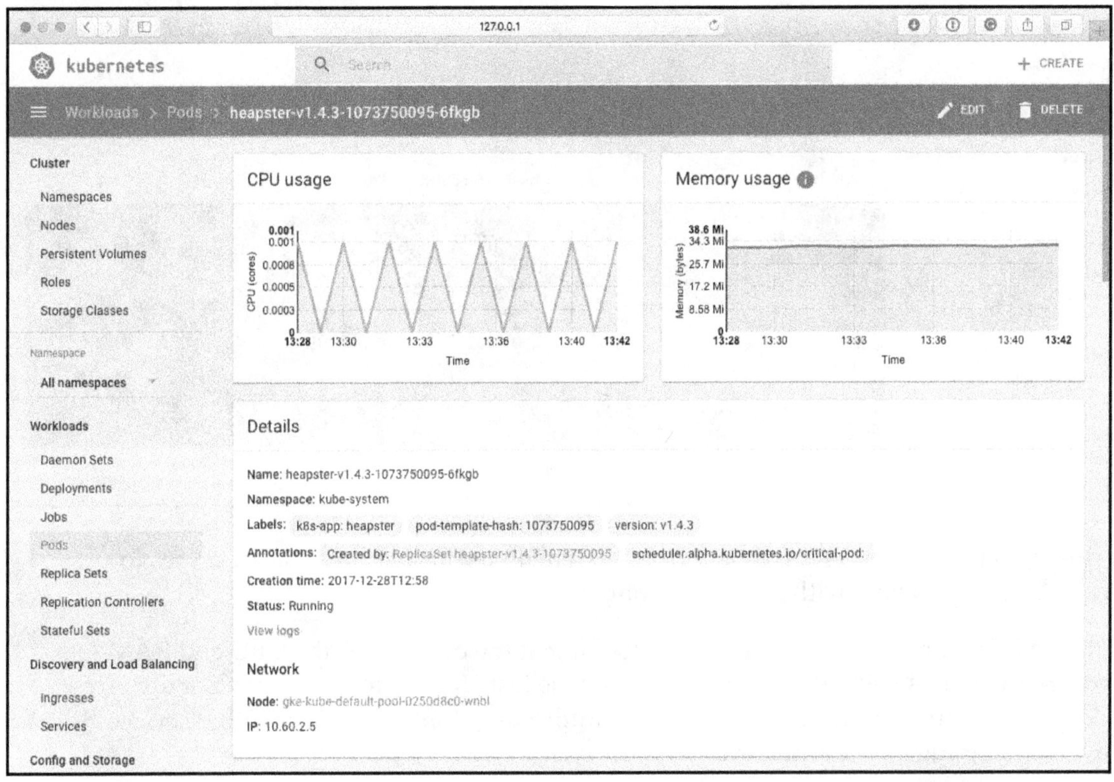

Scrolling down will show you the containers. In the case of heapster, there are three containers in the pod. From here, you can view the logs for each container in real time:

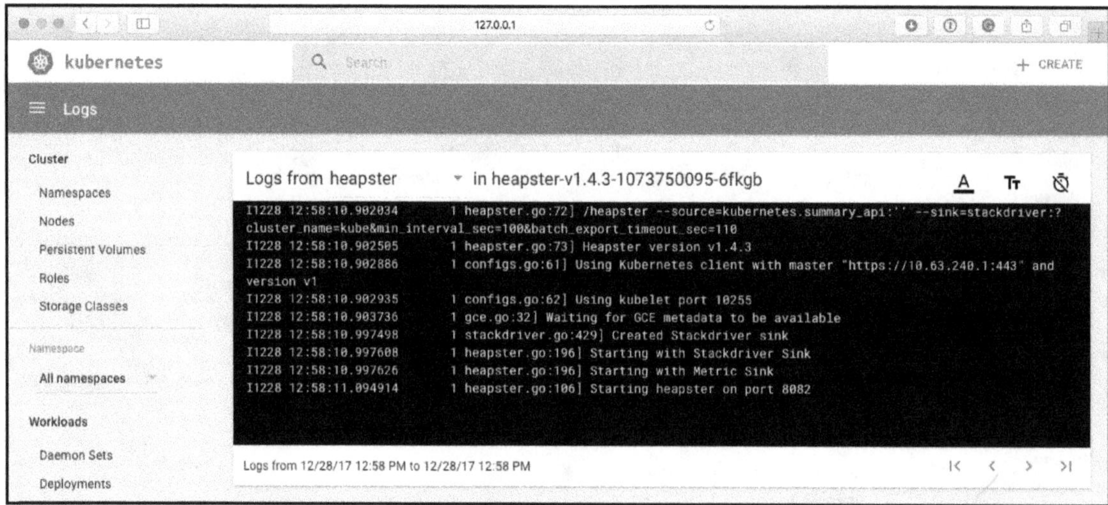

This is, as I am sure you can imagine, an extremely useful feature when it comes to debugging a problem with a running container.

However, you may have noticed when looking at the dashboard the CPU and RAM utilization that is being displayed is only for the last 15 minutes—you can not dig any deeper or go further back. Because of this, information on currently-running services is available through the dashboard.

This makes the dashboard perfect for logging in and getting a very quick overview of your cluster—and what's good is that the dashboard is included with most Kubernetes clusters out of the box, making it very convenient.

Google Cloud

Next up we have Google Cloud. On the face of it, the Kubernetes section of the Google Cloud Console appears pretty much like the Kubernetes dashboard:

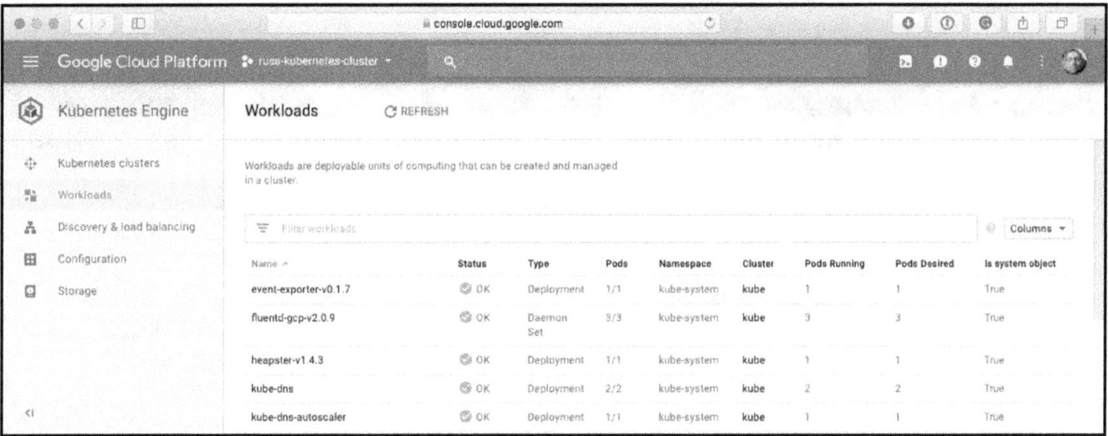

However, as you can see from the preceding screenshot, other than giving a status of **OK** it really doesn't tell you much about what is going on within your cluster. Instead, you need to use Stackdriver, which is accessible from the left-hand menu within the Google Cloud Console.

Google Stackdriver is a Google Cloud service which allows you to record metrics from several sources, including Google Cloud services, AWS, and also individual servers using an agent. The service is not free of charge; a detailed cost breakdown can be found at `https://cloud.google.com/stackdriver/pricing`. We will be using the free trial, but if you have already used Google Stackdriver, the following steps may incur cost.

When you first go to Stackdriver you will be asked several questions. Work through this process and at the end of it you should have a free trial up and collecting logs from your Kubernetes cluster. After a few minutes you should start to see information from your cluster starting to show in the metrics explorer. From here, you can start to build up dashboards such as the following one:

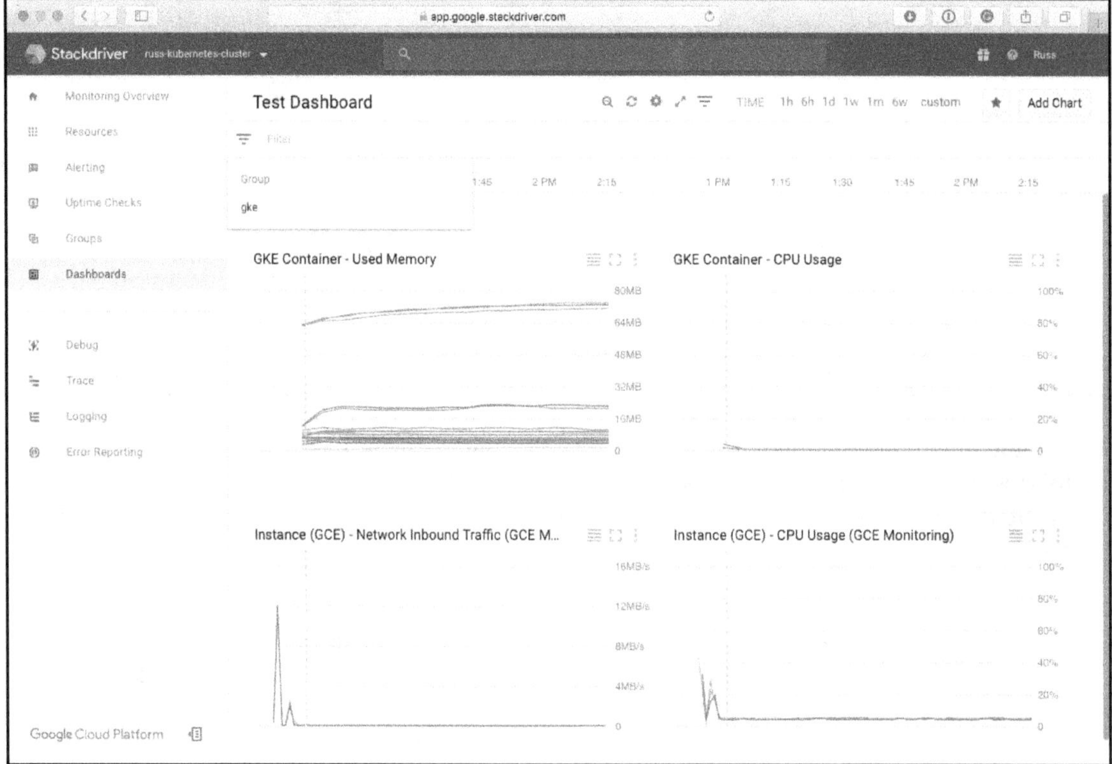

As you can see from the preceding screenshot, we have the option to view more than 15 minutes worth of data—in fact, the dashboard is showing over an hour's worth of data, which is how old the cluster is.

Not only does Stackdriver give you access to metrics about your cluster, you can also access the logs from both your Kubernetes cluster and the containers themselves:

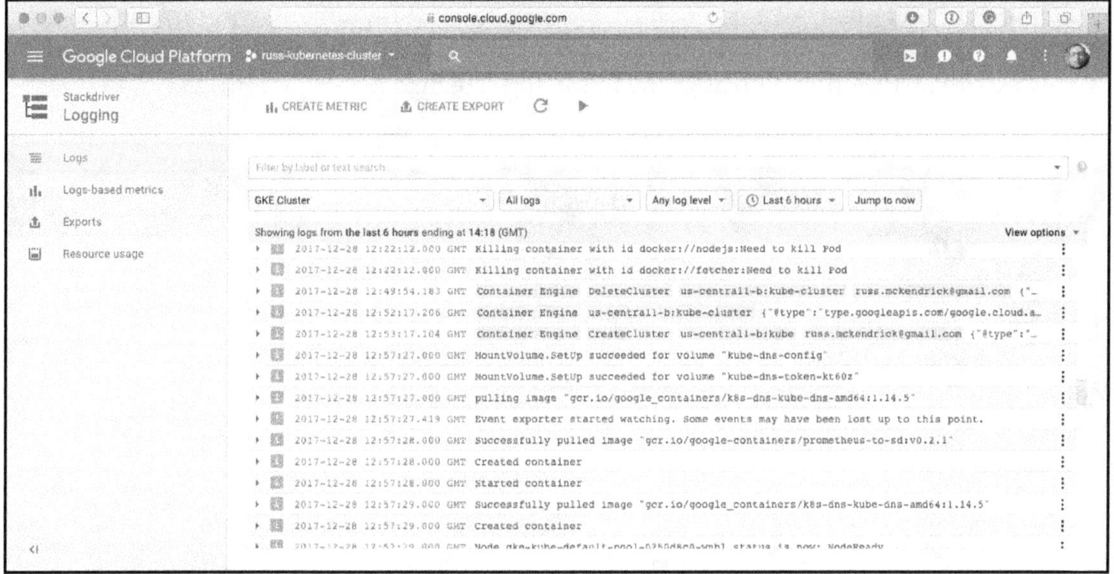

As the logs and metrics are being stored away from your cluster, historical information about your containers is also accessible. If you are running a function in a container which is only live for a few seconds, you will not only be able to see the RAM and CPU utilization for that container, you will also have access to the entire life of the container.

Other features of Stackdriver are daily, weekly, and monthly email reports about your overall usage, as well as the option to configure triggers for when metric thresholds are crossed or when events appear in log files—you can be notified about these via SMS, email, or even chat products such as Slack or Campfire.

Microsoft Azure

Compared to Google Cloud, Microsoft Azure's out-of-the-box insights into your Kubernetes cluster are not that great. You do not have views into what is going on within your cluster, and while there are metrics available they are only the for the host machines—for example, you can see the CPU utilization as in the following screenshot:

Along the same lines, you can launch the Kubernetes dashboard using the following command (making sure you replace the resource group and name with your own):

```
$ az aks browse --resource-group KubeResourceGroup --name AzureKubeCluster
```

Fear not though, there is the Container Monitoring solution; this is an agent-based system that you can deploy on your Kubernetes cluster, which then feeds back information to the Azure portal.

To deploy it, you need to search for the Container Monitoring solution by Microsoft in the **Azure Market**, from within your Azure portal. Clicking on the **Create** button will ask you to create a workspace; I chose to create my workspace in the same resource group and region as my Kubernetes cluster. Make sure that **Pin to dashboard** is ticked and click on **Deploy**.

This is where it gets a little complicated, as you need to get the **WORKSPACE ID** and **PRIMARY KEY**. These are buried quite deep inside a series of links. To get them, go to your dashboard and select your workspace—mine is labelled as **Containers(russ-monitor)**. From there, click on **OMS Workspace**, and then **Advanced settings**. You should see something like the following screenshot:

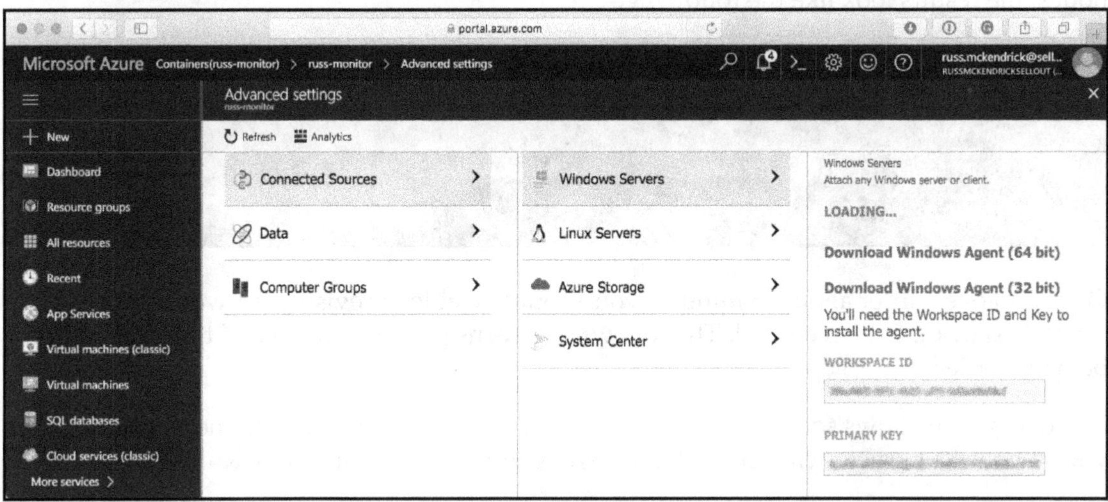

Make a note of the **WORKSPACE ID** and **PRIMARY KEY** (mine are blurred out in the preceding screenshot). In the `Chapter10` folder of the repository that accompanies this book there is a file called `oms-daemonset.yaml`; make a copy of it and update it so that the values in the following `env` section are updated with your actual **WORKSPACE ID** and **PRIMARY KEY**:

```
env:
  - name: WSID
    value: <WORKSPACE ID>
  - name: KEY
    value: <PRIMARY KEY>
```

Once you have updated the file, run the following command from the same folder where you saved the updated copy of the `oms-daemonset.yaml` file to deploy the `daemonset` into your cluster:

```
$ kubectl create -f oms-daemonset.yaml
```

Once deployed, you should be able to run the following command to confirm that everything is working as expected:

```
$ kubectl get daemonset
```

You should see one `daemonset` for each node within your cluster. As my cluster has three nodes, the results look like the following:

```
1. Desktop (bash)
⚡ kubectl create -f oms-daemonset.yaml
daemonset "omsagent" created
russ in ~/Desktop
⚡ kubectl get daemonset
NAME       DESIRED   CURRENT   READY     UP-TO-DATE   AVAILABLE   NODE SELECTOR                 AGE
omsagent   3         3         3         3            3           beta.kubernetes.io/os=linux   1m
russ in ~/Desktop
⚡
```

Once deployed, after about 15 minutes you should be able to revisit your workspace and see stats starting to be recorded. The following screens give you an idea of the information being recorded.

The first screen shows some basic information about the number of containers running within your Kubernetes cluster, with any errors and events recorded by Kubernetes:

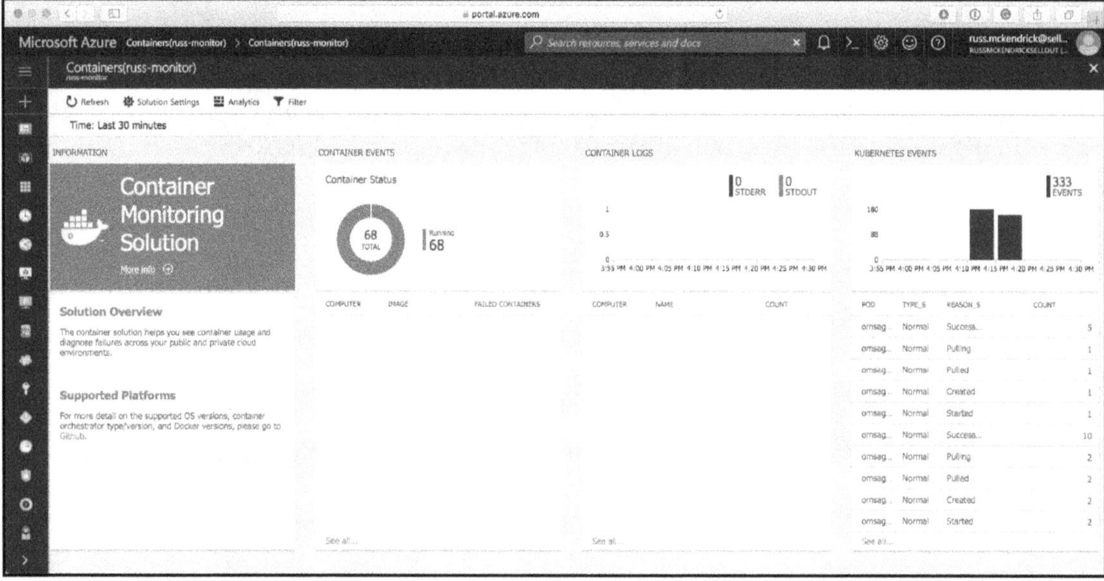

Scrolling to the right will show you more details about your cluster:

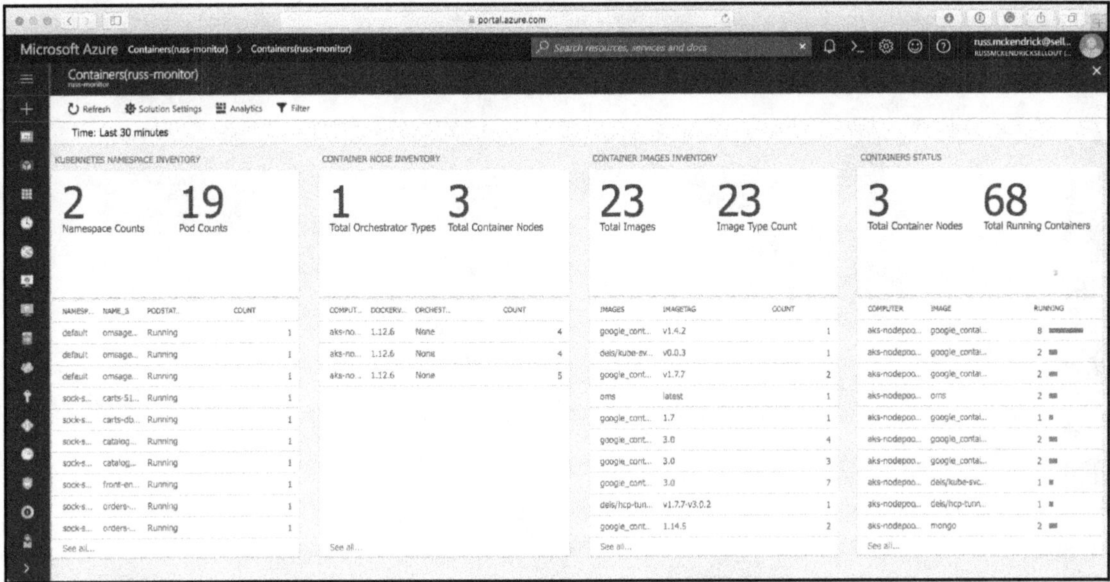

As you can see, we have information pods running in the two namespaces my cluster has, and then we have nodes within the cluster. Following that, we have all of the images that have been downloaded, and details of all of the running containers.

Scrolling right again will show you more information:

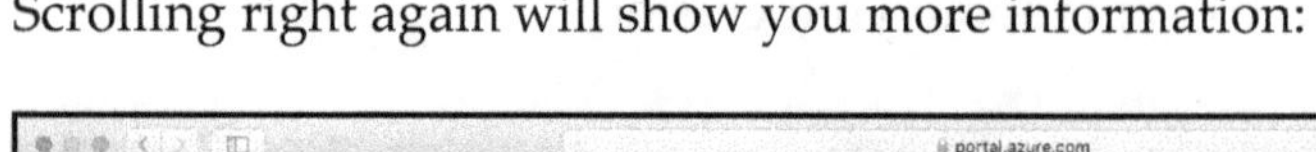

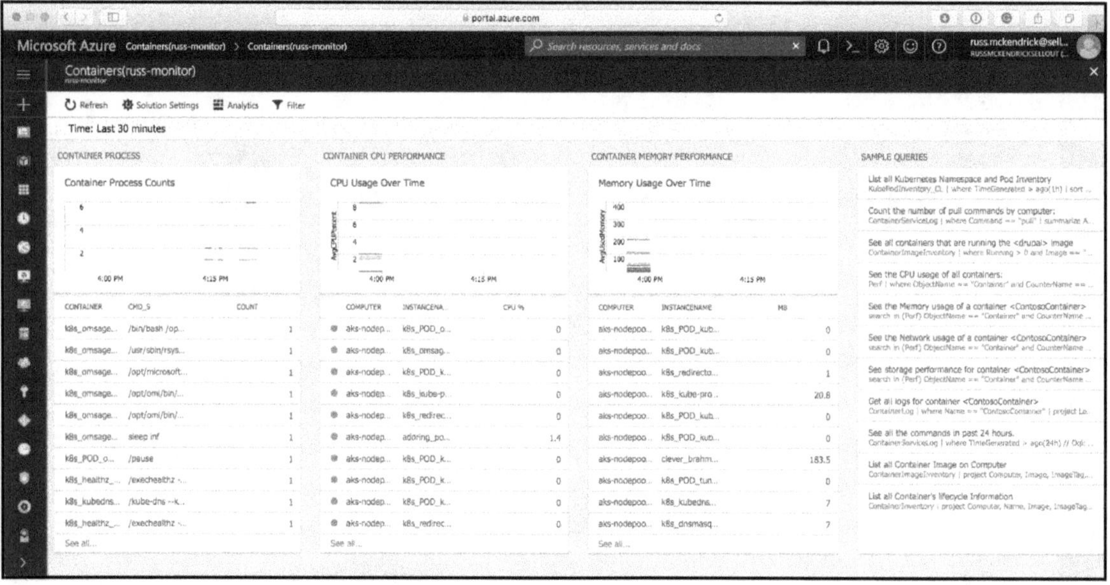

Here we can see the number of processes across all of our containers, the CPU and Memory performance over our chosen time frame, and finally, some example queries we can run on the data we are collecting. Clicking on the link will execute the sample queries, and from there, you will have the option of saving the results as a Microsoft Excel file or exporting the data to Microsoft's Power BI service.

Power BI is a business analytics service provided by Microsoft. It allows you to create dashboards and run some quite complex calculations on your datasets—one of which is the metric data being exported from your Kubernetes cluster into your Microsoft Azure workspace.

As you can see, we have gone from having very little information to being overwhelmed with stats and logs from our cluster. For more information on the Container Monitoring solution from Microsoft, see its product page at `https://docs.microsoft.com/en-us/azure/log-analytics/log-analytics-containers/`.

Summary

In this chapter, we have discussed how our Kubernetes cluster is secured and how to secure the default configuration for each of the serverless tools we have looked at in the previous chapters. We have looked at three ways we can get real-time stats from our Kubernetes clusters using the Kubernetes dashboard and also looked at the monitoring tools provided by Google Cloud and Microsoft Azure for storing and querying metrics from your clusters.

In the next chapter, which is also the final chapter, we are going to be taking a look at how to best run your serverless workloads on Kubernetes, based on everything we have learnt in the previous chapters.

11
Running Serverless Workloads

In this, our final chapter, we are going to talk about a few of the different scenarios where you would want to host your own serverless workloads, and what to consider when choosing a tool. We are going to start by discussing the advantages and disadvantages of working with a technology that is still in its infancy and is still going through quite a lot of active development.

Evolving software and platforms

Pretty much all of the technology we have looked at in this book is currently in development. Some of the projects, as we already discussed, are in the very early stages of development, while others are more mature. Let's start by discussing Kubernetes itself.

Kubernetes

Kubernetes is very much in active development, though it is quite far into its development cycle. I started writing this book at the beginning of September 2017 and now, as I write the final chapter, it is the end of December 2017.

During this period there have been a total of 48 releases, as you can see from the following screenshot:

Releases		
02/09/2017: v1.8.0-beta.0	01/10/2017: v1.5.9-beta.0	20/11/2017: v1.8.5-beta.0
02/09/2017: v1.9.0-aplhpa.0	05/10/2017: v1.7.8	20/11/2017: v1.9.0-beta.0
13/09/2017: v1.8.0-beta.1	05/10/2017: v1.7.9-beta.0	20/11/2017: v1.10.0-alpha.0
13/09/2017: v1.6.10	12/10/2017: v1.8.1	22/11/2017: v1.6.13
13/09/2017: v1.6.11-beta.0	19/10/2017: v1.7.9	22/11/2017: v1.6.14-beta.0
14/09/2017: v1.7.6	19/10/2017: v1.7.10-beta.0	25/11/2017: v1.7.11
14/09/2017: v1.7.7-beta.0	24/10/2017: v1.8.2	25/11/2017: v1.7.12-beta.0
23/09/2017: v1.8.0-rc.1	24/10/2017: v1.8.3-beta.0	01/12/2017: v1.9.0-beta.1
23/09/2017: v1.9.0-alpha.1	25/10/2017: v1.6.12	07/12/2017: v1.8.5

These updates cover everything from the maintenance releases v1.5, v1.6, and v1.7; the actual releases of v.1.8 and v1.9; and the subsequent maintenance releases all the way to the first alpha versions of v1.10. With such an active release cycle, how easy is it to keep on top of the releases?

Well, given the frequency of releases, not as bad as you may think, though it can get complicated. As you can see from the table, each Kubernetes release has a major version, a minor version, and a patch version. For example, the current releases at the time of writing are:

- v1.6.13 (older release)
- v1.7.11 (older release)

- v1.8.6 (current release)
- v1.9.0 (development release)

So, as of *December 12, 2017*, there are four minor versions of the same major release being actively worked on and patched. Kubernetes itself supports three minor versions at a time; namely the current release (v1.8) and two older releases (v1.6 and v1.7). What this means is:

- A master node running the current release is expected to work with nodes that are running the two previous versions. That is, you can have a v1.8 master and a mixture of v1.7 and v1.6 nodes within your cluster.
- A master node running the current release is expected to work with a client, like kubectl, that is one version behind and one version ahead of the current release; this means that we can interact our v1.8 master with the v1.9 and v1.10 client.
- It is recommended that whichever version you are running, you always run the latest patch version, as the patches often contain critical bug and security fixes.

What this support model means is that features that may be present in version v1.6.13 could potentially be unavailable in version v1.9.0. With a new minor release roughly every two months, you have around four months to plan your updates, and then two months to action them—this may mean reviewing and possibly updating existing applications that are deployed in your cluster to make sure that they are not using any functionality that is being phased out of recent releases.

This is where reading the release notes becomes invaluable, as new minor versions always have a *Before Upgrading* section that confirms exactly what potential cluster-breaking changes there have been since the previous release. For example, the current development version is v1.9.0. I know that it will become the current release in about two months, so to prepare for that I need to work my cluster and make sure that I take into account all of the changes detailed at `https://github.com/kubernetes/kubernetes/blob/master/CHANGELOG-1.9.md#before-upgrading`.

Features are only added, deprecated, and removed in minor versions. Patch releases are just that, patches to existing functionality. I also recommend reading through *Kubernetes Depreciation Policy*, which explains the rules for removing/disabling functionality. The policy can be found at `https://kubernetes.io/docs/reference/deprecation-policy/`.

You can list the versions of Kubernetes that can be deployed using Minikube by running the following command:

```
$ minikube get-k8s-versions
```

The supported versions of Kubernetes releases for Google Cloud can be found at `https://cloud.google.com/kubernetes-engine/supported-versions`. Microsoft Azure supports all of the current releases; an example of this support can be found at the AKS introductory blog post at `https://azure.microsoft.com/en-us/blog/introducing-azure-container-service-aks-managed-kubernetes-and-azure-container-registry-geo-replication/`, where the example shows a live upgrade of v1.7.7 to v1.8.1.

Serverless tools

So how does the on-going development cycle of Kubernetes affect the development of the serverless tools we have been looking at, and how does that affect their own development cycles?

To start, let's look at the type of tool. In the last chapter, when looking at security, we found out that there are basically two types of tool. The first adds and extends functionality within Kubernetes, such as Kubeless and Funktion. The second type of tool consumes Kubernetes services by basically sitting on top of Kubernetes and making API calls, such as Apache OpenWhisk, Fission, and OpenFaaS.

The tools that are closely coupled with Kubernetes will always have to not only plan their releases in line with Kubernetes, but also have to keep a very close eye on the path that Kubernetes is taking, as decisions made by the Kubernetes special interest groups will directly affect their own roadmaps.

For example, in September 2017, Kubeless released an update to change from using **ThirdPartyResources** (**TPR**) to **CustomResourceDefinitions** (**CRD**), as TPR was deprecated as of Kubernetes v.1.7 and removed in v1.8.

This does mean that your choice of tool will require a little research. The questions you should be asking yourself are:

- Does the tool I am evaluating work with the version of Kubernetes I will be deploying in my cluster? If in doubt, you can check by doing a few test installations with Minikube.
- Are there any open issues that could affect my deployment? Before you commit to the tool, I recommend looking at any open issues on the tools GitHub project page; do any of the problems sound familiar, and could they be applicable to your installation?

- Is the tool I am looking at deploying in active development, and how frequent are new releases? Does there appear to be a community supporting the tool? Review the releases page on GitHub; how frequent are releases, and does there appear to be any service-breaking releases?
- How secure is the tool? Based on the previous chapter, how secure is the default configuration, and how will making it secure affect how you use the tool?

A collection of useful links that should help you answer the previous questions can be found as follows.

Kubeless

The useful links for Kubeless are as follows:

- **Project homepage:** `http://kubeless.io/`
- **Project License:** `https://github.com/kubeless/kubeless/blob/master/LICENSE`
- **Issues:** `https://github.com/kubeless/kubeless/issues`
- **Releases:** `https://github.com/kubeless/kubeless/releases`
- **Contributing guidelines:** `https://github.com/kubeless/kubeless/blob/master/CONTRIBUTING.md`
- **Docs:** `https://github.com/kubeless/kubeless/tree/master/docs`

Apache OpenWhisk

The useful links for OpenWhisk are as follows:

- **Project homepage:** `https://openwhisk.apache.org`
- **Project License:** `https://github.com/apache/incubator-openwhisk/blob/master/LICENSE.txt`
- **Issues:** `https://github.com/apache/incubator-openwhisk/issues`
- **Contributing guidelines:** `https://github.com/apache/incubator-openwhisk/blob/master/CONTRIBUTING.md`
- **Docs:** `https://cwiki.apache.org/confluence/display/OPENWHISK/OpenWhisk+Project+Wiki`

Fission

The useful links for Fission are as follows:

- **Project homepage:** `http://fission.io/`
- **Project License:** `https://github.com/fission/fission/blob/master/LICENSE`
- **Issues:** `https://github.com/fission/fission/issues`
- **Releases:** `https://github.com/fission/fission/releases`
- **Contributing guidelines:** `https://github.com/fission/fission/blob/master/CONTRIBUTING.md`
- **Docs:** `https://github.com/fission/fission/tree/master/Documentation`

OpenFaaS

The useful links for OpenFaaS are as follows:

- **Project homepage:** `https://www.openfaas.com`
- **Project License:** `https://github.com/openfaas/faas/blob/master/LICENSE`
- **Issues:** `https://github.com/openfaas/faas/issues`
- **Releases:** `https://github.com/openfaas/faas/releases`
- **Contributing guidelines:** `https://github.com/openfaas/faas/blob/master/CONTRIBUTING.md`
- **Docs:** `https://github.com/openfaas/faas/tree/master/docs`

Funktion

The useful links for Funktion are as follows:

Since this book was first started, Funktion has been sandboxed. The source code remains available for anyone to use, or fork their own version to continue development. The authors recommend two alternatives: either Kubeless or Apache OpenWhisk.

- **Project homepage:** `https://funktion.fabric8.io`
- **Project License:** `https://github.com/funktionio/funktion/blob/master/LICENSE.md`

- **Issues:** `https://github.com/funktionio/funktion/issues`
- **Releases:** `https://github.com/funktionio/funktion/releases`
- **Contributing guidelines:** `https://cwiki.apache.org/confluence/display/OPENWHISK/OpenWhisk+Project+Wiki`
- **Docs:** `https://funktion.fabric8.io/docs/`

Future developments

Three months is a long time in technology. There have been a few changes to the Kubernetes ecosystem since I first started writing this book; the most notable two are currently in private beta and are expected to open up for public use in early 2018.

The first is an alternative to running Kubernetes locally using Minikube, which came from an unexpected source: Docker. During DockerCon Europe 2017, it was announced that Docker will be supporting Kubernetes alongside Docker swarm in both the Community and Enterprise Editions of Docker for macOS and Docker for Windows.

You can find out more information on this upcoming release at `https://www.docker.com/kubernetes`, or watch Elton Stoneman's introduction video for the service at `https://www.youtube.com/watch?v=jWupQjdjLN0`.

The second service, which came as no surprise, is the introduction of the **Amazon Elastic Container Service for Kubernetes** service, or **Amazon EKS** for short. Amazon announced this at their yearly re:Invent conference, and as you would expect, it has deep levels of integration with other AWS services such as Amazon VPC, IAM, Elastic Load Balancing, and AWS CloudTrail, to name a few—you can find out more about the service, which is currently in private beta, at `https://aws.amazon.com/eks/`, as well as watching the announcement at `https://www.youtube.com/watch?v=gUFtUU7qvSQ`.

Why Functions as a Service on Kubernetes

In the first few chapters, we spoke about serverless functions and Kubernetes and the advantages of using them:

- **Kubernetes**: the biggest use case for using Kubernetes to deploy your application is that it allows you to develop once and then deploy in a consistent way across multiple platforms, be it self-hosted bare-metal servers, or private clouds running virtual machines on VMWare, OpenStack, KVM, Hyper-V, and more. The same goes for public cloud providers such as Google Cloud, Microsoft Azure, and now AWS, who all offer their own native-managed Kubernetes services all the way through to your local machine running Minikube or the soon-to-be-released versions of Docker for macOS or Docker for Windows.
- **Serverless**: Deploying all or parts of your application as serverless functions can help it scale with ease. All of a sudden, you do not need to worry about whether your virtual machine or container has enough resources to be able to handle a flood of incoming connections, or how those connections are routed to your application. Each request will be sent to an individual or cluster of containers managed where your request will be processed—once complete, that container will either be terminated or recycled for the next request.
- **Kubernetes plus serverless**: As already mentioned, the serverless portions of your application can easily scale—this can combine with Kubernetes, where additional nodes can quickly be spun up and added to your cluster both manually and via scripts. Once the additional resource is part of the cluster, your serverless functions will automatically be scheduled on the new resource, with the need for you make any further changes either to your application routing or code.

Now, couple this with the knowledge that you can pretty much deploy your application in any of the major public cloud providers, and you will get a consistent experience, rather than having to adapt your code to have to work with the provider's own Functions as a Service offerings, such as the ones we discussed in `Chapter 1`, *The Serverless Landscape*.

Your choice of serverless tool will more than likely come down to two factors, the first being what language your application is written in—for example, is your application written in Python, Node.js, PHP, Java, .NET, or Go?

The second factor will be personal preference. You have probably already formed an opinion, while working through the chapters of this book, about which of the tools is best for you, and which will fit in with both your development workflows and your own way of working. Issues such as security will always be a contributing factor, but as discussed in the previous chapter, there are ways of overcoming these.

Fixed points

So far we have been discussing lots of potentially small moving parts. What about big fixed points such as databases and file storage? How do they fit in with FaaS services on Kubernetes?

Databases

There is still debate going on as to whether you should be running your database services in containers—this has pretty much been around since Docker first started to get traction, and unfortunately, there is no simple yes or no answer.

Whenever I approach a project, I tend to look at the usage and what impact the database has on the overall performance of the application itself, and then work back from there.

Kubernetes allows you to run a PetSet; think back to the pet versus cattle analogy from the start of the book. In Kubernetes v1.5, as the feature left alpha, it became known as a StatefulSet. The feature came out of beta in Kubernetes v1.9.

See the following GitHub issue for a discussion about the change of name from PetSet to StatefulSet `https://github.com/kubernetes/kubernetes/issues/27430`.

A StatefulSet allows you to run what would traditionally be quite difficult to run in a clustered service such as Kubernetes. Using a combination of pods and persistent storage, it basically creates a fixed point within your Kubernetes cluster which:

- Has a stable unique network identifier that will persist should the StatefulSet need to move between hosts or the pod need restarting because of error
- Has stable persistent storage that is dedicated to the StatefulSet, useful for storing databases, configuration, and more

- Has ordered and graceful deployment and scaling, deletion and termination, and automated rolling updates, all of which means you have control over the software that needs to be controlled when it is started, moved, or shut down

All of these mean that it is more than possible to host your databases within your Kubernetes cluster. Doing so means that you will be able to connect to your database within the same namespaces, but this solution may not be suitable for all scenarios.

For example, if you have a large dataset, or your database needs to be accessible outside of your Kubernetes cluster by other applications, then you may be better off using the native database services offered by your public cloud provider. These services include:

- **Amazon Relational Database Service** (**Amazon RDS**): This service supports MySQL, PostgreSQL, MariaDB, Oracle, and Microsoft SQL. For more details, see `https://aws.amazon.com/rds/`.
- **Microsoft Azure Database**: There are Microsoft SQL, MySQL, and PostgreSQL options; see `https://azure.microsoft.com/en-gb/services/sql-database/`, `https://azure.microsoft.com/en-gb/services/mysql/`, and `https://azure.microsoft.com/en-gb/services/postgresql/` for further details.
- **Google Cloud SQL**: This supports MySQL and PostgreSQL. See the following link for more information: `https://cloud.google.com/sql/`.

While using these services exposes you to a little vendor lock-in as you will have large parts of your data outside of your Kubernetes cluster, all three offer open source database engines, which from an application point of view means they are still consuming the same database service, be it hosted within your cluster or as one of your public cloud providers services.

For more information about StatefulSets, I would recommend reading through the following two examples on the Kubernetes website:

- `https://kubernetes.io/docs/tasks/run-application/run-single-instance-stateful-application/`
- `https://kubernetes.io/docs/tasks/run-application/run-replicated-stateful-application/`

Please remember that up until Kubernetes v1.9 this feature was in beta, so you may have to check the documentation if your cluster is running an older version.

Storage

Most modern applications should already not be storing files that are being generated on local drives—instead, they should be using an object store. Typically, an object offers an API that allows the application to both write files to the service, and also query the service to find out metadata for the files, including retrieving a URL where the file can be accessed over HTTP.

The big three public cloud providers all offer object storage:

- **Amazon S3**: `https://aws.amazon.com/s3/`
- **Microsoft Azure Blob storage**: `https://azure.microsoft.com/en-gb/services/storage/blobs/`
- **Google Cloud Storage**: `https://cloud.google.com/storage/`

Amazon S3 is the granddaddy of them all; it is more than likely that at some point in the last 48 hours you have accessed a file which has been served either directly from Amazon S3, or indirectly, using a content delivery network where Amazon S3 is the origin for the file.

What if you wish to keep your application within Kubernetes, including the object store? Don't worry, it is possible to run your own object store; in fact, you can run one that has a highlevel of compatibility with Amazon S3, meaning that your application should continue to work with little to no modification.

Minio is a multi-cloud object store that you can deploy to Kubernetes as well as other cloud and service providers; it is even possible to run it locally using Minikube.

For more information on Minio on Kubernetes, see the following link: `https://www.minio.io/kubernetes.html`.

Summary

So, here we are at the end of the book. We have worked through what we mean by serverless, and addressed the confusion about running serverless functions on servers.

We have learned about how Kubernetes started and some of its core concepts, as well as about deploying clusters locally and in public clouds using both tools provided by Kubernetes themselves, and also the cloud provider's native solutions.

Using these clusters, we worked through several tools that all provide Functions as a Service functionality, either by extending Kubernetes with new functionality, or by taking advantages of the Platform as a Service functionality of Kubernetes and installing themselves on top of Kubernetes.

We then discussed potential security issues with these deployments and how to monitor them, before then talking about how we try and keep ahead of an ever-evolving technology, and what you will need to consider when starting out on your own deploying serverless functions on Kubernetes.

Other Books You May Enjoy

If you enjoyed this book, you may be interested in these other books by Packt:

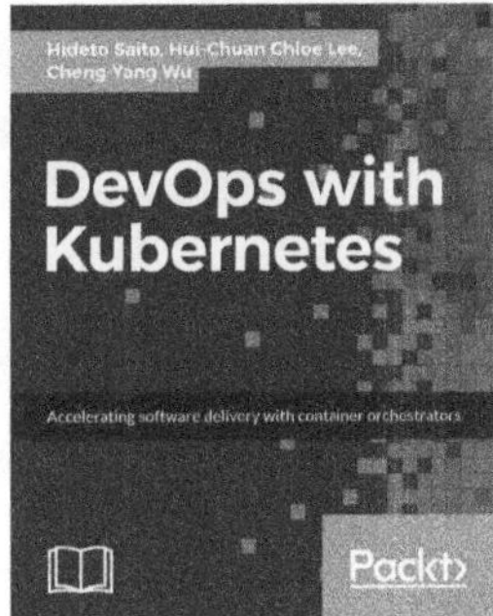

DevOps with Kubernetes
Hideto Saito, Hui-Chuan Chloe Lee, Cheng-Yang Wu

ISBN: 978-1-78839-664-6

- Learn fundamental and advanced DevOps skills and tools
- Get a comprehensive understanding for container
- Learn how to move your application to container world
- Learn how to manipulate your application by Kubernetes
- Learn how to work with Kubernetes in popular public cloud
- Improve time to market with Kubernetes and Continuous Delivery
- Learn how to monitor, log, and troubleshoot your application with Kubernetes

Docker and Kubernetes for Java Developers
Jaroslaw Krochmalski

ISBN: 978-1-78646-839-0

- Package Java applications into Docker images
- Understand the running of containers locally
- Explore development and deployment options with Docker
- Integrate Docker into Maven builds
- Manage and monitor Java applications running on Kubernetes clusters
- Create Continuous Delivery pipelines for Java applications deployed to Kubernetes

Leave a review - let other readers know what you think

Please share your thoughts on this book with others by leaving a review on the site that you bought it from. If you purchased the book from Amazon, please leave us an honest review on this book's Amazon page. This is vital so that other potential readers can see and use your unbiased opinion to make purchasing decisions, we can understand what our customers think about our products, and our authors can see your feedback on the title that they have worked with Packt to create. It will only take a few minutes of your time, but is valuable to other potential customers, our authors, and Packt. Thank you!

Index

D

F

G

H

I

K

L

M

N

O

P

R

S

T

U

V

W

Z

www.ingramcontent.com/pod-product-compliance
Lightning Source LLC
Chambersburg PA
CBHW080625060326
40690CB00021B/4815

* 9 7 8 1 7 8 8 6 2 0 3 7 6 *